"Here I Have Lived"

LINCOLN IN 1860
From a recently discovered
daguerreotype

"Here I Have Lived"

A HISTORY
OF
LINCOLN'S SPRINGFIELD
1821-1865

By Paul M. Angle

A PUBLICATION OF
THE ABRAHAM LINCOLN ASSOCIATION
SPRINGFIELD, ILLINOIS

RUTGERS UNIVERSITY PRESS
New Brunswick, New Jersey

TO LOGAN HAY

ILLUSTRATIONS

CONTENTS

Contents

"*My Friends: No one, not in my situation, can appreciate my feeling of sadness at this parting. To this place, and the kindness of these people, I owe everything. Here I have lived a quarter of a century, and have passed from a young to an old man. Here my children have been born, and one is buried. I now leave, not knowing when or whether ever I may return, with a task before me greater than that which rested upon Washington. Without the assistance of that Divine Being who ever attended him, I cannot succeed. With that assistance, I cannot fail. Trusting in Him who can go with me, and remain with you, and be everywhere for good, let us confidently hope that all will yet be well. To His care commending you, as I hope in your prayers you will commend me, I bid you an affectionate farewell.*"

—Abraham Lincoln at Springfield, Illinois
February 11, 1861

PROLOGUE

IN the spring of 1830 a young man named Abraham Lincoln, with father, mother and other relatives, came from southern Indiana to settle on the Sangamon River in Macon County, Illinois. A year later the young man, now alone, established himself in the village of New Salem in Sangamon County. Six years later he removed to Springfield, the new capital of the state. There he remained until February 11, 1861, when he left for Washington to become the sixteenth President of the United States.

That there are certain relationships between a man's environment and what he ultimately becomes is obvious. If a community refuses to support a portrait painter, and the portrait painter refuses to find another home, he either chooses a different occupation or he starves. And so, in this most fundamental of all human endeavors, Lincoln owed a debt to Springfield and the area which centers in it, for it afforded him a living in the profession of his choice.

Moreover, the community responded only less generously to his other ambition—political advancement. He made only one unsuccessful attempt at office-holding, and then his neighbors gave him four terms in the state legislature and, after a short interval, two years in Congress. Not until the slavery question shattered all loyalties did old friends turn away from him, and even then the city of his home remained faithful, though by the narrowest of margins.

"Here I Have Lived"

But these are hardly more than the conditions of existence, and need no demonstration. More interesting are the influences which defy proof, and can only be suggested. Could Lincoln, for instance, have attained high standing at the bar if he had not resided at the one city in the state where the high courts sat? Could he have become a power in Illinois politics if the legislature and the courts had not drawn the political leaders to his home at regular and frequent intervals? Could he have learned to gauge the temper of the people as surely as he did learn to gauge it had he not been forced for years to evaluate the conflicting sentiments which these men were constantly reporting? Could he have attained to the mastery of political manoeuvre that was his had he not had years of association with venturesome and skillful politicians, both as friends and opponents? Could he have held to his faith in political democracy if he had not lived in a city where economic opportunity was a fact? Could he have understood, and solved, the problem of the Border States without a quarter-century's association with neighbors whose backgrounds and prejudices were closely akin to those of the people of Kentucky and Missouri? How much of his own cautious sureness resulted from the conservatism of these same neighbors? What part of his insistence upon maintenance of the Union could be traced to the necessity of keeping open the Mississippi in order that the produce of the farms of central Illinois might find its natural market at New Orleans? To what extent were the Southerners of his home city responsible for his refusal to adopt a policy of vengeance towards the conquered section?

When Lincoln said farewell to the people of Springfield he gave his own answer to these questions. "To this place, and the kindness of these people, I owe everything." Spoken out of deep emotion, the words can hardly be expected to convey exact, cold-blooded truth. Yet one shrinks from an analysis. To attempt to formulate a detailed statement of the

Prologue

debt seems not only foolhardy, but also, for a resident of the city which owes so much to him, ungracious. Rather than that, the picture of the community itself is presented, and readers may draw from it such inferences as they choose. If some phases of a personality not yet completely understood are illuminated, its major purpose will have been realized; if it fails in this respect, perhaps it will still have value as a footnote to the history of fifty years of American life.

"Here I Have Lived"
A History of Lincoln's Springfield
1821-1865

CHAPTER I

A Little Cluster of Log Cabins

ANYONE who knows the steaming summers of central Illinois will have difficulty in realizing that there was a time when ice hundreds of feet thick covered most of the state. Yet, as geologists measure time, it was not long ago—perhaps 150,000 years—that the Illinoisan glacier, the third of the great ice-masses which moved downward from the vicinity of Labrador and Hudson's Bay, reached its southernmost limit on the slopes of the Illinois Ozarks.

The fact is of more than casual interest. For one thing, it meant a radical change in the landscape. Rugged hills were planed off and deep valleys filled, so that when the ice receded it left behind a land of level surfaces and gentle slopes. More important, however, was the fact that it marked the first step in the formation of the state's greatest asset—soil.

For soil does not just happen. On the contrary, it is the result of natural forces acting over thousands of years. When the Illinoisan glacier receded it left a deposit of boulder clay, twenty, forty, even eighty feet in thickness, the pulverized remains of the rocks which the ice had carried with it. After intervals of thousands of years two more ice caps came down from the north. Both stopped near the northern boundary of Illinois, but as they melted and receded, immense quantities of finely ground rock were carried southward and deposited in the flood plains of the rivers. Winds distributed this material more widely and more evenly. Gradually it decomposed, vegetation grew upon it, decayed and grew again, and deep soil of wonderful fertility was formed.

Nowhere in the state was this soil richer than in the valley of the Sangamon River, the quiet stream which rises in Champaign County and empties into the Illinois a hundred miles above the latter's junction with the Mississippi. And nowhere in the Sangamon valley was the land finer than in that part of it which the pioneers came to know as the "Sangamo country." Here, where now the counties of Sangamon, Logan, Menard, Mason and Cass[1] are to be found, fine groves of forest trees lined the water courses and dotted prairies tall with grass and flowering weeds. Game abounded, and the Indians knew it as a land of plenty.

French explorers, missionaries and fur-traders, passing back and forth over Illinois since the latter part of the seventeenth century, must more than once have crossed the Sangamo country and noted its attractiveness. Americans, slowly trickling into Illinois in the first years after the Revolutionary War, certainly visited it. By 1812, when Governor Edwards and his rangers swept through it on their way to the Indian village on Peoria Lake, its reputation was well established.

[1]The description is only an approximate one. The present counties of Sangamon and Menard are the heart of the old Sangamo country, which extended indefinite distances from them.

For settlement, however, it had to wait until the mass-movement of western expansion reached it.

Before the end of the Revolution settlers were crowding through the passes of the Alleghenies to the virgin lands beyond the mountains. The danger of Indian massacre, the grinding work of clearing land and building farms, the absence of all except the bare essentials of life failed to deter them. Down the Shenandoah Valley of Virginia, through the Cumberland Gap, then west and northwest came a stream of settlers, to make Kentucky a state by 1792 and Tennessee another four years later. Over the mountains and down the Ohio came other homeseekers, contributing to Kentucky's population and bringing Ohio into the Union in 1803.

From the early years of the eighteenth century there had been permanent settlements in Illinois, Frenchmen living for the most part in the villages strung along the Mississippi in the "American Bottom." Here, after Clark's conquest during the Revolution, came a few Americans. Growth was slow, however. The census of 1800 showed fewer than 2,500 people in Illinois; that of 1810 enumerated only 12,282. In the same years both Kentucky and Ohio had gained 185,000 inhabitants. Even in 1818, when Illinois became a state, there is not much doubt that it lacked the 40,000 inhabitants who were supposed to be a prerequisite to statehood.

Nevertheless, settlers were coming at a rapidly increasing rate. Most of them were Kentuckians, generally by adoption, sometimes by birth, although the eastern states made sizable contributions. But regardless of origin, they came from the south. For several years Shawneetown on the Ohio River was the gateway to Illinois, with roads radiating throughout the southern tip of the state. As the country filled, the wave of settlement moved northward. By 1818, the year of statehood, it had traversed perhaps the lowest fourth of the state.

The compact line of advance, however, was still far to the south when Robert Pulliam built the first cabin in what is now

Sangamon County. It was October, 1817, that Pulliam, accompanied by two or three hired men and the wife of one of them, erected a shelter about twelve miles south of Springfield and four miles southeast of Chatham. It was not meant to be a permanent habitation, but merely a covering while the men tended a herd of cattle and a few horses which they had brought up for better grazing from St. Clair County. The winter over, they went back home.

When Pulliam came back in the spring of 1819, bringing his family with him, there were others where before he had been alone. Living in the cabin which he himself had built were Zachariah Peter and his wife and family. Nearby were other cabins, occupied since the preceding spring by William Drennan and several relatives. To the north, the Kellys were building cabins where Springfield now stands. The settlement of the Sangamo country had, in fact, begun. Ferdinand Ernst, a German traveler, heard so much of its fine land that he decided to see it for himself, and found sixty farms on Sugar Creek alone when he passed along its fifteen-mile course in September, 1819. In the early summer of the same year Gershom Flagg wrote from Edwardsville that two hundred families had settled north of that town in the last year, and that some were as distant as 120 miles. All the talk, in fact, was of the marvelous fertility of the Sangamo country. Hunters said that it was the finest honey country on earth, that eight or ten swarms of bees could be found in a day. Word went out that the first crop of sod corn stood fifteen feet high. Henry R. Schoolcraft, traveling up the Illinois in 1821, heard so much of its productiveness that he called it almost proverbial.

With such a reputation the population increased rapidly, and by 1821 the legislature decided that it was sufficient for a county government of its own. On January 30 of that year the county of Sangamon was created. It was a gigantic tract of land in the shape of a rough triangle, with the Illinois

River—or at least as much of it as lies between the present cities of Beardstown and Peru—forming its diagonal boundary. Provision was made for the election of three county commissioners whose first duty should be to select a temporary county seat as near the center of population as possible. A hint was dropped a week later when it was enacted that the election of commissioners and other officers of the new county should be held "at the house of John Kelly on Spring Creek."

In due time the commissioners were elected—Zachariah Peter, William Drennan and Rivers Cormack. On April 10 Peter and Drennan met at Kelly's cabin, drove a stake into the ground and called it Springfield. Recording the transaction, they stated that after a full examination of the county's population they had "fixed and designated a certain point in the prairie near John Kelly's field on the water of Spring Creek at a stake marked Z D as the temporary seat of Justice." John Kelly's cabin stood on what is now the northwest corner of Second and Jefferson streets, and the stake was driven close by. The name, Springfield, was doubtless suggested by the adjacent creek, although it is not unlikely that Peter's long residence in Washington county, Kentucky, which also has a Springfield for a county seat, had something to do with its selection.

Three years earlier a bachelor named Elisha Kelly left North Carolina to settle in Illinois. He built a cabin in Macoupin County, but since he was very fond of hunting he ranged the country for many miles in all directions. One day he wandered into a ravine in which a small, clear stream ran northward to empty into Spring Creek. Large numbers of deer passed up and down, and Kelly thought it a hunter's paradise.

The following year he induced his father, Henry, and four brothers—John, Elijah, William and George—to come with him to the spot he had discovered and settle there. All built cabins. By 1821 others had settled in the same locality. It was, in fact, the most thickly settled spot in the whole immense county; the only place, it was said, where families lived close enough to provide food and lodging for those who would attend court sessions in the new county seat.

The little settlement was attractively located. Zimri Enos, who remembered the surroundings from his boyhood, wrote of the "handsome undulating prairie nook" in which John Kelly's cabin stood—"a mile in length east and west and a half mile north and south, thoroughly drained by never-failing spring branches and bordered on the north and west by heavy timber and on the south by a number of beautiful groves of young forest trees, of pin oak, elm, cherry and hackberry, which were festooned with grape vines and fringed with plum and haw bushes, crab-apples, hazel nuts, elders and blackberries, and encircled by millions of strawberry vines."

Having located the county seat, the commissioners promptly attacked the housing problem. A contract was made with John Kelly for the erection of a court house—a log building twenty feet square and one story high, with a plank floor, good roof, door and window cut out. Kelly went at the job in leisurely fashion, so that it was not until early June that it was finished and a warrant for $47.50 was issued to him for his work. The commissioners then arranged with Jesse Brevard for chinking the structure and furnishing it with door, window and fireplace. At the same time a contract for a jail was made with Robert Hamilton. Springfield was now ready to function as a county seat.

The town, however, was anything but securely started. Eight settlers lived within two miles of the court house, but every one of them was a mere squatter with no legal right whatever to be there. The land had not even been surveyed, and it would be at least two years before the government would put it on sale. At that time anyone might buy it over the settlers' heads and evict them. So far as an increase of population was concerned, the location of the temporary

county seat had attracted only one settler. He was Charles
R. Matheny, who had been induced to locate there by the
offer of all the county offices except that of sheriff. Even he
was finding it difficult to live on the fees of his combined offices. It was at least an even chance that the little village, thus
prematurely born, would live out a listless existence of a year
or two, and gradually disappear.

That this did not happen was due to a twenty-five year
old Kentuckian named Elijah Iles. The son of typical pioneers, Iles had learned self-reliance at an early age. By the
time he was twenty he had accumulated $600 by raising cat-
tle in Bath County, Kentucky. It was then that he heard of
the fine lands in Missouri, where a man could have "large,
square cornfields" instead of the "little zig-zag ones" which
were all that he knew. So he took his money and started for
this farmers' paradise. He remained for three years, clerking
in a store long enough to learn something about frontier
storekeeping, exploring the country, buying and selling land,
saving his money. But he failed to take root. Missouri, he
thought, would remain frontier throughout his lifetime.

Early in 1821, while crossing Illinois after a visit to his
family in Kentucky, he heard of the Sangamon valley and its
fertile soil. Accompanied by a step-brother, he swung from
his direct route to visit a part of it. He liked what he saw, so
as soon as he had settled his affairs in Missouri, and got his
step-brother established in a store there, he "pulled up
stakes" for Illinois.

In the late spring of 1821 Iles crossed the Mississippi at
Louisiana, Missouri, went southward almost to the mouth
of the Illinois, swam his horse across that river and struck
the trail from St. Louis to the Diamond Grove, where Jacksonville is now located. There the Island Grove timber was
pointed out to him. "I crossed the prairie without a trail,"
he wrote, "found no one in the grove, and kept on the west
side until I struck a trail running east to where it was said a

temporary county seat was located. Following this trail I found the place, on the east side of Spring Creek timber. Charles R. Matheny had just moved to the place, and had erected a cabin of one room, in which he was residing with a large family of little children. He had been appointed clerk of the circuit and county court, judge of the probate, clerk of his own court, and county recorder, although there were no deeds yet to be recorded . . . John Kelly resided in the vicinity, and I stopped with him for the night."

The following day Iles explored the country. It more than confirmed his first impression, and he decided to stay. But what was he to do until the land should be put on sale? He remembered his experience as a clerk in Missouri, thought of the money he had saved, and decided to open a store.

"I hunted around and found the stake that had been stuck for the beginning of a town named Springfield," he related, "and then bargained for the erection of a store house, to be set near the stake, eighteen feet square, with sheds on the sides for shelter. The house was to be of hewn logs, covered with boards, with heavy poles laid on to keep the boards from blowing off." The contract made, he set out for St. Louis to purchase a stock of goods. When he had what he wanted he chartered a boat and hired five men to tow it up the Illinois to the mouth of the Sangamon. The trip was made without serious accident, and the merchandise unloaded on the shore where Beardstown now stands. Nearby was a vacant cabin. In it Iles stored his goods, and then started for Springfield on foot. Before he had gone far he found two wagoners going to the river, and since neither had full loads for the return trip, he induced them to take the first instalment of his stock. In a short time his store was open for business.

Trade was good. Wheat was ripe in the fields, and Iles had a goodly supply of the whiskey without which harvesters found it almost impossible to work. Iron castings, nails, stoneware, salt and coffee were also in demand. Many customers came seventy-five and eighty miles to make their purchases, for the store was the sole trading place in a territory of perhaps 10,000 square miles. Indians bought about as much as whites. Trade was mostly by barter. The Indians paid in furs, undressed deer skins and blue grass seed; the whites in homemade jeans, cotton and linen cloth, beeswax and honey. Ordinary farm products—grain, butter, eggs—were of little use as a medium of exchange, since the cost of transporting them to the nearest market exceeded their entire value.

A profitable business established, Iles began to make plans for the future. He had come to Illinois as a prospective land-buyer, not as a storekeeper. And so, when the land was surveyed later in 1821, he made it known that he intended to purchase the land on which his store-house stood as a town site. He made it known also that if he succeeded in buying the land, he would give each settler the lot on which his cabin stood. A town was in the making.

Nevertheless, for the first year or two its fate was doubtful. Settlers—in the surrounding country as well as in Springfield—risked the loss of every improvement they made, for no preemption system existed by which they could establish a claim prior to the land sales. In actual practice, however, it was infrequent that anyone outbid the man who lived on the land and forced his eviction—at least without paying him a fair price for his buildings and for his labor in bringing the land under cultivation.[2] When the squatter himself wanted to stay, settlers were likely to deal roughly with an outsider who

[2] In a letter to the Commissioner of the General Land Office, written May 8, 1826, Pascal P. Enos, who was then the receiver of the Springfield Land Office, described the sort of thing that happened at the government "auction"; "And here permit me to remark Sir that there has never been an instance during either of the two land sales at this place of any person biding more than the Govt. prices, or any persons biding agt. a person that held by possession. Tho there was many instances in which individuals threatened to do it, in consequence of some old grudge or quarrel that existed. One in particular I will mention, a Mr. Kirkpatrick and Wm. Broadwell made a settlement. K. afterward stated that B. had cheated him out of $14 in the settlement and unless he did pay him back the $14 he would positively bid against him when his land came into the market. Wm. S. Hamilton on learning this determina-

was presumptuous enough to bid more than the minimum government price of $1.25 an acre; while if he wanted to move on to less crowded regions, the possibility of being ridden on a rail usually brought a fair payment for improvements from the purchaser. Still, the possibility of eviction existed, and did something to deter settlement.

Moreover, many of those who were building cabins in the Sangamo country were not of the sort who meant to stay. Wherever there was a frontier a hardy, adventurous, half-nomadic class who lived by a combination of hunting and crude agriculture were to be found. A cabin, a few rude farm implements, a horse and perhaps a yoke of oxen, together with a small herd of half-wild hogs, made up the sum of their possessions. They cultivated a patch of corn and allowed their stock to run wild. When the population increased to a point where cattle had to be fenced in, and where it was necessary to buy land in order to live on it, they moved on. It was a common saying among them that when one could see the smoke of a neighbor's chimney the country was too crowded for comfort. Industry was not one of their characteristics. "They do the least work I believe of any people in the world," a disgusted Yankee wrote.

Naturally, a town surrounded by a population of this sort was not going to develop into a metropolis over night. Still, settlers were pouring into the surrounding country, and some of them found their way to the county seat. By the autumn of 1823, when the land was put on sale, there were perhaps thirty families living in Springfield. They resided in log houses, scattered, for the most part, along Jefferson Street

tion of K. and at the time of the sales went to him and paid him the $14 and on his return stated that he had settled the difficulty between those two men but whether B. gave him the money to pay or whether he paid it out of his own pocket, I do not know. But the inducement that led him to compromise this difficulty he stated on his return to be this that he was affraid that if they once began to bid that they would continue to bid, and might be the means of his losing his mills in Morgan county. These mills he and his partner had lately purchased the possessory right to for which they gave a large sum."

from First to Fourth streets. A small public square had been set apart for the court house at Second and Jefferson. Elijah Iles was still without a competitor, but three tavern keepers were obliged to divide the patronage of the neighborhood. A postoffice, named "Sangamon," had been established early in 1822, with Stephen Stillman as postmaster. Pascal P. Enos had opened the government land office in a two-story log cabin on the northwest corner of Third and Jefferson streets. Thomas Cox operated a horse mill and a distillery at the western edge of town. Gershom Jayne, the physician, had a double log cabin in which he kept travelers over night.

The town was still a frontier hamlet, however. Peter Cartwright, who first saw it in 1823, said that it contained "a few smoky, hastily-built cabins, and one or two little shanties called 'stores,' " the contents of which he could have carried away on his back in a few loads. Another visitor described it as "a little cluster of log cabins." Squads of Kickapoo and Potawatomi still visited it frequently.

Nevertheless, Elijah Iles held to his plan of making the straggling settlement into a city. The land on which it stood had been surveyed in 1821. Early in the following year he laid out the streets: Jefferson, Washington, Adams and Monroe running east and west, with six others, unnamed, intersecting them at right angles. Soon he found allies in John Taylor, the sheriff, Thomas Cox, the register of the land office, and Daniel Pope Cook, congressman for the district, each of whom bought the settlers' claims to a quarter-section. In September, 1823, Pascal P. Enos, fifty-three years old and a Yankee by birth, came to Springfield as receiver of public moneys at the land office. He too was impressed with the possibilities of the place, and was allowed to buy a share in the venture. Together the proprietors agreed that Iles and Enos would each enter one of the two quarter-sections on which the town stood.

On November 6, 1823, the first land sales took place. The

next day Iles and Enos made their entries. To the former went the southwest quarter of Section 27, within which was included most of that part of the town which lay north of Washington Street. Enos' entry was for the northwest quarter of Section 34, adjoining Iles' purchase on the south. Both tracts were struck off without opposition for the minimum price of $1.25 an acre. On the same day Thomas Cox entered the southeast quarter of Section 28, on which the few cabins west of First Street and north of Washington were located. Thus title to the land on which the original village of Springfield was situated passed from the United States of America to three individual "proprietors." [3]

The first act of the proprietors was to change the town's

[3]There were only three proprietors of record. That Taylor and Cook were also interested appears from a detailed account of the transaction which Pascal P. Enos wrote in May, 1826, when William S. Hamilton charged both him and Cox with improper conduct. "Some time previous to the first Land sale at this office," he wrote, "I came here with a desire to provide some place for my family the county then being new with abt. 6 or 8 little cabin houses in the place. I then learnt that a Mr. Iles had purchased the improvements to a Qr. Sec. of Land abt. 2 years previous for $200—Mr. Taylor had purchased another quarter abt. a year after for which he gave $130. That Danl. P. Cook our Rep. in Congress obtained the possession of another quarter, on which he had erected a cabin house and put 10 acres under farm, which cost him $130 or 40, and the R. [Cox, the register] either had or was abt. to purchase another quarter for which he gave $200 for the possession. At this time I felt anxious to possess a little land in the place where I thought it probable that I should remain a few years in case I was honest and faithful in the discharge of my duties as a public agent. These proprietors learning that I was desirous to obtain some land in the place informed me that I might have a share of theirs on the same terms which they gave for it; as they had more than they wanted in case they obtained it, and in case, they did not, the loss would not be as great. My remark to them was that I would not like to purchase the possessory right to real estate. That when I did purchase my object would be to procure the title as well as the possession—and stated further to them that I was affraid that it would be received by some evil disposed person, as an unfair transaction. They said no, that it could not be so considered—that Mr. Cook gave it as his opinion that it would be a fair transaction between me and the Govt. as long as the door would be open for every man to bid that had an intention. I reflected a little upon it, and as I could not satisfy myself that any possible injury could occur to the Govt. as long as any person that had a wish to purchase the whole or any part of these lands would have an opportunity of so doing at the land sales. Accordingly I purchased a part, and in case I have done any one act or thing to prevent third persons from going forward at the sales and biding for these lands I admit that I ought to be displaced from office." Two months later Hamilton retracted his charges.

name. "Colo. Cox, Mr. Enos, and Maj'r Iles has purchased Springfield," James Latham wrote to Ninian Edwards, "and have altered the name to Calhoun with the general satisfaction of the people." John C. Calhoun of South Carolina, the statesman thus honored, was then at the peak of his popularity, especially in the West, where the ardent nationalism of his early career was entirely in keeping with popular sentiment. In 1823 his name was prominently mentioned for the Presidency. "Mr. Calhoun is growing in popularity very fast here," wrote Latham.

The proprietors' next act was to have a survey made of the town. On December 5 there was recorded the plat of the Town of Calhoun. It was a rectangular tract, bounded on the north by Madison Street, on the east by Seventh, on the south by Monroe and on the west by First. Twenty-three blocks and a public square, located as now, were laid out. All the recorded plat was on the quarter sections entered by Iles and Enos.

Lot sales commenced as soon as the plat was recorded. Since the center of settlement was on Iles' property, the first conveyances were from him. Mordecai Mobley, who kept one of the taverns, was among the first purchasers, paying $50.00 for a lot on the north side of Washington Street between Fourth and Fifth. Ordinarily, however, sales were for lower prices. Thus on December 8 a lot on the southwest corner of Jefferson and Third streets was sold to John Messersmith of Ohio for $25.00, and within the next month or so others located no less advantageously were disposed of for as little as $15.00 and $20.00.

The truth was that the proprietors were not embarrassed by a crowd of prospective purchasers. The town's future was still a question mark. For one thing, it had drawn no great number of settlers. Besides, the county offices—the chief reason for its existence—had been located there only temporarily. Rival towns were being founded in the surrounding country, and it was not unlikely that in the end the county government would be located at one of these. Sangamo Town, a small but thriving settlement near the Sangamon River seven or eight miles northwest of Springfield, was making a bid for the county seat; and William S. Hamilton [4] was working hard for the selection of a "paper town" of his own five miles north of the temporary county seat. It was high, dry, and well located, and the fact that not a single building graced its site was only a minor disadvantage.

Knowing that the General Assembly of 1824-25 would make provision for a permanent selection, the rivals gathered at Vandalia. Hamilton had already stolen a march, for in the summer of 1824 he had succeeded in getting himself elected as Sangamon County's representative in the legislature. The proprietors of Springfield countered by sending Jonathan Pugh, whom Hamilton had barely defeated, to the capital to look out for their interests. Neither party won a clear victory, for the law which the legislature passed, on December 23, 1824, appointed commissioners and directed them to meet at the court house in early March and select a permanent seat of justice for Sangamon County on the basis of "the geographical situation of said county, its present and the future population and permanent interest." Actually, the outcome was a defeat for Hamilton, for at the close of the session one of Enos's friends who had been in Vandalia informed him "that if it had not been for Mr. Pugh's strenu-

[4] William Stephen Hamilton was the fifth son of Alexander Hamilton. In 1816, when he was eighteen years old, he secured a position on the staff of William Rector, surveyor general for Illinois and Missouri. About 1822 he left St. Louis, where he had been residing, and settled at Springfield. In 1825 he removed to Peoria, and shortly afterward to the lead mine region around Galena, where he became a prominent figure. After residing in Wisconsin for more than a decade the lure of the gold fields drew him to California, where he died in 1850.

Defending himself against Hamilton's charges in 1826, Enos wrote that "he does not possess one single good trait that shown so conspicuous in his fathers character but he possesses all his bad ones, and a most spiteful and revengeful disposition in the bargain." Many other associates, however, have testified to his ability and personal popularity.

ous & unsparing exertions . . . the county seat of Sangamon
would have been removed according to Hamilton's wishes."

In accordance with the law, four of the five commissioners—James Mason, Rowland P. Allen, Charles Gear and
John R. Sloo—appeared in Springfield about the middle of
March. Being conscientious men, they were determined to in-
spect all the sites in spite of the mud and water left by the
spring thaws. With not a little guile Andrew Elliott, the
North Carolinian who kept the Buckhorn Tavern, volunteered to guide them. Elliott had lived in the neighborhood
for six years and was a fine woodsman, but try as he might
he was unable to get the commissioners to Sangamo Town
without passing through eight or ten sloughs, not to mention
overflowed and marshy prairies. The commissioners agreed
that it was an excellent site, but most difficult of access. The
latter opinion was more than confirmed by their return trip
over a different route, worse if possible. They reached Springfield entirely exhausted, thankful that their lives had been
spared, and determined to take no chances by visiting the
other prospective site. For Andrew Elliott—and Springfield—it was a good day's work.

On the following day Elijah Iles and his wife accomplished
all that remained—Mrs. Iles when she prepared a royal feast
for the weary commissioners, and her husband when he tactfully let it be known that he stood ready to cash their state
warrants at par if they should see fit to select Springfield. (In
actual value the warrants were worth about twenty-five cents
on the dollar.) The result was that the commissioners lost
no time in reporting that Springfield —the name Calhoun had
already been dropped in popular usage—should be the permanent seat of Sangamon County.

In the law providing for the location of the county seat
the legislature had stipulated that the proprietors of the
town selected should donate not less than thirty-five acres to
the county, to be divided into lots and sold to defray the ex-

pense of the public buildings. Iles and Enos promptly complied with the requirement, and deeded to the county the present public square with the blocks immediately north and south, as well as a tract between Washington and Madison streets and extending east from Sixth to a line midway between Eighth and Ninth streets. The county court, with some irony, commissioned William S. Hamilton to make a survey of the acquisition, but Hamilton, disgusted with the day's proceedings, refused the job.

The county officers lost no time in making arrangements for their first lot sale. It was decided to offer thirty lots to the public on the first Monday in May, and Charles R. Matheny, county clerk, was directed to insert a notice to that effect in the Edwardsville *Spectator* and the *Illinois Intelligencer* of Vandalia, offering a credit of three, six and nine months.

In his advertisement Matheny showed not a little familiarity with the arts of the publicity man. "Springfield," he wrote, "is now the permanent seat of justice of Sangamon county, situated within 4½ miles of the Sangamon river, in the heart of perhaps the most beautiful and flourishing county in the state of Illinois. The number of lots are supposed to exceed one thousand. The town site is delightfully situated on the border of a handsome prairie, and in the immediate vicinity of a large quantity of good timber. The population exceeding two hundred souls, furnishes an opportunity of testing its health, which has never yet been denied by the candid mind or intelligent physician. It is an object of enterprise which equally becomes the actual settler or the speculator, to become interested in purchasing property in this place."

The thirty lots offered for sale were disposed of in three days at prices ranging from $10.25, which Charles R. Matheny paid for the northwest corner of Monroe and Seventh streets, to $40.50, given by Elijah Iles for the southeast corner of Sixth and Adams. All the lots were 80 feet front and 157 feet deep. What is now the finest business property in the city went for a few dollars. Thus James Adams bought the northeast corner of Fifth and Monroe streets for $13.75, while Garret Elkin, James C. McNabb and Elijah Iles bought the four lots which made up the south side of the square for a total of $90.50. (A sad sequel to the first lot sale came six months later, when the county commissioners ordered that "the notes and accounts for the sale of lots in the Town of Springfield be put in the hands of John Taylor Sheriff for collection.")

Nevertheless, the lots were all sold—a fact which indicated that a growing number of people were convinced that the town was there to stay. Their confidence was soon justified, for in the following year its population more than doubled. When Charles R. Matheny composed a second advertisement early in 1826, he was able to announce the presence of 500 inhabitants "in a prosperous and thriving condition," and to assert, in calm confidence, that "if town property is to be valuable in any county town in the Western Country, it doubtless must be here."

CHAPTER II

The Town Takes Root

IN the Springfield of a century ago and more, the fundamental problem of obtaining a place to live was a simple one. All a settler needed was an ax, some timber and the will to work, for everyone, in town as well as country, lived in log cabins. Generally they were small—not more than fifteen by eighteen feet—but as time went on enterprising owners doubled capacity by adding an upper story or by building a second cabin adjoining the first. Often "houseraisings" were held for the benefit of newcomers, while weddings were a signal for the entire community to join in the work. Early in the morning the men gathered with axes, saws and adzes, and by night the cabin was ready for occupancy—ready, that is, except for the housewarming, with its feasting and drinking and dancing "to wear the splinters off the floor."

For the first few years clothing too was mostly hand made. "We raised cotton sufficient to supply our wants . . ." wrote one early settler. "We had several cotton gins and our wives and daughters with their spinning wheels, cotton cards and looms supplied us with most of our wearing apparel." Wild animals were abundant, and many families made hats and clothing of their pelts.

The same primitiveness was reflected in the settlers' food. "During my first year in Springfield I boarded with old Grandfather Kelly, and I think of it as the most luxurious living of all my days," wrote Elijah Iles, reminiscing in a pleasant glow. "It consisted of Venison, Turkey, Prairie Chickens, Quail, Squirrel, beef and enough pork to season; honey and the best of milk and butter, and the never-to-be-forgotten corn dodger, and the hoe cake." If fresh venison were wanted for breakfast a deer could usually be killed in the grove where the Governor's mansion now stands. Hickory nuts and walnuts were abundant in the timber around the town, while in summer there was a profusion of wild strawberries, blackberries and plums.

To commence housekeeping, even for the town's leading citizen, was a simple matter. Elijah Iles thus described the preparations for his marriage with Malinda Benjamin, which took place in 1824. "To enable her to do her part, I furnished her bed-ticking, feathers, and sheeting, to be made up for a bed which was to be placed in a room above my little store. She was a brisk worker, and soon had them ready. For my part, I built a shed and brick chimney, with open fireplace (this was before the days of cook stoves), attached to the rear of the store, for a cooking and dining place, until I had time to build a better. I soon had cooking utensils and table ware, and was prepared. After supper we called in a preacher, who married us, and our bridal trip was across the street to our bed room."

Social intercourse was without formality. When a young lady wished to entertain company she simply placed a lighted candle in her window. In a few minutes she would have as her guests most of the young men of the village, who collected nightly at the four corners at Second and Jefferson streets. John T. Stuart, who came to Springfield in the fall of 1828, thus described his initiation into the custom. "Miss Clarissa Benjamin, now Van Bergen, placed her candle in the window of the parlor room, above the store of Major Iles. Phil Latham gave notice by exclaiming: 'Boys, Clarissa's candle is in the window; let's go over.' The young men assembled there, and found Miss Clarissa Benjamin, Misses Hannah and Margaret Taylor, the Misses Dryers, and Miss Jane Bergen. It was a pleasant, social evening, and these ladies were as handsome, refined, and entertained as well and gracefully, as the young ladies of the present day."

In the long winter evenings families gathered around the huge fireplaces, often six feet or more in width. A back log so big that it had to be rolled over the floor and put in place on skids glowed red, while small wood piled around it kept the cabin warm. Everyone had an abundant supply of nuts. "In our family we added the parching and roasting of pop-corn and yellow corn," said Zimri Enos. "The latter, when well browned and ground and served in a bowl with rich, sweet milk, is a dish I could enjoy even now."

Sometimes less pacific occupations were indulged in. On Saturdays, when the farmers came to town, the little square at the intersection of Second and Jefferson streets was likely to be the scene of considerable brawling. There the young men of the Sangamo country demonstrated their physical prowess by the time-honored method of blacking each other's eyes. Neighborhood quarrels were settled in the same way. Now it would be South Fork and Flat Branch against Richland and Clary's Grove; now Spring Creek against Lake Fork. Sometimes a dozen battles were in progress at the same time.

Springfield was, in truth, a frontier town, and many phases of its life revealed the small gap which separated it from the uninhabited prairies of a few years before. James Adams received an amusing demonstration of this fact soon after he settled there in 1821. Bitten by a rattlesnake, he wanted to obtain some snake oil as a remedy. Seeking speedy relief, he let it be known that he would pay fifty cents for the first rattler offered him and twenty-five cents for each additional one. In a short time a man appeared with a snake and collected his fifty cents. A few minutes later he came back with two more, and received the stipulated price of twenty-five cents for each of them. Then he asked Adams to go with him to his wagon. The bed was a tangled mass of rattlers, one hundred and twenty-two of them! Adams finally compromised by paying $5.00 for the lot.

In the country around the town evidences of newness were everywhere. As late as 1833 an observant traveler wrote that even in the neighborhood of Springfield "the cultivated fields form a mere speck on the surface of the prairie," while government land remained unsold within a mile of the town. Most farms were located on the edge of the timber. In the beginning settlers had looked upon the prairies as sterile—if trees wouldn't grow upon them, how could crops be expected to thrive? The fallacy of this belief was soon demonstrated, but land bordered by timber remained desirable by reason of the ease with which wood for building, fencing and fuel could be obtained. "A settler regards the distance of half a mile from forest an intolerable burden," wrote one observer.

The unbroken prairie, however, was more than mere wasteland; it was a thing of such beauty that few remained insensitive to it. In the summer tall grasses and brilliant flowering weeds, rippling in the wind like waves, stood as high as the head of a man on horse-back; while horses' hoofs and fetlocks turned crimson with the juice of wild strawberries. In the winter the very immensity of its brown barrenness was not to be forgotten. Never was the prairie so majestic, however, as when it was afire. Through the dry grass the blaze sped faster than a horse could run, a quivering, leaping rush of flame. Smoke rose in heavy clouds, and night became light. Men not known to possess a particle of poetry in their natures became lyrical in describing the sight.

On the farms, which were the chief reason for Springfield's existence, the methods were those of agriculture in its early stages. Once the prairie was broken—a hard job which required four or five oxen—little attention was paid to the crop until it was harvested. At the first planting corn was dropped in every third or fourth furrow and covered with the next turf. The resulting crop, known as sod corn, often yielded fifty bushels to an acre. Afterward corn was sowed in hills four feet apart. Machines to lighten work were unknown. Hay forks were made of forked sticks; hay was raked into rows with hand rakes. Wheat was cut and bound by hand, and threshed with a flail or trampled out by horses. In the spring, when ground was to be prepared for planting, corn stalks were cut off with a hoe and piled into heaps to be burned. Fences for keeping cattle in were made of rails split by hand, and hogs were allowed to run wild in the timber.

Throughout the first decade of settlement, each farm was almost entirely self-sufficing. This was necessarily so, for little money could be obtained from the sale of crops. The people of Springfield and other villages consumed only a small part of the farmers' surplus, and the cost of transportation to more distant markets often exceeded in value what remained. The experience of a settler named Thomas Beam, who lived near Rochester, was typical. In 1830 Beam raised a good crop of corn. He determined to sell it, take the proceeds and remove to Galena. He found that he was unable to get a cent of money. The best he could do was to trade the entire crop for a barrel of whiskey, which he traded in turn for a three-year old steer. Finally he sold the steer for $10.00.

What produce was sold for cash brought low prices. Throughout the decade corn brought from five to eight cents a bushel in the field. Butter could be bought for five cents a pound, eggs for three cents a dozen, venison hams for twenty-five to forty cents a pair. Prairie chickens had no value at all. Pork sold from $1.00 to $1.50 per hundred; while beef cattle three or four years old were worth $8.00 to $10.00 each. Milch cows brought from $5.00 to $10.00.

In the stores of Springfield produce was exchanged for goods more often than for cash. Old settlers told of trades they made in the early days—of exchanging thirty bushels of oats for eight yards of calico, or a winter's bag of 'coon skins for two hundred pounds of salt, or a bolt of homespun cloth for a set of china dishes. Money was scarce, and of uncertain value. Bank notes might be worth anywhere from nothing to 100 cents on the dollar, and even specie was treacherous, since there were many counterfeits and "shaved" coins in circulation. The currency situation, however, was of small importance to good traders, who found storekeeping the surest way to make money. "That business is the best that can now be engaged in, in this part of the State," a Springfield man wrote in 1828.

For several years even postage was often paid in poultry, jeans, or beeswax. Charges—usually twenty-five cents a letter—were collected from the recipient rather than from the sender. Mails came so infrequently that the arrival of the carrier was a big event. All the inhabitants of the town—and often of the country for many miles around—gathered at Iles' store, where the postoffice was located for a number of years, to see the mail distributed. John Williams, Iles' clerk, called out the names of the addressees, but letters were not delivered until the postage was paid, unless, of course, the person was "good for it." Williams told of a Scotchman who devised a system of skinning the postoffice. This man, who had relatives in the East, would meet every mail, but it was seldom that he accepted the letter which always came for him. Instead, he would take it, look it over longingly, and then remark, "I wude luve to read it but siller is too hard to get to be spent on a feckless letter." But now and then he would pay his twenty-five cents and accept it. Their curiosity aroused, Iles and Williams discovered that the clan had devised a cypher system of innocent looking marks on the outside of the letter. If the marks told the Scotchman that all was well with his correspondent he refused the letter; if they informed him that something was wrong, he accepted it. Needless to say, after this discovery the canny settler was compelled to pay cash before even a look was permitted him.

As time went on and Springfield slowly became larger, the occupations of its inhabitants began to cover a wider range. After the general store, the tavern was the next business to make an appearance. In 1821 Andrew Elliott opened the Buckhorn, and in early March, 1822, Elijah Slater and Thomas Price were both licensed to keep "public houses of entertainment" in Springfield. Prices were strictly regulated. Thus, for "victuals," a charge of 37½¢ could be made; lodging for the night was 12½¢. The sort of accommodations available can be guessed from the fact that the charge for stabling a horse for the night, without feed, was 50¢— four times the rate charged mere humans. Brandy and wine were to be sold for 25¢ per half pint, gin for 18¾¢ and whiskey for 12½¢.

One by one craftsmen appeared. Jacob Ellis had done blacksmithing even before Iles' store was built, but it was some years before other skilled artisans located at the town. Thomas Strawbridge, who came in 1824, was the first saddler, and Jabez Capps, who arrived shortly afterward, the first shoemaker. Not until 1829 did a hatmaker set up an establishment. By that time a considerable diversification of industry had taken place. "We have four public houses of entertainment (poor things)," Enos wrote in 1828, "five dry goods stores with good asortments for a new country three groceries well supplyed, which operates to the injury of the morals and purses of the Inhabitants—a post office a printing office a carding machine and power grist mill two blacksmith shops, two first rate shoe makers, and several coblers—three cabinet shops where good cherry work can be obtained at a pretty extravigant price—Carpenders, joiners and other mechanicks in the same proportion."

Keeping pace with the craftsmen were representatives of the professions. Gershom Jayne, the first physician, settled in Springfield in 1823. Shortly afterward Garrett Elkin, a Transylvania graduate, appeared. By 1828 there were four physicians living in the town. "They were men of intelligence . . . ," said John T. Stuart, who arrived in that year, "besides they were men of splendid physique, and able to endure the arduous labor of the practice of the day which required them to ride night and day, on horseback or in the sulky, for fifty miles around."

Stuart, himself a lawyer, found five other members of his profession living in Springfield at the time he settled there. All except James Adams were young men, and Adams was only forty-three. Court met only twice a year in Sangamon County, but by visiting the courts in the other counties within traveling distance it was possible for them all to make a living.

The presence of craftsmen, doctors and lawyers was significant. Keen observers of the American frontier recognized successive stages in its development. First came the "bee-hunters"—the restless adventurers who hunted for a living, indulged in a little crude farming, and moved westward when real settlement commenced. In the Sangamo country this class had ceased to predominate at the time when Springfield was founded. In their place came the first settlers, differing from their predecessors only in the extent of their possessions and in their somewhat greater stability. By 1825, however, a different class of men was arriving in number. A contemporary writer characterized this class as "enterprising men from Kentucky and the Atlantic States. This class consists of Young Doctors, Lawyers, farmers, mechanics &c, who found towns, trade, speculate in land, and begin the fabric of Society. There is in this class every *gradation* of *intellectual* and moral character; but the general tone of Social manners is yet too much relaxed. There is too much reliance upon personal prowess, and the laws have not yet acquired sufficient energy to prevent violence." The description fitted Springfield in the latter part of its first decade, and throughout the second.

It is difficult, however, to draw a line between successive stages of development. From the beginning some characteristics of a settled society were apparent. Schools are a case in point. One was established during the town's first winter, and never afterward were the children without the opportunity of learning their a b c's.

They were primitive affairs, of course. The first one was held in a log house located in a clearing on the north side of Washington Street between Pasfield and Lewis. Light was admitted from windows made by leaving out a log and inserting glass in its place. The pupils sat on backless benches made of log slabs with sticks for legs. There were no desks, the little writing required being done on a shelf around the wall. Later on facilities were better. One term of school was held in the old Masonic Hall, located in the upper part of a two-story cabin on the south side of Jefferson Street between Second and Third, and, after 1825, several terms were held in the frame court house on the northeast corner of Sixth and Adams. Admission was by subscription only, parents paying the schoolmaster a stipulated sum per week for each child.

As late as 1827 one individual was supplying the educational needs of the town, for in the spring of that year Enos informed an applicant for a school that the town already had a teacher. "We have a teacher of the english language . . . ," he wrote, "and as long as he keeps, it would not be possible to procure scholars for another school, besides Sir, the Citizens of this town have no idea of giving but little more to an instructor than to a hired man—of course more than two hundred and twenty five or fifty dollars could not be obtained for the year—Provided that we were without a teacher at the present time."

No one will ever know how much the first schoolmasters of Springfield contributed to the intellectual enrichment of their pupils, but it can be said with certainty that at least two of them aided in relieving the monotony of the town's existence. One Mendel, who had an excessive fondness for the product of Thomas Cox's distillery, was the source of much amusement. His most famous exploit took place during a term of court. While both school and court were adjourned for dinner, and Mendel was fortifying himself for the afternoon's work, his scholars tied a calf to the judge's chair and put twelve geese in the jury box. When the judge and lawyers returned, they found the schoolmaster in the midst of an excited speech, earnestly addressing the calf as "the honorable judge" and the twelve geese as "gentlemen of the jury." Erastus Wright was another personality, but in a different sense. To the citizens, his outspoken abolitionism—he was a New Englander—was a strange and dangerous doctrine; while the youngsters found a perpetual source of wonder in the trained elk which he rode and drove in harness.

The school's twin institution, the church, lagged behind in early Springfield. Itinerant preachers, like the famous circuit-rider, Peter Cartwright, held services, and at an early date a Methodist Society was formed, but no churches were built and no permanent preachers secured until near the end of the first ten years.

The reason was economic, for there is evidence of plenty of interest in religion. In February, 1825, for instance, the Edwardsville *Spectator* reported that the Sangamo Sabbath School Society, organized at Springfield nine months earlier, had brought ten schools into existence in Sangamon County and one in Fulton. Two superintendents and seven teachers had charge of seventy "learners." With naïve confidence in the numerical measurement of religion, it was said that 6,435 verses of Scripture and 755 verses of hymns had been recited. Another indication of popular feeling may be found in the action of the county commissioners who, in the autumn of 1826, ordered the purchase of a Bible and hymn book for the use of the occupants of the jail.

Since 1821 the Methodist Society had been holding meetings, usually in the home of Charles R. Matheny. More than once they talked of building a meeting house, but in the end they permitted the Presbyterians to beat them to it. A missionary of the latter denomination had organized a congregation in Springfield early in 1828, and when John G. Bergen, Princeton graduate and Presbyterian minister, settled there later in the year, he induced the congregation to undertake the building of a church. In all, $1,200 was subscribed, and it was decided that the building should be of brick. Accordingly, a brickmaker was imported from Alton, and preparations commenced. Not until the summer of 1830 was the building completed. It was located on the east side of Third Street, between Washington and Adams. Peter Cartwright called it a "little brick shanty," but his estimate was probably colored by jealousy, since the Methodists had been aroused to similar activity by the example of their rivals. Their structure, a frame building at the corner of Fifth and Monroe, was built on two lots which Pascal P. Enos had offered as an alternative to a subscription of $50 in cash. It was completed soon after the first services were held in the Presbyterian church.

In other spheres there were gropings on the part of Springfield settlers for the way of life of older communities. Fourth of July celebrations made an early appearance, the first one being held in 1823. At that time the citizens of the "Sangamo county" gave a dinner to Governor Coles and Daniel Pope Cook "as a mark of respect due them on account of their firm, independent, and uniform *republican* conduct." Two years later a second celebration was held "at the Spring of Col. Cox, in the suburbs of Springfield," where dinner was served and numerous toasts were drunk.

The toasts on both occasions reflected the modes of thought which prevailed in the Sangamo country. Ardent republicanism was evident not only in the orthodox Independence Day toasts—to Washington, the Revolutionary patriots, the Constitution—but also in the sympathy expressed for other aspiring peoples. Grecian independence was toasted several times; Bolivar, the South American patriot, was lauded; while the Holy Alliance came in for a rap in the following words: "May the bitterest tincture of the Bohun Upas be the mildest drink of their infamous brotherhood."

Toasts on both occasions revealed the place in the social scheme which the men at least thought the women ought to occupy. "The Fair of Illinois—May housewifery and proper economy ever be their delight," was the final toast at the dinner in 1823; while two years later nine cheers were given to the sentiment: "The Fair of Illinois—May they adorn their minds with useful knowledge, and their bodies with the fruits of their own industry."

At the first celebration the attitude of the settlers on the question which was then agitating the entire state—that is, whether a convention should be called to amend the constitution so as to permit the introduction of slavery—was made clear. One would naturally expect to find sentiment in favor of the change. Most of the settlers came from states below the Ohio River, and made no secret of their antipathy toward Yankees and Yankee prejudices. Moreover, in Springfield itself Negroes were held in practical bondage through the harsh indenture system permitted by the constitution. Nevertheless, the citizens were outspoken against the calling of a convention. Eleven cheers greeted the toast, "The Tree of Liberty, planted by the Ordinance of 1787, nourished by Ohio and Indiana—May Illinois never cut it down." Others of like tenor were greeted no less cordially.

Nine months later the attitude of the people on the slavery question was given expression in an address issued by fourteen of the eighteen men empaneled for the April grand jury. Expressing the belief that they represented "the feelings and sentiments of much the greater portion of the people of Sangamo," these men proclaimed: "We hope and trust the virtue and good sense of the people of Illinois will save them from the evils with which they are now menaced (the introduction of slavery) and we call upon the friends of freedom throughout the state to array themselves under its banner, and to sustain with all their energies the edifice of our political rights as it now stands."

The election, held in August, 1824, proved that these sentiments were an accurate expression of popular opinion. In Sangamon County 722 votes were cast against a convention as compared with 153 in favor of one. In the Springfield precinct the count was 373 against a convention to 75 in favor of one.

From the first, the Sangamo settlers took an interest in politics. Years afterward a voter described the first election held in Springfield for members of the General Assembly. "I was present at the general election, August 1822," he wrote. ". . . The voters were chiefly emigrants from the East and South, though a large portion of the men present were Indians and Darkies, they of course not being allowed the right of suffrage. The voting portion of the community were then called the Yankees and white men. Three men named Kinny, Parkerson and Edwards, had a long bench ranged along the Court House, on which they set their liquors. The polls were held in the interior. We all got plenty to drink. The white men sang songs, the Indians and darkies danced, and a general frolic occurred; but what has surprised me, as I have reflected upon those early days, we had no fighting. The great evil was, that every candidate had to fill his portmanteau with whiskey, and go around and see and treat every voter and his wife and family with the poisonous stuff, or stand a chance of being defeated."

Two years later the presidential campaign of 1824 aroused considerable enthusiasm. In Springfield John Quincy Adams and Henry Clay were the favorite contestants. Both were toasted at the Fourth of July celebration in 1823. As the election approached, the leaders became active. On September 11, 1824, Clay supporters held a meeting in Springfield, elected James Turley chairman and Thomas M. Neale secretary, and chose Neale, Elijah Iles and James Strode delegates to a larger meeting to be held in Carrollton later in the month. On the same day an Adams meeting was held in Alton, with Thomas Cox, Charles R. Matheny and William Harrison in attendance as Sangamon County's delegates.

At the election the two favorites stood almost even, 125 votes being cast for Adams and 123 for Clay. Only 37 out of the total of 294 were given to Jackson electors. Four years later, however, it was a different story. By that time Andrew Jackson's popularity had increased mightily, and he had no difficulty in polling nearly 700 of the county's 1,100 votes.

The election statistics furnish a rough measuring stick by which the growth of the Sangamo country can be gauged. Nearly four times as many votes were cast in 1828 as in 1824, and this in spite of the fact that during these years Sangamon County lost more than half its original area, while at the same time a large exodus to Galena and the lead mines took place. Of course, more lively interest may account for part of the increased vote, but even so, settlement was increasing rapidly. In the autumn of 1825 the editor of the *Illinois Intelligencer* of Vandalia counted the wagons passing through there on their way to Sangamon County, and estimated that in five weeks 650 persons must have been added to its population. And this was only one of the routes used by emigrants!

The arrival of new settlers added zest to life in the town of Springfield, for not much happened there to break the routine of daily living. Occasionally, however, an event took place which seared itself into memory so deeply that men never forgot it. Such was the Van Noy hanging.

On August 27, 1826, a blacksmith named Nathaniel Van Noy killed his wife in a drunken fit. He was arrested at once. The next day the circuit court met in special session and his trial commenced. On the 29th a verdict of guilty was returned, and the murderer was sentenced to be hanged on November 26. A large crowd assembled for the event, men coming twenty-five and thirty miles and bringing their families. At the jail a long procession formed—wagons filled with men, women and children, men and boys on horseback and on foot. Passing west on Jefferson Street, the crowd turned south on First to a gallows in the hollow north of the present State House. The wagon containing Van Noy was driven beneath the posts, the noose was slipped around his neck, and then the horses were started. And for many years thereafter events were dated by "the fall Van Noy was hung."

The Winnebago War was another event long to be remembered. In the summer of 1827 word came to Governor Edwards that the Winnebago Indians were committing depredations and that the miners in the vicinity of Galena were in serious danger. Edwards ordered Thomas M. Neale, the Springfield lawyer and surveyor who commanded the 20th militia regiment, to muster 600 volunteers and proceed to the scene of the disturbances.

Late in July the first volunteers from Sangamon County gathered in Springfield, and formed in a ragged line at the northwest edge of town. They were not a martial-looking group, but Colonel Neale's splendor made up for their deficiencies. Dressed in braided blue, with "epaulets, cock hat and plume, sword belt and spurs," he galloped up and down before his men—and so dazzled the boys of the town that they played soldier until winter set in.

A few days later the *Sangamo Spectator* recorded the departure of the troops. "On Friday last Col. Neale, with about

230 mounted volunteers, left this place for Peoria," Hooper Warren, the editor, wrote. "Other troops, which were not in readiness to go with the Colonel, will depart to-morrow, to join him at that place. Among these is a new company of riflemen, organized for the occasion, and commanded by Captain Edward Mitchell, Jr."

The expedition, thus bravely started, developed into something of a farce. At Peoria the regiment chose its officers. James D. Henry, Springfield storekeeper, was elected adjutant. Elijah Iles, elected major, was dubbed the "mule major" because of his mount. Gershom Jayne was chosen surgeon and William Smith, another Springfield man, quartermaster. After various difficulties—with provisions, not Indians—the regiment reached Gratiot's Grove near Galena, but being unable to find either Indians or the federal troops who were known to be in the neighborhood, Neale disbanded his command and the men straggled home.

The outstanding event of pioneer days, however, was the deep snow of 1830-31. Before it, in the memory of early settlers, all else shrank to insignificance. Births, deaths and weddings were dated by it, while stories of its vagaries passed into the folklore of the prairies.

After weeks of mild weather, snow commenced to fall on Christmas Eve, 1830. On Christmas Day it was a foot deep, and everyone was jubilant. Then the weather turned bitter cold, and the snow continued. Day after day it fell, until even on the level surfaces it was four and five feet deep.

For the youngsters of Springfield it was a time of hilarity. Sleds and sleighs were improvised and tied behind the cutters of Doctors Todd and Jayne, famous horsemen and fast drivers, until the doctors tired of the sport and discouraged it by driving headlong into uncleared streets. Sleighing parties were organized—to Sangamo Town for a barrel of flour, to Jacksonville to rescue snowbound friends or just for the fun of the trip. "Though the description of these rides, as given at the time, is vivid in my recollection," wrote Rev. John G. Bergen with ministerial reticence, "I shall leave them to the imagination of the reader, with the rough roomy sleigh, covered with buffalo robes, filled to overflowing with hale, happy companions, behind four fiery horses, champing their bits in the cold, ready for the plunge. The driver cracks his whip, the bells jingle as the merry parting sings out, and they are off—sometimes in deep drifts, where they flounder, snow within, snow without, snow everywhere, cold cutting the face, drifts blinding the eyes, horses rearing and plunging, and at times drawing their 'slow length' wearily along."

In many places there was suffering. Often it was impossible to get to a mill for flour, and in that case the snowbound family had to live on homemade corn grits. Hogs froze to death in the woods, and game animals died in great numbers, so that it was hard to obtain fresh meat. It was a serious matter when the wood supply ran low, for horses were not strong enough to drag logs through the drifts.

That Springfield escaped without hardship was due to Pascal P. Enos and his fondness for fine oxen. He had two large teams, and with them he broke the way to mill and wood lot. Throughout the weeks when the town was snowbound, he could have been seen almost daily, "with wolfskin cap on head, a Yankee frock buttoned close to the neck behind, reaching below his knees, belted over a great coat beneath, with legging protectors and ox-goad in hand," hauling huge logs to the doors of those who were destitute.

In the spring, when the streams were swollen with the melted snow, three young men of Macon County floated down the Sangamon to the Springfield landing, and came into town to meet the man who had hired them to take a flat-boat to New Orleans. Twenty-nine years later one of them, Abraham Lincoln by name, wrote that this was "the time and the manner" of his first entrance into Sangamon County.

CHAPTER III

County Town

THE year of the deep snow was a notable date in the history of Springfield. As definitely as dates ever can, it marked the end of frontier days and the beginning of years of thriving growth as a county town.

In 1831 and the years which followed, the population of Springfield increased rapidly. The *Sangamo Journal,* newly founded, reflected on the attainment of a population of some 800 or 900 and predicted great things for the future. "Our short residence in Springfield," said the editor in the first number, "does not enable us to speak with certainty of the comparative improvement of the place in the last with former years. We see enough, however, to convince us, that the advantages which Springfield offers to the merchant, the mechanic, and other professions, will not be much longer overlooked. Our population is rapidly increasing. A considerable number of buildings were erected last summer—many are now being built—and a still greater number are projected for the ensuing year."

Early in 1832 came news of an undertaking which raised the hopes of the populace to peaks of optimism. The greatest bar to the progress of Springfield, and all inland towns for that matter, was the lack of adequate transportation facilities. Agriculture was the foundation upon which all economic life was based, and the prosperity of agriculture depended entirely upon whether the farmer's grain and hogs could be shipped to the markets at St. Louis or Cincinnati or New Orleans at a cost low enough to leave him anything for the work of raising them. The farmer's income went up exactly as the cost of freight went down. Money in the farmer's pocket, moreover, meant prosperity for the merchants and lawyers and doctors and craftsmen who had goods and services to sell him. The cost of transportation affected everyone, and everyone was aware of the fact.

So far as Springfield and the Sangamo country were concerned, it was the first stage of transport—the trip by wagon to Beardstown or Alton—that absorbed a disproportionate share of the market price. Freight charges to Beardstown, a distance of forty-five miles, equalled the cost of shipping from Beardstown to Louisville, approximately 700 miles by water. Naturally, everyone was jubilant when Vincent Bogue, who owned a mill on the Sangamon seven or eight miles from Springfield, announced that he intended to open navigation on the river as soon as the ice broke up. Early in January, 1832, he wrote from Cincinnati to Edward Mitchell, the postmaster, asking that merchants reserve their freight for him. "I shall deliver freight from St. Louis at the landing on the Sangamo river, opposite the town of Springfield, *for thirty-seven and a half cents for 100 pounds,*" he promised. This was less than half the overland charge.

In the weeks which followed Bogue's announcement the people of Springfield caught at news of his progress with enthusiasm. The Cincinnati *Gazette* announced on January 19 that "the splendid upper cabin steamer *Talisman,* J. M. Pollock, Master, will leave for Portland, Springfield on the Sangamo River, and all the intermediate ports and landings, say Beardstown, Naples, St. Louis, Louisville, on Thursday, Feb. 2d;" and when a copy of the paper found its way to Springfield three weeks later, a public meeting was called at once to consider what measures should be taken to aid the enterprise. Bogue had asked that ten or twelve men with long-handled axes, and also a pilot who knew the channel, meet him at the river's mouth, so E. D. Taylor, Washington Iles and Thomas M. Neale were delegated to carry out his wish; while Thomas Moffett, Gershom Jayne and David Dickingson were charged with taking a subscription to defray expenses.

On February 22 the *Talisman* arrived at St. Louis. From that point on, her progress was exasperatingly slow. The axmen met her at Beardstown, but the cutting of overhanging timbers proved to be a harder task than was anticipated, while a disconcerting number of shoals were discovered in the river's channel. Nevertheless, on the 24th of March, she finally tied up at Portland, or Bogue's mill, on the Sangamon half-way between the present Alton and Illinois Central bridges. The townspeople crowded the river banks, while boys and sturdy settlers who had never seen a craft more pretentious than a scow swarmed through her cabin, dazzled by its magnificence. Hopes bounded upward. "We congratulate our farmers, our mechanics, our merchants, and professional men, for the rich harvest in prospect," the editor of the *Sangamo Journal* proclaimed; "and we cordially invite emigrating citizens from other States, whether they be poor or rich, if so be they are industrious and honest, to come thither and partake of the good things of Sangamo."

Enthusiasm was too great to be expended in mere words, so a ball was held to celebrate the emergence of Springfield as a river town. Prose proved to be too heavy a medium for the description of its glories, but the local rimesters rose to the occasion. Doubtless there was poetic license in the romantic rumor,

> And twenty bachelors they say,
> Were strung in Hymen's noose that day,

but in all probability the economic footnote,

Jabez's gude liquors went off slick,
Some for the cash but most on tick,

was literal truth.

Only one discordant note was evident, and that was not fully discernible until the following morning. Skipper Pollock, foreseeing a long and lonesome voyage, had taken care to provide himself with feminine companionship. At the ball the somewhat gaudy female he introduced was accepted for what he said she was—his wife—but doubts were raised when she exhibited too great a fondness for "Jabez's gude liquors" and became unduly demonstrative in her relations with the captain. The next morning the truth got out—the "quality" of Springfield had had as its guest a woman of easy virtue.

The revelation might have been taken as an omen. After the *Talisman* had lain at Bogue's mill for a week, her officers finally heeded the warning of the rapidly falling waters and pointed her nose down stream. Only by a combination of skill and good luck was she able to get away undamaged. The sponsor of the voyage was not so fortunate. He had operated mainly on credit, and when his notes came due he was unable to meet them. He solved the problem by disappearing, leaving his creditors to pay for the glory of opening a water highway to Springfield.

In spite of the failure of the enterprise, the people of the Sangamo country were unwilling to see an end to their hopes of cheaper transportation. It was natural that Abraham Lincoln of New Salem, announcing his candidacy for the legislature, should devote most of his address to the voters to an argument for the improvement of the Sangamon, for the address was issued two weeks before the *Talisman's* arrival, when the excitement was at its height. Three months later, however, other candidates were no less confident than Lincoln that the river could be made navigable. George Forquer urged it as an internal improvement certain of accomplishment, and Thomas M. Neale thought that it would take a mere $2,000 to make the Sangamon accessible for boats of sixty tons at least four months a year.

Close after the *Talisman* excitement came an event which deferred for a few months the realization of the hopes which the steamboat's arrival had aroused—the Black Hawk War. Early in April Governor Reynolds ordered Thomas M. Neale to muster 600 men of his brigade at Beardstown on April 22, to become a part of the force raised to defend the northwestern part of the state against Black Hawk and his braves. Three companies from Sangamon County answered the first call. The mounted volunteers went overland to the Yellow Banks (Oquawka) while the infantry was conveyed to the same place by boat. By the middle of May all were at Dixon's Ferry, within striking distance of hostilities.

From April until August the *Sangamo Journal* was filled with accounts of Indian battles, some real, more imaginary. Most of the Sangamon troops saw little fighting, and few casualties took place among them. Nevertheless, the lion's share of the war's glory settled on a Springfield man, James D. Henry, who exhibited real military capacity where the other commanders, of the regulars as well as the militia, exhibited a lamentable lack of it. Almost overnight he became a hero. A local poet celebrated his exploits in verse,

> Brave Henry, foremost in the fight,
> To him we owe the meed of might.
>   The Bard his deeds should tell,
> And proud our Sangamo should be
> That boasts a warrior such as he!

while upon his return to Springfield the citizens honored him and the officers under his command with a public ball at Miller's Hotel. Two years later an apparently irresistible movement to elect him governor developed. Meetings everywhere were held to place his name in nomination. All the while Henry was in New Orleans, struggling with advanced tuberculosis. He died March 4, 1834, weeks before his fellow citizens ceased to hold meetings in his behalf.

The war over, settlers crowded the roads to Illinois. "Strangers are constantly traversing our country, and examining it, with a view to settlement. . . ." said the *Sangamo Journal* in October, 1832. "Our taverns are constantly filled with strangers, and our stages are running full." Where before the great majority had come from Kentucky and Tennessee, there were now large numbers from Ohio and New England as well. "Emigrants are coming by thousands into Illinois," said the *Journal* in the autumn of 1833, "and from all quarters of the Union. On Friday last fifteen large wagons from St. Lawrence County, N. York, loaded with emigrants, arrived in our village, and drove up in front of the market house, in grand style. These emigrants had been about ten weeks on the journey, and enjoyed good health during the time. They design to settle in Sangamo County—to which we bid them welcome.—A few days previous a company of emigrants from Vermont for Green County, passed through this place. Our northern counties are daily receiving inhabitants from New York, Ohio, and the Eastern States." Settlers continued to come from the south, while many Illinoisans, lured to Arkansas by exaggerated tales of fertile land, were returning.

There were those in the Sangamo country, incidentally, whom no one could outdo when it came to talk of fertile soil. Simeon Francis, the editor of the *Sangamo Journal,* could become almost lyrical over turnips so large that only two could be put into a half-bushel measure, and words were inadequate when he came to describe "the tender, rich, crisp, twenty pound cabbages of Sangamo!" "The greatest difficulty our farmers apprehend is that they will not be able to harvest the produce of their farms!" he boasted in the summer of 1833. "This is the solemn truth. Hear it ye delvers on the worn-out lands of the east, and continue to

delve, if you have not ambition enough to make one effort
to secure a comfortable independence."

Francis was not the only one to shout the glories of the
Sangamo country. Travelers did their share of press-
agenting. Maximilian, Prince of Wied, wrote in 1834 that
in the neighborhood of Springfield the soil was so rich that
it was "scarcely necessary to do more than hoe the ground"
in order to obtain yields of eighty bushels of corn and fifty
bushels of wheat from an acre.   Others lavished praise on
the scenery. One visitor wrote from Springfield to the *Hartford Review* that "the vale of Arno is not more beautiful
than the valley of Sangamon, with its lovely groves and mur-
muring brooks and flowry meads," and enforced the point
with verse:

> Oh Italy, sweet clime of song, where oft
> The Bard hath sung thy beauties, matchless deemed,
> Thou has a rival in this western land.

It is impossible to measure the effect of such chants as
these on the hard-headed farmers and merchants and the
ambitious young professional men who were looking for
new homes in the West. The fact remains that they came to
Springfield and Sangamon County in increasing numbers.
A census taken in 1835 enumerated 17,573 people in the
county, a gain of nearly 4,000 in four years. Springfield,
with a population of perhaps 850 in 1831, counted 1,419
inhabitants in 1835. In the single year which followed an
increase of 460 took place. It was typical of a new community that the men should outnumber the women in the
ratio of five to four.

Even the fear of virulent disease failed to deter the emigrants. Anxiously throughout the latter part of 1832 the
people of Springfield followed the ravages of the cholera,
watched it approach closer and closer. In October cases were
reported at Chicago and Rock Island, then at St. Louis.

Late in November the first case appeared in Springfield. A near panic followed. The physicians published an open letter on the treatment of the disease, a makeshift hospital was fitted up for travelers and the indigent, and the town braced itself for a harrowing experience. Fortunately, the epidemic failed to materialize. Weeks passed without a case being reported, and the tension slowly eased.

The next year the experience was repeated. Throughout the spring and summer the *Sangamo Journal* was again filled with reports of the cholera in Ohio and Kentucky, and then as close home as Alton, Quincy and Jacksonville. In Jacksonville the epidemic was particularly severe, and for weeks all activity except the mournful business of burying the dead ceased. Anson G. Henry, a young physician who had just settled in Springfield, showed no little heroism when he spent a week in the neighboring town to observe the disease at first hand. Late in August it appeared in Springfield, but after causing two or three deaths, it suddenly abated.

The final scare, and the only visitation approaching epidemic proportions, took place in August and September, 1834, when seventeen deaths occurred in less than a month. Then, as before, the disease suddenly disappeared.

With growth, Springfield's appearance changed. Prior to 1831, the town centered about the small square at Second and Jefferson streets, where Iles' store and the first court house were located. Most of the houses were scattered along Jefferson Street. To the west, they commenced with the Town Branch timber (about Klein Street) and extended east to Fourth Street. There were only a few houses on Washington Street. Standing out from all others was the two-story frame residence of Dr. John Todd, the best house in town, which stood alone on the south side of the block between First and Second. The present square was on the fringe of settlement. Dr. Garret Elkin lived on the southwest corner of Sixth and Adams, while diagonally across from him, on the site of the present Illinois Building, stood the two-story frame court house which the county commissioners had built in 1825. On the west side of the square was a solitary two-room frame house. The square itself, swampy and grown over with weeds, contained only the whipping post, a gruesome monument which stood bare and awesome across from the present Marine Bank. North of Jefferson Street, east of Sixth and south of Adams, all was virgin prairie and timber except for the home and small farm of Charles R. Matheny near the intersection of Sixth and Cook streets and the small tract which Edward Mitchell cultivated north of the present Illinois Central freight house.

With the melting of the deep snow in the spring of 1831, changes commenced. First in both importance and influence was the new court house, located in the center of the present square. Brick, two stories in height, with a hip roof surmounted by a cupola, it was the most pretentious building in town. Soon after it was finished a brick market house was built at the northwest corner of the square. The completion of two good buildings was an incentive to further improvement. A plank fence, with stiles, was built around the court house, a public well was sunk and a pump erected, and the entire square sown with grass.

These improvements were the cause of a shift in the direction of the town's growth. Buildings began to appear on Fifth Street (then known as Main Street) and on Washington Street north of the court house. Most of them were one story in height and built of wood, but some were brick. A row of three two-story brick stores was built on Fifth Street south from the corner of Washington in 1831, while in 1835 Hoffman's Row of six two-story bricks, extending northward from the same corner, was constructed. The north side of the square was less fortunate. There, through the decade and afterward, stood a row of small ramshackle shops with wooden awnings over the sidewalk, known as "Chicken Row" from the fact that chickens and country produce were sold there.

In spite of the new court house and its improved surroundings, several years elapsed before Springfield as a whole outgrew the appearance of frontier rawness. Observers compared it with Jacksonville and found it inferior. William Cullen Bryant, who passed through both towns in the summer of 1832, wrote that "the houses are not so good (as those of Jacksonville), a considerable proportion of them being log cabins, and the whole town having an appearance of dirt and discomfort." (Jacksonville he had found "a horribly ugly village, composed of little shops and dwellings, stuck close together around a dirty square, in the middle of which stands the ugliest of possible brick court-houses.") Fifteen months later Patrick Shirreff, a Scotch traveler, saw it as "an irregular village of wooden houses," inferior in "buildings, arrangement, and situation" to its neighbor to the west. The rapid influx of newcomers in 1835 and 1836 resulted in the construction of many new houses and stores, but not enough to remove entirely the vestiges of its early crudeness. Even in 1837, after the legislature had designated it the future capital, an observer charitable enough to describe the public square as "a green pleasant lawn," and to call the structures which faced it "handsome edifices" was compelled to confess that many of the buildings in the town were small and that "the humble log cabin, the abiding place of some of the first settlers," was still much in evidence.

Growth and building activity were only two of many evidences of the rapid development which took place in Springfield in the years following the deep snow. Equally significant were the multiplication of businesses and the greater range of commodities for sale.

Advertisements in the first numbers of the *Sangamo*

Journal show that by the end of 1831 nine stores were selling
dry goods and groceries in Springfield, and there were probably others whose owners were as yet unconvinced of the value
of advertising. There was considerable variety in the goods
offered for sale. Thus Mather, Lamb and Co. announced
in November, 1831 that they were opening in "Mr. Enos'
New Store House on Main Street," a large stock of merchandise from New Orleans, Philadelphia and New York,
and specified, among others, the following commodities:
dry goods, groceries, hardware and cutlery, glass and china
ware, iron and castings, fur and wool hats, books and stationery, boots and shoes. The advertisement of McNeely
and Radford shows that in addition to liquors—cognac,
peach brandy, whiskey, Madeira and Malaga wine—groceries were stocked with molasses, brown sugar and loaf
sugar, all kinds of spices, tea and coffee, candy and chocolate,
raisins and even oysters. In addition, there was at least one
book store—that of William Manning, Jr.—while Edward
Mitchell, the postmaster, was authorized to take subscriptions for the *Lady's Book, Atkinson's Casket* and the *Saturday Evening Post.*

Craftsmen were increasing in number. Two hatters and
two cabinet makers were advertising in the *Journal* in 1831,
and William Kirkman, tailor, was offering to make "Gentleman's Clothing, and Ladies' Habits, in the most fashionable,
or in a plain style, as he shall receive directions." A potter
was already operating, and in 1833 John Hay set up an
establishment for the manufacture of yarn. Representatives
of the building trades were numerous.

With every year new merchants opened stores, new shop-
keepers appeared, new lawyers and new doctors came to
Springfield. By 1836, when a new census of the town was
taken, there were nineteen dry goods stores, six retail groceries, one wholesale grocery, four hotels, four coffee houses,
four drug stores, two clothing stores and two shoe stores.

Among the craftsmen represented were hatters, tailors, shoemakers, tinsmiths, painters, carpenters, blacksmiths, wagonmakers, saddlers, watchmakers and one barber. Eighteen doctors ("including steam doctors") and eleven lawyers resided in the town. The beginnings of domestic manufacture were evident in the enumeration of one foundry, one mill, four carding machines and five brick yards. An occupation now become archaic—at least in its original form—was suggested by the inclusion, among the buildings erected during the year, of "1 Bath House, Cost $5,000."

Yet the occupational field was far from adequately covered. Like most other mid-western towns, Springfield grew without plan, in haphazard fashion. In its making there was nothing of the colonizing process—the system of settlement by which whole communities, supplied in advance with doctors and preachers and blacksmiths and shoemakers, were transplanted to a new locality. No matter how essential to social welfare an occupation might be, the community had to wait for its benefits until some individual learned— or perhaps convinced himself—that an opportunity existed. Thus items like the following frequently appeared in the *Sangamo Journal:* "Springfield wants a Tallow Chandler and Soap Boiler; and it is believed would be able to give to a person who could unite the two professions, steady and profitable employment." In 1836 Richard H. Beach wrote from Springfield that buildings could not be put up for want of workmen, that the field was open for carpenters, masons, tinners and other skilled mechanics. It was almost impossible to obtain laborers and domestic servants. A good farm hand received $120 a year and his keep; a mediocre one $100. One hotel keeper told Patrick Shirreff in 1833 that he paid "two female helps" each two dollars a week, and added the perennially pertinent comment that "if it were not for a desire young girls have for fine clothes, he could not get one on any terms."

Some idea of what two dollars a week meant in real wages may be had from the commodity prices which prevailed. Butter sold for eight cents a pound, eggs for six cents a dozen. In small quantities dressed beef brought three cents a pound and pork two cents; by the carcass both were much cheaper. Due to the long distance they had to be hauled such articles as coffee and sugar were expensive, the former selling at twenty cents a pound, the latter at half that price. Still, one could live at the best hotel in the town, board and room both, for $3.00 a week for short periods and $2.50 for longer periods. A "French bedstead" sold for between $8.00 and $10.00, a "cherry table, turned legs with halves," brought $7.00—prices which were reputed high. The measure of all values, however, was land, and plenty of good land was still available at $1.25 an acre. Thus, with the proceeds of a year's work, a good farm hand could acquire an eighty-acre farm, and have something left with which to commence its improvement.

Land, at least that which was bought from the government, had to be paid for in money, but barter was still an accepted basis of trade so far as most commodities were concerned. All the merchants advertised that they would take country produce in exchange for goods, and some even preferred it to cash. Under the stress of necessity, and in spite of the lack of transportation facilities, an export business was being developed. In 1833 one merchant alone shipped 14,000 pounds of butter from Sangamon County. In 1840 Thomas Lewis, "at the sign of the Big Boot," made known his wants for the year: "20,000 good Dry Hides; 30,000 Deer Skins; 16,000 'Coon Skins; 1,000 barrels of Flour, and any quantity of Butter, Eggs, Lard, Beeswax &c." Except in the months when ice closed the Illinois River, produce taken in by the merchants was hauled to Beardstown, where it was loaded on shipboard for the large markets. When the Illinois was closed to navigation, Alton was Springfield's port.

The farmers were getting around the transportation problem in a different way. Freight charges on grain might be confiscatory, but cattle and hogs could be driven to market. It was a tedious task and a costly one, but less expensive than other methods of carriage. As a consequence, men of vision and resources turned more and more to stock raising. In 1835 George Power, near Athens, drove a herd of 800 cattle all the way to Philadelphia. Three years later it was estimated that 25,000 hogs were driven to markets out of the county in twelve months' time. Sheep were being introduced in large numbers, not to be sold for meat, but because both wool and tallow were easily transported and commanded a ready sale at good prices.

While merchants and farmers were making advances in spite of transportation difficulties, facilities for the carriage of passengers and mail were undergoing great improvement. In 1831 mails from all directions reached Springfield once a week. The following year mails from most nearby cities arrived twice a week. In 1835 mail from St. Louis came daily, from Jacksonville every other day, from Beardstown twice a week. Stage routes for passengers showed a corresponding increase in number and speed.

At best, however, travel by stage was a slow and costly way of getting anywhere. Under ideal conditions, it required three days to go to Chicago and cost $25 in gold. Under the worst conditions, one stayed at home. In the winter of 1836, for instance, the roads became so bad that all communication between Springfield and Vandalia was cut off for more than two weeks. When the creeks rose in flood times, stages simply had to wait until the waters subsided, for as late as 1835 there was not a single bridge in Sangamon County, which then included Menard and most of Logan and Christian.

At the same time that these breaches in the wall of isolation were being made, life in Springfield was becoming more interesting. Things happened more frequently than before. During the winter there would be a ball or two and sleighing parties, and perhaps, if the snow were deep enough, wolf hunts in which horsemen ran down the prairie wolves and clubbed them to death. In the summer of 1835 a circus came to town. Farmers and townspeople both were terrorized by the giant anaconda and fascinated by the bespangled girl who stood upright on a horse's back as she rode full speed around the ring.

Although no freak of the weather was ever to sink so deeply into memory as the deep snow, natural phenomena continued to excite interest. In the fall of 1833 a "meteor shower" aroused both wonder and fear. In the small hours of a November night myriads of "shooting stars" lighted the skies. Word of the spectacle spread, and a crowd gathered on the roof of the market house where a good view could be obtained. Many thought the heavens afire, and there were timid souls, familiar with the Book of Revelations, who believed—temporarily—that the end of the world had come.

Occasionally a dash of villainy spiced the local scene. Old settlers were fond of talking about the complete honesty of men in the early days, but stray items in the *Sangamo Journal* indicate that human frailty was just as marked in the Springfield of a century ago as it is today. There were the two Hoosiers, for instance, who showed up in the summer of 1833 with a "Portable Gas Lamp" which would furnish better light than candles at a fourth of the cost. They found a purchaser for the patent, and gave him the secret of the business in a formula for compounding a lighting fluid of whiskey, camphor, turpentine and pearlash. It cost him three dollars to find out that the mixture was no more inflammable than soft soap—and by that time the swindlers had vanished. A notice published in the summer of 1834 yields further evidence. "A meeting of the citizens of Springfield," it read, "will be held in the Court House on this afternoon, (Saturday) at 4 o'clock, for the purpose of devising means to suppress Gambling in this place. All persons friendly to the object are invited to attend."

Fourth of July celebrations were more elaborate than those which were held in the town's infancy. The advent of Independence Day, 1835, was marked by a "feu de joie" fired by Captain Merryman's Springfield Artillery. At eleven o'clock a procession formed at the Court House and marched to the Methodist Church, where the Rev. John G. Bergen offered prayer and Dan Stone delivered an oration "replete with just and patriotic sentiments." Afterward there was a dinner at Alden's Hotel, followed by the usual succession of toasts. The next year's observance was even more elaborate. In addition to the Artillery there were the Sharp Shooters, while a ball at the Court House and a fireworks display were added features.

The military companies were the most spectacular among the organizations in which Springfield citizens were beginning to find relief from tedium. The Artillery was organized in 1835, the Sharp Shooters—E. D. Baker, captain—the following year. They were composed of young men who drilled weekly and had a general good time. An exchange of visits with the Jacksonville companies made the year 1835 a memorable one for those who participated in it. On a Monday morning in late July the Springfield companies, with baggage wagons, tents and full equipment, set out for the neighboring town. The next evening they camped a short distance east of their destination. On the following morning Captains Hardin and Happy, with the Jacksonville cavalry and infantry, escorted them to a camp site on the prairie between the town and college hill. "The appearance of the Springfield troops was strikingly opposing," said the Jacksonville paper generously. "Their uniforms, the one red and blue, the other black and green, surmounted by appropriate plumes, were rich and showy; their arms bright as sunbeams, their officers gallant, military-looking men, and music full and harmonious."

Two exciting days followed. First came a dinner at Major Miller's Hotel, with "brimming bumpers, compliments and comic songs." The next day Governor Duncan reviewed the troops, and gave them a dinner on the lawn of his residence, with "the usual finale of good wine, good toasts and good feeling," and eloquent speeches by Baker and Hardin. After the dinner a sham battle was fought. The final event was a military ball "which, for numbers, music, decorations, brilliancy of dress and beauty of belles, has never been equalled, we make bold to say, in this state."

Three months later the Jacksonville companies returned the visit. On the day of their arrival they were dined at Captain Ransdell's tavern, and on the following day a barbecue, got up "in the true Kentucky style," was given in their honor. A military ball concluded the festivities.

Many Jacksonville girls had come to Springfield for the ball. When they left, the ladies of Springfield escorted them several miles on their way. The parting gave a writer in the *Sangamo Journal* an opportunity to display the sentimentality which all seemed to consider appropriate whenever the activities of women were mentioned. "It was on one of the loveliest mornings in this delightful, though melancholy season, Indian summer," he wrote. "Descending from their carriages to take their affectionate leave of each other, after three days intercourse as though they were all members of the same family, they formed a ring, hand in hand, and sang several appropriate parting songs. Then the last adieus were sighed—or looked, words being unutterable. It seemed like rending the bonds which link together, in sweetest friendship, an affectionate sisterhood." Whereupon the writer, having exhausted the possibilities of prose, turned to rhyme, and in nine stanzas lamented the departure of the "Maids of Morgan."

Shortly after the formation of the military companies another organization for the employment of leisure time was founded. It was the Thespian Society, organized in November, 1836. The first performance, a melodrama called "The Charcoal Burner," was given on December 7. So well was it received that a second performance was given a week later, and other productions were planned to follow. Nevertheless, there was an undercurrent of criticism. The Thespians recognized it, and tried to render it innocuous by pointing out that "many of the oldest and most respectable citizens of our town and county" had attended the first performance, and also by stressing the fact that the proceeds would be devoted to objects of charity or public utility.

At the same time that the Thespians were deriving amusement from amateur dramatics the Young Men's Lyceum was undergoing rejuvenation. It had been formed in the winter of 1833 by a group which included Simeon Francis, John T. Stuart, John Williams, Dan Stone and Thomas Moffett, but after the first year interest abated and meetings were held only occasionally. By 1836, however, it was functioning actively, its members debating such questions as "Do the signs of the present times indicate the downfall of this government?" and listening to addresses by doctors, lawyers, preachers and schoolmasters on subjects of moral and political interest.

Self-improvement was the purpose of the Young Men's Lyceum. Most of the town's organizations, however, went further, and aimed at the improvement of others also. There was the Colonization Society—formed in 1833 with Charles R. Matheny as president and John G. Bergen, Edmund Roberts and John T. Stuart vice-presidents—which sought to solve the slavery question by purchasing the freedom of slaves and inducing them to settle in Liberia. There was the Springfield Temperance Society, organized in 1832, which had as its purpose the promotion of total abstinence through voluntary association. There was the Juvenile Temperance Society, which took young people as its particular province. Finally, there were the organizations interested in the free distribution of the Bible—the Sangamon Bible Society in which the ministers of the town were the active leaders, and the Female Bible Society, headed by Mrs. Eliza Lowry.

With societies such as these coming into existence, one would expect to find a corresponding development in religious organization. Such a development did, in fact, take place. A revival held in 1833 made so many converts to Methodism that the Springfield church, until then served by circuit riders, engaged a resident minister. The Presbyterian congregation also grew, but in 1835 the basic weakness of Protestantism asserted itself, and thirty members of the First Church seceded to form the Second Presbyterian Church. In the same year Bishop Philander Chase organized St. Paul's Episcopal Church. Meanwhile, other sects had formed congregations. A Baptist society, formed in 1830, grew until at the end of its first ten years it had its own church and a membership of more than a hundred. Josephus Hewett, a well known Christian, or Campbellite, evangelist, had held a revival in 1832 and had made enough converts to organize the Christian Church of Springfield. So far Protestantism was alone in the field of organized religion, although throughout the decade Roman Catholic services were held by visiting priests in the home of William Alvey for the benefit of the communicants who lived in the town and surrounding country.

Religion, humanitarianism, self-improvement and mere amusement might all claim attention at one time or another, but the questions in which all the people were always interested were economic. The scarcity of capital, the price of public land, the cost of transportation—these affected everyone too directly to be long out of mind.

Candidates for public office reflected in their campaign

announcements the thought of the people. Until a law limiting the rate of interest to 12 per cent. per annum was passed in 1833, usury legislation was a subject of particular concern. Abraham Lincoln recommended it in 1832, while George Forquer, running for the state senate, observed pithily that he favored the passage of "a law limiting interest to some reasonable rate, which would require men who have but two or three hundred dollars, to go to work, instead of lounging about our streets and making their living by extorting off of the farmers, mechanics and laborers." Reduction in the price of public lands, distribution of the proceeds of land sales among the states, and the passage of a general preemption law were planks in many platforms. Several candidates recommended the establishment of a system of free public schools.

Transcending all other questions, however, was that of transportation. Farmers might drive their stock to market, and merchants become exporters in spite of freight costs, but the people wanted quick, cheap transportation for all. And if eastern capitalists, their vision unclouded by imperative need, failed to see profits in railroads and canals in central Illinois, that was a small matter: the people themselves would build them. Communities between Beardstown and Springfield were intent upon constructing a canal connecting the two places, and chartered a company for that purpose. In Springfield, however, a railroad to Alton was the project which aroused most enthusiasm. In March, 1835, more than a thousand citizens attended a meeting to further the enterprise, and appointed a committee to solicit funds for a survey of the route. Six months later the survey was made public, along with statistics to show that the road would be highly profitable when finished. A company was formed, and stock subscription books opened. "With railroad facilities to carry the immense surplus products of this country to market, our farms will quadruple their value, and our town will soon rival Lexington in population, wealth and importance," Editor Francis proclaimed.

Nevertheless, it was soon apparent that local capital was inadequate for this or any other similar undertaking, and that if anything were to be accomplished, it would have to be done, in large part at least, by the state. To bring this conviction to the notice of the legislature, an internal improvement convention was called to meet at Vandalia early in December, 1836. Springfield was represented by sixteen delegates. The convention divided on the question of whether the state alone should make all improvements, or whether it should limit itself to encouraging private enterprise by subscribing for large blocks of stock. The final decision—a compromise—was of small importance, for the convention had already accomplished its real purpose by demonstrating to the legislators that the people of the state were in earnest about railroads and canals and river improvement.

For nearly three months the legislators tussled with the problem. A large majority favored the creation of a system of internal improvements at state expense, but trouble in plenty came when the matter narrowed down to the specific projects of which the whole was to be composed. Every town and county wanted a railroad, a canal, or an appropriation for river improvement, and threatened to oppose the entire scheme unless its wants were satisfied.

Every county, that is, except Sangamon. Although the lack of transportation facilities had for years been its greatest problem, its nine shrewd delegates—the "Long Nine"— were silent on its claims. The reason for their attitude was to be found in the fact that they were seeking an even greater prize, and that if they won it, Sangamon County's transportation problem would take care of itself.

In 1820 the capital of Illinois had been removed from Kaskaskia to an uninhabited spot on the Kaskaskia River which was named Vandalia. The legislature expected that the state, which owned the entire site, would take a large profit from the sale of town lots, but the hope proved to be futile. Population increased slowly, the town gained a reputation for unhealthiness, and frequent complaint was made of the lack of adequate accommodations for the legislators. As a consequence, agitation for a new seat of government commenced long before the expiration of the twenty year period for which the location at Vandalia had been made.

The question first received the serious consideration of the legislature during the session of 1832-33, when it was enacted that at the next election for the General Assembly, that is, in the summer of 1834, a popular vote on the matter should be taken. Six places were nominated: Alton, Jacksonville, Peoria, Vandalia, Springfield, and an undetermined, uninhabited site called the Geographical Center of the state. The place receiving the highest number of votes should, in the words of the law, "forever hereafter remain the seat of government for the state of Illinois."

The people seemed to have recognized in advance the futility of the proceeding, for only 25,000 votes were cast— nearly 8,000 less than the number cast for governor at the same time. Their apathy was justified in the result. Alton led with 8,157, Vandalia came next with 7,730, while Springfield, with 7,075, was third. The other three received only a few hundred each. With so even a division between the three leading contenders, few were naïve enough to accept the result as final.

Springfield lost no time in laying its plans for the future. The *Sangamo Journal* and the *Illinois Republican,* founded in 1835, devoted columns to proving her superior claim to the honor. Candidates for the legislature, regardless of political affiliation, pledged themselves to do all in their power to secure the prize for their constituents. As a result, the Sangamon delegation approached the crucial session convinced that success was possible, and determined to attain it.

The game was played under the leadership of Abraham Lincoln, now risen to a position of influence in the House. The major stratagem was to defer positive action on the capital question until the internal improvement system should be finally adopted. For it was on the jealousy and cupidity of the counties and towns which wanted railroads of their own that Lincoln had based his plan of campaign. Sangamon County had nine votes, and those nine votes were available for a railroad here, a canal there, and grants of money to those who got neither, provided only that votes for Springfield as the capital were pledged in return. There were times when it seemed that the legislators could not be held away from the capital question, but in the end Lincoln was successful. On February 25, 1837, the law locating the capital by popular vote was repealed. In its place it was enacted that the location would be made by majority vote of the legislature on February 28, when it was certain that the internal improvement system would be out of the way. On the first ballot Springfield received 35 votes, more than twice as many as Vandalia, its nearest competitor. Its lead increased on both of the next two ballots, while on the fourth it attained a majority. In two years it would be the state capital.

When the news reached Springfield there was wild rejoicing, culminating in a huge bonfire built around the whipping post on the east side of the square. There were doubtless aching heads in the days that followed, for the groceries were doing a record business, but these were as nothing against the general belief that the town's fortune was made. Simeon Francis distilled into words the feeling of all when he wrote that "the owner of real estate sees his property rapidly enhancing in value; the merchant anticipates a large accession to our population, and a correspondent additional sale for his goods; the mechanic already has more contracts offered him for building and improvement than he can execute; the farmer anticipates, in the growth of a large and important town, a market for the varied products of his farm; indeed, every class of our citizens look to the future with confidence that we trust, will not be disappointed."

CHAPTER IV

Political Pot Bubblings

SIX weeks after the passage of the seat of government act the young New Salem law maker who had steered it through the legislature packed his scanty belongings in his saddle bags, rode into Springfield and arranged with Joshua Speed to share the latter's room above his store. On the same day the *Sangamo Journal* announced the formation of a new law partnership, John T. Stuart and A. Lincoln.

Although Lincoln, more than any other individual, was responsible for Springfield's new-found glory, the first weeks in his new home were depressing ones. The "flourishing about in carriages" which he noticed deepened his dejection at his own poverty and made him painfully sensitive of his social shortcomings. Three weeks after his arrival he moodily summed up his feelings: "This thing of living in Springfield is rather a dull business, after all; at least it is to me. I am quite as lonesome here as I ever was anywhere in my life. I have been spoken to by but one woman since I have been here, and should not have been by her if she could have avoided it. I've never been to church yet, and probably shall not be soon. I stay away because I am conscious I should not know how to behave myself."

But the mood soon passed. Within a short time the political pot was bubbling briskly. In stirring it Lincoln found an absorbing occupation, found also congenial friends and a

59

number of not-unworthy opponents.

In Sangamon County, as in the state as a whole, politics were nearing the end of an epoch in 1837. It was an epoch in which political parties, in the modern sense, had not existed. To be sure, men favored Jackson or Clay for the Presidency, called themselves Jackson men or Clay men and held meetings to further the cause of their favorite candidate, but that was about the limit of party organization. When a man wanted to run for the legislature, for instance, he either announced his candidacy or inspired a group of friends to call upon him to run. In the campaign which followed, the party label played no part. The candidate made no mention of his Jacksonism or anti-Jacksonism, but counted on personal popularity or persuasiveness in advocating internal improvement or usury laws to bring him success.

That is not to say that political campaigns were genteel, colorless canvasses. Frequently they were anything but that. When a man relied on personal popularity to bring him office, it was natural that his opponents should direct their attacks at his character and personal habits. And when personalities entered, there was no limit to insult and vituperation.

Consider, for instance, the congressional campaign of 1834. The contestants for representative from the third district, which included nearly half the state, were William L. May of Springfield and Benjamin Mills of Peoria, both Jacksonians. The campaign was calm enough until six weeks before the election, when a writer using the signature of "Illinois" opened fire in the Jacksonville *Patriot*. May, he charged, was morally unfit for office. During a previous residence in Edwardsville he had been indicted for burglary and had escaped conviction only by inducing the complaining witness to leave the state. Moreover, in 1825 he had seduced a woman living in Greene County, had promised to pay her $200, and then had bought her off for an old horse and a side saddle, representing that they were his only possessions.

May replied in the *Sangamo Journal,* paying for the space at advertising rates. He frankly admitted the seduction, but brought forth evidence to prove that he had dealt fairly with the woman. For the burglary indictment he had a neat explanation. It was secured under a misapprehension of the facts. True, he had been caught in a house in the middle of the night, but he had been there at the invitation of a woman of the household for the purpose of illicit intercourse, not robbery. When the truth was ascertained, the prosecution was dropped. "I have freely acknowledged," he asserted, "that in youth, and in early manhood I have committed many follies and indiscretions, and have been led by an ardent temperament to do what I have long and sincerely regretted, and for which I trusted I had long since made some atonement by an upright moral deportment before my fellow citizens."

May's complacency stung his opponents. "Yes, you were a boy," their representative, now calling himself "Agricola," retorted, "—a hot-blood mettlesome boy, just about arrived at the tender and innocent age of *thirty,* before the experience of years had taught you courage and discretion, just as the piping treble of your voice was deepening into manly bass and the tardy down began to adorn your chin." The "burglarly" incident was embellished. It was asserted that while he lived at Edwardsville May had fallen into such disrepute that all his friends but one had cast him off. That one was the man whose home he had entered; the woman in the case was his friend's wife. Thus to the offense itself was added the obloquy of betraying a friend and destroying his home.

Making no attempt at denial, May counter-attacked with a roar of vituperation. "Who is this 'Agricola' "? he demanded. "Some *puling,* sentimental, *he* old maid! whose cold liver and pulseless heart, never felt a desire which could be tempted, except for getting money, for fawning on the great and feasting his malice on slander and detraction, who fawns, flutters, lies and cheats, and

'Compounds for sins he is inclined to
By damning those he has no mind to'—

some spindle-shanked, toad-eating, man-granny, who feeds the depraved appetites of his patrons with gossip and slander!" The defense was good enough for the people of the district, who elected him by an ample majority.

Soon, however, other considerations than personal ones were to be deciding factors in even the most unimportant elections. The Jackson men, calling themselves Democrats, were building a party organization on lines which have endured to this day. Its central feature was the convention— the meeting of party representatives in which the party creed was stated and candidates selected. With the convention came a new conception, that of party regularity. Henceforth independence of thought and action were to be incompatible with good standing in the organization. The lay member of the party must vote only for the candidates selected by the convention; the candidate must subordinate his own opinions to the principles stated by the convention; the office holder must carry out only the measures approved by the convention. To violate these rules meant sacrifice of party membership.

In Springfield and Sangamon County there was lively opposition before the convention system was firmly established. The presidential campaign of 1836 was the occasion for the first test. It began early, eighteen months before the election, when Martin Van Buren was nominated by a convention held in Baltimore. Many Democrats whose Jacksonism could hardly be questioned refused to acquiesce in the nomination and came out in support of Hugh L. White of Tennessee, behind whom the old Clay-Adams following was reluctantly rallying. In so doing, they claimed the right of independent judgment, asserting not only that they were original Jackson men, but that their candidate represented the fundamental principles of Jacksonism better than the old General himself, who had wavered sadly in his old age. These were the men who drew the heaviest fire from the Van Buren supporters. Archer G. Herndon, most prominent among them, was singled out for particular attack. The *Illinois Republican,* newly founded Democratic paper, pointed battery after battery at him, but all to no purpose. In August, 1835, he was elected to the state senate over his opponent, John Calhoun, by a sizable majority.

To the anti-Jackson men, now beginning to call themselves Whigs, the convention system and its attendant doctrine of party regularity were hateful heresies. When, in the spring of 1836, the central group of Springfield Democrats picked a legislative ticket instead of waiting for individuals to announce their candidacies, the *Sangamo Journal* voiced the attitude of the opposition. "Heretofore the voters of this County have been accustomed to vote as they please," said the editor. "There are but few individuals here who have not, time and again, supported candidates of both parties; but this will be no longer permitted to Van Buren men. They must give up their private judgment—and be led up to the polls by a twine through the gristle of the proboscis. So says the caucus." No less reprehensible was the effort to extend party discipline to the presidential election. "The political contest in this State," said the *Journal,* "is between the friends of Judge White and Martin Van Buren. Jacksonism or Clayism has not, justly, anything to do with the matter."

Nevertheless, the organization of the Democratic party proceeded steadily. Impetus was given to it late in the campaign, when a movement for the election of William Henry Harrison gathered considerable force. In Illinois, where

White had never been a popular candidate, Harrison's name attracted many. Before long it was proposed that the anti-Jackson electors should cast their ballots for the man receiving the largest popular vote, White or Harrison. Since there could be no doubt of Harrison's affiliations—he had been a consistent opponent of Jackson—the recalcitrant Democrats who had clung to White were left out on the end of the limb.

The result of the campaign, in which Van Buren, unpopular though he was, carried the state by a safe majority, was a general clarification of the political atmosphere. Faced with the necessity of supporting the convention system and Van Buren on the one hand, or of opposing the system only to contribute to Harrison's election on the other, most of the independent Democrats surrendered their prejudices and reunited with their old associates. In so doing they gave greater unity to the Whig ranks, and at the same time carried to the opposition leaders the conviction that closer organization was essential unless they were willing to remain permanently out of office.

By early 1837, when Lincoln came to Springfield, local political lines were pretty clearly drawn. Moreover, within each party a small central group was in control. The nominal head of the Democracy was William L. May, the congressman, but actual leadership rested with George Forquer, long a lieutenant of Ninian Edwards, and only recently,—since 1834—a Jackson supporter. In John Calhoun, Forquer had a trusted supporter. Schoolteacher, lawyer, surveyor, Calhoun was a man of excellent mind and a political debater second only to Stephen A. Douglas. Douglas himself joined the group in April, 1837, when he took office as register of the Springfield land office. In spite of his youth—he was only twenty-four—he was already a power. Upon Forquer's death in 1838, and May's subsequent defection to Whiggery, he became the dominant figure in the Springfield clique.

Prominent among the Whigs were a number of native Kentuckians: John T. Stuart, handsome, courtly, a skillful political manipulator; Stephen T. Logan, small, eccentric, already a leading lawyer; Ninian W. Edwards, cold, reserved, distrustful of democracy; and William Butler, reputed to be the canniest political forecaster in the county. Active also were Edward D. Baker and Anson G. Henry. Baker, a native Englishman who had lived in Springfield since 1835, was known both for his egotism and his oratorical ability. Henry, a physician, was a fiery fighter with a capacity for making two bitter enemies for each warm friend. In temporary alliance was Archer G. Herndon, a hot-headed Virginian and one of the old settlers, who was soon to return to his original affiliation with the Democrats.

Each party had its newspaper. The *Sangamo Journal,* with Simeon Francis as editor, was the Whig organ; the *Illinois Republican,* under George R. Weber, was Democratic. In 1839 it consolidated with William Walters' *Illinois State Register and People's Advocate* of Vandalia, which followed the seat of government to Springfield, and was thereafter known as the *Illinois State Register.*

In the spring of 1837 an era of good feeling in local politics was coming to an end. For months a tacit truce had been in effect—the struggle to secure the capital for Springfield had required the united effort of all. Now that that was over, the good feeling which success had generated was wearing off. Both Whigs and Democrats were beginning to itch for a fight.

An election for several county officials furnished the occasion. Among the places to be filled was that of probate justice of the peace—the forerunner of the modern probate judge. The office itself was of no great importance, but when the Whigs put up A. G. Henry as a candidate, one of the bitterest personal and political fights that Springfield has ever witnessed was precipitated.

Henry—one of those positive individuals to whom men cannot long remain indifferent—was a gad-fly to the Democrats. Since settling in Springfield he had taken an active part in politics, and more than once his stinging articles in the *Journal* had brought blood. When he was rewarded by an appointment as one of the three commissioners to superintend the construction of the new state house, his political opponents were angered. When he became a candidate for the probate justiceship they determined to administer a spanking defeat.

At first the usual charges and counter-charges were handed back and forth, but in mid-June the Democrats opened up in earnest with an attack in the *Republican*. Henry, it was charged, had been appointed State House Commissioner on account of the "dirty work" he had done for the Whigs, and now the people were paying the price. To pay $700, as he had done, for the removal of the court house was absurd— $160 would have been ample. "The people are paying dear for the services of a desperate, reckless adventurer to write for the *Journal,*" said the editor. "At the rate he is progressing, it is probable that the $50,000 the people of this town have to pay, will about pay the expense of the foundation, and the Building itself will not cost the State more than $500,000, if A. G. Henry is allowed to superintend it."

The Whigs countered effectively. The *Journal* charged that the *Republican's* article was inspired by partisan malice; Henry called a public meeting and asked that his conduct be investigated. John T. Stuart was elected chairman and Robert Allen, a Democrat, secretary. Lincoln offered a resolution providing for an investigating committee, bi-partisan in make-up, which soon published a report in which Henry was entirely vindicated.

From the Democratic standpoint the Henry episode was a bad tactical error. Papers in towns jealous of Springfield pounced on the charge of extravagance, and called for repeal of the capital law. The Whigs saw their opportunity and seized it at once. The *Republican* and its supporters were traitors, enemies of Sangamon who would strike at the heart of their city for partisan advantage. Elect John Calhoun to the seat in the house which Dan Stone had resigned?—John Calhoun, "the candidate of those who bear a deadly hate to our County?" Never! On the first of July E. D. Baker won an easy victory.

Meanwhile, there had been other developments. Garret Elkin, the sheriff, had cancelled his subscription to the *Republican* when the article on Henry appeared. The *Republican* retaliated by printing some uncomplimentary remarks about Elkin. Elkin demanded the author's name, and when it was refused, took out his spleen on George R. Weber, the editor, with a horsewhip. As soon as Weber's brother learned what had happened he armed himself with a knife, found Elkin and a friend named Cutright and stabbed them both. Attackers and attacked were placed under arrest, but the newspaper war continued until the following notice, addressed to John B. Weber, appeared in the *Journal:* "Sir: In the last *Republican* you have made false statements about myself. You state, too, that you will maintain those statements 'any where and in any way.' I fully understand this information; and now inform you that your proposition is accepted. Call on me either personally or otherwise and the proper arrangements shall be made. It will soon be seen whether your 'honor' is a more valuable material than your 'statement of facts.' D. Cutright." Weber declined the challenge.

If the Whigs had been content to let the Democrats flounder in the unpopularity their state house charges had brought them, all would have been well. But that was a tame procedure for a group of mettlesome young politicians. James Adams, Henry's opponent, was too vulnerable a target to be neglected. Three days after the *Republican* had opened on Henry, the *Journal* printed a short letter signed "Sampson's Ghost." If the truth were known, the writer intimated, Adams would stand revealed as the author of the attack on Henry. But let him be careful. "Before he assails the conduct of other men, he should take a retrospective view of his own conduct—official as well as private. He must know that his own house stands upon disputed ground."

For six consecutive weeks communications from Sampson's Ghost—the shade of a man named Sampson who had once owned the land on which Adams lived—appeared in the *Journal*. With each letter the insinuations became more pointed, in spite of Adams' vehement denials and charges of persecution. Two weeks before the election, which was to be held on August 7th, the Ghost became explicit. "I must again ask you to give some account of your trade with me," he wrote, as if addressing Adams, "—how you came to take advantage of me and draw from me a lease of two lots for ten years, for the great consideration of ten dollars—so as to place beyond my control for ten years, two lots, which I had purchased for my own especial benefit. I must also, again, ask you to refer me to some of the respectable citizens of Springfield who knew of that lease, before I can believe that I could have been so crazy as to give you such a lease. I wish to leave my memory purged from the charge of insanity."

The next week Sampson's Ghost added a second charge. "There is another subject which the People wish to understand," he wrote. "I allude to the case of *Joseph Anderson*. You are aware that a lot of land of ten acres, or thereabouts, which appears to be deeded to you on the Record Books of this county, is claimed by the heirs of the said Joseph Anderson—that they have brought a suit against you in the Circuit Court of this County for the said land."

Just before the election a long hand bill on the Anderson land emanated from the press of the *Sangamo Journal*. Addressed to the public, the author gave as reasons for issuing it the existence of "considerable excitement" in regard to certain of Adams' land titles, and the assertion of the General that "the whole has been gotten up by a knot of lawyers to injure his election." The hand bill was unsigned, but the *Journal* editor was authorized to give the writer's name to anyone who might request it. Lincoln was quickly revealed as the author.

According to Lincoln's statement, the widow and son of one Joseph Anderson had come to Springfield in the spring of 1837 to sell a ten acre lot of ground which they claimed as the property of the deceased husband and father. Finding the land claimed by General Adams, they had retained Stuart and Lincoln to start suit for its recovery. Lincoln at once commenced an examination of Adams' title. Discovering a flaw in the record, he asked Talbott, the recorder, to get the original papers from Adams. Talbott complied, found that the flaw was only a copyist's error and took the original deed to Lincoln. When Lincoln unfolded it a paper fell out. It was an assignment of a judgment by Anderson to Adams—a necessary link in the latter's title. Yet it was dated several months prior to the date of the judgment, it was in Adams' hand-writing, and it appeared to be freshly written. Lincoln concluded—although he stopped short of making the explicit charge—that Adams had forged it.

The election followed before Adams and the Democrats had time to circulate a reply. The Whigs, however, had overshot. To many people Adams was the object of a persistent persecution. As a consequence, he received 1025 votes to 792 cast for Henry.

The Whigs were bitterly disappointed. Some of them, however, were able to laugh at one of Lincoln's stories which was going the rounds. Several years ago, Lincoln said, he had been traveling to Springfield when he met a resident of the place who was going in the opposite direction.

"Good evening, friend," said Lincoln; "how far is it to Springfield?"

"Well, I guess it's about five miles," the other answered.

"Are you just from there?"

"I am."

"What's the news there?" Lincoln asked.

"Well," the Springfielder replied, "there's nothing of any account but a sad accident that happened the other day—you don't know Gineral Adams?—Well, the Gineral went to stoop down to pick some blackberries, and John Taylor's calf gave him a butt right——"

"You don't say so! And did the General die?"

"No, by God, but the calf did!"

In years to come malicious Democrats might have turned Lincoln's story against himself, for, while he escaped the sad fate of John Taylor's calf, he failed to make any impression on the General's popularity. The Whig lawyers, convinced that Adams was a malefactor who deserved exposure, refused to let the matter drop. Two weeks after the election the *Journal* reprinted Lincoln's pre-election hand bill, and with it a blanket denial of wrong-doing from Adams. For four months the newspaper controversy continued, a bewildering succession of charges, counter-charges and denials. Into it were drawn Elijah Iles, Benjamin Talbott, Logan, Stuart and A. G. Herndon. Bitter animosities developed; friendships of long duration were broken.

Finally, in November, the *Sangamo Journal* went the limit and published an indictment for forgery which had been brought against Adams while he was a resident of New York. When even this failed to shake the townspeople's confidence, the Whigs gave up. Adams was twice re-elected probate justice, and died in office in 1843. In the courts the suit which the Whig lawyers had brought against him on behalf of Anderson's heirs never came to trial, and was finally dropped when Adams died.

While the Adams controversy had been running its length, a sharp attack against Springfield's prospective glory as the capital had been made and beaten off.

Early in 1837 financial panic suddenly struck the country. The speculative mania and the era of extravagance which had loaded Illinois with the internal improvement system collapsed. Financial houses failed in rapid succession. In April the State Bank at Springfield suspended specie payments. Early in June the *Journal* summed up the business situation with a wail: "One loud, deep, uninterrupted groan of hard times is echoed from one end of the country to the other."

The state was in a bad way. Large sums of state money were in the state banks, whose charters were forfeit when they suspended specie payments. Yet they had been forced to do so, hoping that they would receive legislative approval of their action in the near future. Moreover, panic conditions were making it practically impossible for Illinois to secure loans for the internal improvement system. Governor Duncan, summoning the legislature to meet in special session on July 10, called for appropriate legislation—for legalization of the banks' suspension and for a repeal of the internal improvement system. But the Sangamon delegation, well aware of the intimate connection between the system and the capital law, expected trouble on that score as well. It came early in the session when W. L. D. Ewing of Vandalia introduced a bill to repeal the seat of government act. Springfield's "arrogance" was not to be endured; she had "sold out" to the internal improvement men, had secured the passage of the law by "chicanery and trickery," said Ewing. Lincoln made sharp reply, and the delegation, under his leadership, killed the repeal bill.

The session lasted less than two weeks. The banks were given a breathing spell, but instead of following the Governor's advice on internal improvements, the legislature administered a stinging rebuke and directed the commissioners in charge of the system to proceed immediately with surveys and construction.

This, together with the defeat of the capital repeal bill, was "a faithful performance of official duties" so far as the people of Sangamon County were concerned. When, after adjournment, a number of the legislators stopped in Springfield on their way home, the citizens invited them to a public banquet at Spottswood's Rural Hotel. After a "sumptuous dinner" the cloth was removed, and toasts to Illinois and the legislature were drunk. Orville H. Browning of Quincy spoke of the Long Nine— "their judicious management, their ability, their gentlemanly deportment, their unassuming manners, their constant and untiring labors for your interests"—whereupon they were toasted: "Well done good and faithful servants." There followed a long series of toasts in which the future of Illinois, to be made incomparably prosperous through the railroads and canals of the improvement system, and also Springfield's glory as the capital, were viewed in the rosiest optimism.

Once more Springfield was to be the object of attack before she was to rest secure in her claim to the capital. The occasion came during the legislative session of 1838-39, when Lincoln introduced a bill to appropriate $128,300 for the completion and furnishing of the state house. Orlando Ficklin of Coles County immediately moved two amendments—that the amount requested should be donated by individuals, and that at the next legislative election the people of the state should be given the opportunity of voting for or against the removal of the seat of government to Springfield. Both were voted down. Immediately a Vandalia delegate moved an amendment directing the Governor to reconvey the public square to Springfield and providing that the people should express their preference for the capital site in the next election. The amendment was decisively defeated. But the contest was not yet over. A motion to defeat the appropriation bill was made and lost; another to subject it to popular vote was defeated. Finally, after all means of stopping it had failed, Lincoln's bill passed. With it serious opposition to the location of the capital at Springfield ceased.

However, in clinching her hold on the capital, Springfield had to take a dose of bitter medicine in the loss of county territory. It was inevitable, of course, that the huge area with which Sangamon County was originally endowed would be speedily curtailed as settlement progressed, but by 1825, after the present counties of Morgan, Scott and Cass had been cut from her western limits and most of the territory bordering on the Illinois River had been severed, her people hoped that her limits would remain unmodified. But in the years which followed, agitation for further division gained momentum. Residents living near the boundaries complained that it took two days, and often longer, to travel to Springfield and return to their homes; and proprietors of town sites which aspired to be county seats abetted their discontent. Springfield protested, tried to send to the legislature men who were pledged against county division. By 1838, however, the movement was too strong to be resisted, and the session of that year saw the creation of Menard and Logan to the north and Dane, now Christian, to the south. Springfield made a wry face, but finally took consolation in the fact that the limits of Sangamon County, though curtailed, were still extensive enough to permit her to be called the Empire County.

Meanwhile, the ceaseless activity of stone cutters, brick masons and carpenters in the public square was a constant reminder of the day when Springfield would be a town apart. No time had been wasted in commencing work on the state house. On March 11, 1837—less than two weeks after the passage of the bill transferring the capital—the county commissioners conveyed the public square to Governor Duncan.

In April advertisements offering a premium of $300 for a plan for a new building appeared in the leading papers of Illinois and neighboring states. By the end of May the court house had been removed. By mid-June excavation was almost completed, and piles of limestone rock and sand were standing on the square.

On the Fourth of July the corner stone was laid with elaborate ceremonies. The military companies, including Capt. Thomas M. Neale's newly organized cavalry, fired a salute at sunrise and spent the morning in parading. In the afternoon the members of the Mechanics' Institute formed in procession and marched to the Methodist Church, where Edmund R. Wiley delivered an address. The citizens then gathered at the state house. When the corner stone was edged into place, E. D. Baker mounted it and delivered the oration of the day. "At the close of the address the welkin rang with huzzas—a salute was fired—and the people and military retired, highly gratified with the proceedings of the day."

Throughout July long queues of oxen, ten and twelve to a team, drew heavy blocks of stone to Springfield from the quarry south of Cotton Hill. And as people noticed its warm buff color, the feeling grew that this was the proper material for the building. The original plans—the work of Springfield's baker-architect, John F. Rague—had called for a brick superstructure on a stone foundation. Late in July the *Sangamo Journal* reported the preference for stone: "The members of the Legislature, and other distinguished citizens, who have passed through here . . . have strenuously urged upon the Commissioners, the propriety of constructing the walls of this beautiful material." As the months passed and the foundation neared completion, the conviction spread that the use of brick would be a mistake. Finally, in December, when outdoor work was stopped for the winter, the commissioners announced their decision—the building would be constructed of stone. It was a wise conclusion, for, aside from its graceful lines, the chief charm of the old building as it stands today is the soft buff color of its walls.

Work on the State House continued throughout 1838 and 1839. Early in 1840 it was ready for partial occupancy, but years were to elapse before it presented a finished appearance. In 1843, for instance, one of the newspapers commented on the fact that the roof leaked, and that much of the stone intended for the front columns was lying about the yard, where it was in daily danger of injury. Not until 1853 was the building completely finished.

For the people of Springfield it turned out to be a costly structure. They had willingly accepted the provisions of the capital law requiring them to convey the square to the state and donate $50,000 toward the cost of the state house, but when panic struck the country a few weeks later the second part of their obligation seemed staggeringly large. Nevertheless, by various expedients the money was raised. One-third of the amount was assessed property owners, who borrowed the money from the State Bank on the understanding that they would be given five years to pay their notes. By this means the city treasurer was able to make the first payment of $16,666.67 in December, 1837. When the second instalment fell due in the spring of the following year, the city, which had undertaken to pay it, had no money. In the emergency one hundred and twenty-nine of the leading citizens executed a joint note to the State Bank for the amount due, the city promising to reimburse them in case they would be called on for payment. The final instalment, which had been assumed by Sangamon County, was ultimately discharged in internal improvement scrip, worth about fifteen cents on the dollar.

The construction of the state house attracted many workmen to Springfield. Among them was Jared P. Irwin, a brick mason of Philadelphia. Irwin, a serious young man with a strong religious bent, kept a diary. From its yellow pages much can be surmised about the daily flow of life in Springfield nearly a century ago.

Irwin reached Springfield in the first week of June, 1837, having traveled from Alton to Naples by steamer and thence through Jacksonville on the stage. "My journey from Naples here was very interesting," he noted, "—it being prairie nearly all the way and the first I ever saw. The sight of a large prairie is sublime to a person unaccustomed to seeing them."

A few days later he recorded an event of more than passing interest—the visit of Daniel Webster, first of the distinguished visitors to be attracted to the future capital. Webster, touring the West with his family, was escorted into Springfield on the morning of June 19 by a detachment from the military companies. In the afternoon he attended a barbecue. Then came the inevitable toast: "Daniel Webster: The able defender of a sound circulating medium, in opposition to mere paper money on the one hand, and an exclusively metallic currency on the other." Webster responded in a speech which lasted an hour and a half. The next day he departed for Tremont, leaving the Whigs at least flushed with pride.

For the most part, however, the entries in the diary had to do with the ordinary occupations of a sober, industrious citizen. Those which follow are typical:

June 22, 1837. I this day commenced laying the foundation of the *Capitol,* or *State House,* at $2.50 pr. day.

July 4. This afternoon we laid the 'corner stone' of the State House, after which an Oration was delivered suitable to the occasion. The whole passed off with much eclat.

August 15. Returned from a Camp Meeting held 6 miles west of Town—a poor concern when compared with those of the *East*.

October 18. This evening our beloved stationed Preacher, '*H. Crews*' preached his valedictory sermon and in the morning takes his departure for his new Appointment. He has had the pleasure of closing his labours here in such a revival of religion as I never before witnessed. It has lasted about 5 weeks, and about 130 souls professed to have experienced justification by faith in the atonement. The Shout of the 'King in the Camp' was heard at morning, and noonday and at night.

December 25. I've spent the evening very agreeably at the house of a friend (Rev. Jonas Whitney a Presbyterian preacher) at a little *singing party*.

Then, in early March, 1838, came a note of tragedy. Upon returning from a short visit to Alton, Irwin recorded: "Since I left here the Rev. Dr. J. N. Early (a friend of mine) was *Shot* by H. B. Truett, it has caused a great excitement and it is generally thought he will be hanged."

The Early killing, one of the exciting episodes in Springfield's past, was the outcome of a political quarrel. Truett was a son-in-law of William L. May, Early a physician and Methodist exhorter. Both were Democrats. Friction between them arose when a Democratic convention at Peoria passed a resolution disapproving of Truett's nomination as Register of the Land Office at Galena. Truett blamed Early for the censure. On the evening of March 7 he entered the parlor of Spottswood's Hotel in Springfield, where Early and several other men were sitting. One by one the others left. When the last had gone, Truett asked Early if it were true, as he had been told, that he was the author of the Peoria resolution. Early declined to answer unless Truett gave him the name of his informant, which he refused to do. Hot words followed, Early picked up a chair to defend himself, Truett drew a pistol and pulled the trigger. Early fell, mortally wounded.

Popular feeling was strong against Truett. Nevertheless, at the trial which took place six months later, the skillful defense of Stuart and Lincoln secured his acquittal.[1] "The

[1] In the *Illinois State Register* for Nov. 17, 1855 is to be found a footnote to this episode: "H. B. Truett, formerly of this state, fought a duel with Ashton E. Smith, at San Francisco, on the 19th ult. Smith was slightly wounded,

evidence against him was *clear and conclusive,*" Jared Irwin noted in disgust.

For the remainder of his residence in Springfield the entries in Irwin's diary reflect a community reaching for the amenities of a cultured life, but with the shadow of the frontier occasionally falling across it.

September 15, 1838. Today a caravan or company of 'Mormons' with 67 waggons numbering about 800 Souls passed through this place on their way (as they say) to the 'Promised Land' west of Mississippi. The sight was quite imposing.

September 30. Today a remnant of the Tribe of Pottawatomie Indians passed through town on their journey to their new homes west of the Mississippi. . . . The number was about 800 souls, each one having a horse (save the sick, they being in waggons.)

December 25. For 3 nights past I have been greatly entertained with a course of Lectures to the Young by Rev. Dr. Perry formerly of Phila. but now President of a College in this State. His Lectures were very edifying—he was eloquent.

December 31. This being the last night of the year we held a Temperance Meeting in town, address by Mr. Denman, Merchant of Phila. (being here on business) it was good & I for the first time attached my name to a 'Temperance Pledge.'

January 24, 1839. For 4 nights past I have sat with great delight & heard Col. Lehmanowsky, formerly an officer in Napoleon's army, lecture on the character, disposition, manners of Napoleon & Josephine Empress & first wife of Nap—his wars & their reasons from the first campaign of Italy till the Battle of Waterloo—his fall & exile to 'St. Helena'—his & Madam Josephine's death. Also a short history of his (Lehmanowsky's) own life etc. His lectures were highly interesting, so much so that I have taken notes. He is Polander, 6 feet 3 inches high. He is now a preacher of the Lutheran Church & preached 3 times for us last Sunday.

April 8. This evening heard with pleasure Porter Clay Esq. (Bro. of the Hon. H. Clay) deliver his first lecture in behalf of the 'Colonization Society,' he was recently been appointed agt. of the 'great valley' & has this evening commenced upon the duties of his

and Truett's trousers were torn. This is the same Truett who, eighteen years ago, killed Dr. Early, in this city."

mission, intending to lecture & form Societies throughout the length
& breadth of the Valley. He is quite eloquent.—May success attend
him.[2]

So far as the people of Springfield were concerned, colonization was the respectable way of dealing with the slavery
question. The local society had been functioning for several
years, and numbered many of the town's leading citizens
among its members. But let the opponents of the "peculiar
institution" go further, let them even mention with approval
the dread word "abolition"—and sharp rebuke was quick
to follow. In mid-October, 1837, when the Rev. Jeremiah
Porter announced his intention of speaking on slavery in the
First Presbyterian Church, a crowd collected and swore that
it would mob him. E. D. Baker finally persuaded them to
allow the speaker to talk, and after the address Edward
Beecher, President of Illinois College at Jacksonville, induced the angry citizens to permit Porter to leave town un-
harmed.

But the people were determined not to let the matter
drop until they had given uneqivocal expression to their feelings. A few days later a public meeting was held in the court
room. With Judge Thomas C. Browne in the chair, the following resolutions were passed:

Resolved, That the efforts of abolitionists in this community, are
neither necessary or useful.

Resolved, That as citizens of a free State and a peaceable community, we deprecate any attempt to sow discord among us, or to
create an excitement as to abolition which can be productive of no
good result.

Resolved, That in the opinion of this meeting the doctrine of
immediate emancipation of slaves in this country, (although pro-
mulgated by those who profess to be christians), is at variance with
christianity, and its tendency is to breed contention, broils and mobs,

[2]On the day after this last entry Irwin left Springfield, not to return
until 1857.

and the leaders of those calling themselves abolitionists, are designing, ambitious men, and dangerous members of society, and should be shunned by all good citizens.

Fourteen days after the passage of these resolutions Elijah P. Lovejoy fell before the mob at Alton. In all probability, Springfield citizens deprecated the outrage, but so far as it is possible to ascertain today, not one word of condemnation was spoken publicly. Even Abraham Lincoln, speaking before the Young Men's Lyceum three months later on the evil consequences of mob action, carefully refrained from alluding to the Lovejoy murder, although it would have been a better illustration of his thesis than any of the incidents he cited.

In the light of the southern origin of most of them, the attitude of the townspeople on abolition was a natural one. The puritanism occasionally evident in the discussion of other subjects must be explained on other grounds. Probably it was the religious revival, noted by Jared Irwin, which was responsible for the frame of mind which counted condemnation of the theater and novel reading a moral duty. The evangelical theology of the day was almost unbelievably narrow, and perfectly capable of seeing the hand of the devil in either activity.

Moralists had not seriously challenged the amateur dramatics of the Thespian Society, but when professionals made their appearance there was consternation among them. Isherwood and MacKenzie, the experienced producers who fitted up the dining room of Major Iles' new American House for a series of plays to commence in February, 1838, must have been aware of the criticism they would encounter, and doubtless had something to do with the newspaper puffs which began to appear—brief items calling attention to the way in which the theatrical company emphasized "the beauties of virtue and the hatefulness of vice."

To one such comment, signed "Philo Drama," a writer in the *Illinois Republican* replied with an intemperate screed in which all the prejudices of the rigid moralists found expression. "I challenge Philo Drama to point to the spot where Christianity has looked with a tolerating eye upon the stage," he proclaimed, " . . . it is a school of vice, a hotbed of iniquity, a pander to pollution and death. . . . Does Philo Drama wish Springfield to become what some of the eastern cities are—a sink of pollution, a hole of every foul spirit? The stage has always flourished in proportion to the increase of corruption and depravity in society. . . . The theatre, above all other places, is the spot where the bonds of virtue are first loosened, and finally dissolved."

A tabu even stranger to modern opinion was given forceful expression when C. Birchall and Company of the Springfield Book Store announced that if they could secure one hundred subscribers at $5.00 each per year they would open a circulating library. In all innocence they announced that in addition to the classics contained in the hundred volumes of Harpers' Family Library they would provide the works of such authors as Scott, Cooper, Irving, Maryatt, Bulwer, Fielding and Smollet, "together with the Novels of the most popular authors of the day." To H. A. P., writing in the *Sangamo Journal,* this was gambling with eternal damnation. Novel reading was an unqualified evil. "But, 'say you, has my author ever read Scott, Bulwer, Cooper, Maryatt, etc.?' " he asked oratorically, after quoting a tirade against the reading of fiction. "Yes, he has read them all, and with too much care. He knows every rock and every quicksand; and he solemnly declares to you, that the only good he is conscious of ever having received from them, is a deep impression that men who possess talents of such compass and power, and as perverted in their application, must meet the day of judgment under a responsibility which would be cheaply removed by the price of the world."

Attitudes such as these, however, soon lost whatever force they originally possessed. Opposition to the theater failed to keep large and enthusiastic audiences from attending performances, while even in the best of families Scott and Dickens could be indulged in without fear of broiling in the hereafter. Springfield was small, its streets were unpaved, its homes and buildings for the most part unpretentious, but by the time the state offices were located there it had at least made a start in the direction of occupations and diversions in keeping with the position it was soon to assume in the life of the state.

CHAPTER V

A Young State Capital

ON June 20, 1839, Gov. Thomas Carlin issued a
proclamation ordering the state officers to remove from Vandalia to Springfield. The Board
of State House Commissioners, he recited, had
notified him that suitable rooms were ready. By the terms
of the proclamation the removal was to be completed by
July 4th.

Immediately the new capital exhibited unaccustomed activity. In its first issue after the removal of the state officers
the *Sangamo Journal* printed a long list of guests at the
local hotels. The next number of the paper contained the
names of forty-three lawyers from twenty-one Illinois towns,
in addition to seventeen local attorneys, who were in Springfield to attend the courts in session there. In one week in
October 158 persons registered at the American House
alone. When the legislature convened in early December
the town was so crowded that many of the visitors had difficulty in finding accommodations.

The influx marked the beginning of Springfield's position
as the central city of the state—a position which followed
directly from her capture of the seat of government. The
functions of government were few and simple, but they
were restricted almost entirely to the capital. There the
legislature met; there the state supreme court convened;
there the United States courts for the district of Illinois

were held. To attend the court sessions came the leading
lawyers from all over the state; while the legislature drew
other local political leaders and numbers of business men
seeking corporate charters.

Moreover, having come, they stayed. Travel was slow,
costly, and often dangerous. During the winter it was almost
impossible for a legislator who lived at any distance from
the capital to return to his home during the week-end periods
when the General Assembly was not in session. (In fact,
the constant presence of members in Springfield was taken
as such a matter of course that that body sat all day on both
Saturdays and Mondays, and contented itself with a single
day's vacation at Christmas!) For a lawyer with cases in
the higher courts not to remain in the capital for the entire
term was hardly less feasible. Lacking means of speedy communication as well as transportation, there was no way by
which he could learn when his cases were to be called for
trial. His only course was to come at the beginning of a term
and stay until his work was finished.

These prolonged visits, lasting sometimes for two and
three months, could hardly be called a hardship. Men whose
lives were confined in the main to the farms and villages of
a newly settled country welcomed the opportunity for human companionship which the gatherings at the capital afforded. Besides, small as it was, Springfield offered contacts
with the outside world—in music, lectures, and amusements
of many kinds—far beyond those which their own communities afforded. Round after round of private parties,
with the visitors as honored guests, marked the sessions of
the legislature and courts. The serious businesses of law
making and litigation went forward in a sort of holiday
atmosphere.

The knowledge that a good time might be expected, together with a natural disinclination to endure alone the
loneliness and boredom which their husbands were escaping,

brought many wives of lawyers and lawmakers to Springfield. At the same time every marriageable, pleasure-loving girl in the state made a winter in the capital one of her major ambitions. Relatives, no matter how remote, were carefully cultivated in the hope that the coveted invitation would be extended. As a result, social life in Springfield had zest and liveliness beyond that of any other city in the state. Socially, as well as in law and politics, it was the capital of Illinois.

Let us see, therefore, what sort of a place this was in which so much of the state's life centered. Fortunately, there were visitors who recorded what they saw. Among them was an Ohio editor who wrote with such glowing enthusiasm that one is inclined to suspect him of an investment in Springfield real estate. At any rate, this is what he recorded after a visit in the early autumn of 1839.

Springfield lies on the edge of a large prairie. On the left, as you enter the village from the South, is a delightful grove, where the rills are more lively, and the ground more undulating than usual. . . . Approaching the southern part of the town, you leave a great sweep of verdant landscape behind you, and behold almost as great a natural meadow to your right. No one can conceive the grandeur and beauty of the scenery, unless he has wandered through a prairie country, at a season when an immense carpet, spangled with very bright yellow and vermilion flowers, and fringed along the line of the horizon with a darker timber, is spread over a very gracefully rolling surface, beneath a vast sky half covered with lowering clouds painted by the sun, and the other half as serene and clear as if no vapor had ever stained its azure.

But in the suburbs of Springfield there is a paradise in miniature, which compensates for the loss of the boundless prospect left behind. Small clusters of infant trees, which nature has planted with all the regularity, and more than the taste of art, rise like bowers of romance to hedge in the village with beauty. They extend, like arms from the main grove, not continuously, but like a chain of islands, gradually diminishing in size, and sheltering from a powerful noonday sun, the softly chiming rivulets. Here the man of leisure comes to steal pleasant thoughts from the cool shade, and the man of business for a while gives his care to the refreshing breezes that always carry on a rapid commerce over the heated plains. On Sunday the shady retirements are thronged with visitors in fine broadcloth, who find a place[1] most inviting to contemplation.

Passing them reluctantly, you glance forward at the throng of stores, taverns, and shops, some wearing their titles on their fronts, some on long arms projecting from their sides, and some in the usual style of tavern signs, beneath the picture of a bird or beast, on a black board swinging from a miniature gallows. Before reaching the centre of business, you behold to your right an agreeable assemblage of dwelling houses very neatly painted, most of them white, and situated somewhat retiringly behind tasteful front yards. To the left, at a distance, are seen more showy edifices,[2] the principal expense of which seems to have been their decoration, standing rather proudly apart from the throng of neat but humble mansions. Passing a modest-looking meetinghouse,[3] which speaks more for the simple piety of the inhabitants, than the ostentatious taste of the citizens, you now approach an area fenced from the street by a long stone-cutter's shop, eloquent with the music of scores of pick axes, shaping the rudiments of the new State House. . . .

Turning to the east you see the comfortable buildings, apparently young and certainly tasteful, gradually dwindling in size and becoming more scattered until the town melts away into the level monotonous plain. Several miles across the prairie is seen another grove, and along its margin clever farmhouses are strung in quite a picturesque manner. Toward these centres of rural felicity, narrow black paths wind through the desolate green. Along this edge of the town runs the Central Railroad,[4] now under contract. Follow this, in a northerly direction a short distance and then turn to the left, and new clusters of neat little dwellings attract your attention,[5] many of them labelled as the residences of dealers in pills and legal

[1] The author was probably describing the grove which stood where the Governor's Mansion is now located.

[2] Probably the homes of Ninian W. Edwards, Lawrason Levering, and others at the south end of the present State House grounds.

[3] The Methodist church, on the site of the Ridgely-Farmers Bank Building.

[4] On the right of way of the present-day Wabash.

[5] Jefferson Street.

advice. Towards the grove, the town assumes a more consolidated and antiquated appearance. Here is seen the rarest of all landscapes; crowded squares alive with shrubbery and tasteful ornaments, decorating alike the little remnant of twenty years ago, and costly edifices of last year. Every house is separated from the street by a neat front yard, and from its neighbor by a clean little garden; roses greet the visitor with a blush as he enters the gate, and pushing the door, he finds himself under a bower of honeysuckles.[6] Old shackly buildings are concentrated as the temples of Flora. The sun of contentment and happiness seems to shine on all, and gives the abodes of simple elegance a charm to which mere magnificence must be a stranger.

The new State House, even though unfinished, dominated the town. Although two years had elapsed since the cornerstone was laid, the second story was not yet completed; while tool sheds and stone piles littered the square. Still, thirty or forty men were at work, and the clinking of their hammers was merry music to the young capital.

Of scarcely less interest, especially to the visitors, were the hotels and taverns. Typical of most of these was the Globe Tavern,[7] a plain, two-story wooden structure which also served as an office for several of the stage lines operating through Springfield. Whenever a stage arrived, or a private conveyance for that matter, the clerk would ring a large bell mounted on top of the house, and the stable men would run out from the rear to take charge of the horses.

Completely overshadowing such a modest structure as this was the American House, which Elijah Iles built on the southeast corner of Sixth and Adams streets. Its size alone created a sensation. When it was opened, in November, 1838, two hundred citizens dined with the manager, J. Clifton, "late of Boston." The Ohio editor who wrote so kindly of Springfield commented on it with mixed awe and irrita-

[6]The writer is describing the older section of Springfield which centered about Second and Jefferson streets.

[7]On the north side of Adams Street between Third and Fourth streets.

tion. "Near the State House," he wrote, "is a gigantic building, called the *American House,* intended perhaps as the
tavern proper for the Legislators.—Politics and politeness
hover round this splendid affair. Everything inside puts you
in mind of the Turkish splendor, the carpeting, the papering,
and the furniture, weary the eye with magnificence. The
building itself is distinguished more for the harmony and
simplicity of its proportions, than the richness of its exterior.
A fine place for those who are troubled with a superabun-
dance of silver."

The situation which caused this tart concluding comment
was probably what led to the opening of other and less pretentious taverns during the next year—Joel Johnson's City
Hotel,[8] which boasted "a good table, and faithful ostlers";
and Torrey's Temperance Hotel,[9] which had accommodations for fifteen or twenty boarders and promised the best
table the country afforded. But these were only two of many
new ventures. In spite of the general prostration following
the panic of 1837, Springfield was experiencing a boom. In
the summer of 1838 a Chicagoan asserted that real estate
was as high as in his own speculative city, and cited as proof
the fact that a lot on the public square, 20 by 157 feet, had
been sold at public auction for $1600 on the preceding day.
Moreover, it was a boom which continued steadily, though
not feverishly. In the summer of 1840 it was said that no
less than one hundred buildings were erected, and the town's
population was estimated at more than 3,000. Progress was
constant during the next two years—witness Simeon Francis,
combining the roles of reporter and prophet.

Notwithstanding the depreciation of the currency, and the pressure of the times, Springfield continues to improve. About one
hundred buildings went up last year [1841], and among them some

[8] On Washington Street between Fourth and Fifth.

[9] On Adams between Fourth and Fifth.

beautiful and costly residences, and extensive business houses. The stores occupied by Mr. Grimsley and Messrs. Jewett & Hitchcock, will compare with any in the Western country. The commission house of Messrs. Grubb & Lewis, on the east side of the square, and those now building by Mr. B. S. Edwards and Mr. Dormady, on the north side of the square, capacious and well built stores—the splendid building, the State Bank, which has taken the place of a pond of water—have been built within the last year.[10] Of the residences, those of Messrs. Iles, Irwin and Birchall, in the south part of the city, make the best appearance. The southwest quarter of the city has been nearly covered over with houses within the last year. The south part, and all that quarter of the city on the east along the line of the rail road from Cook to Washington streets, has been spread over with new buildings; and the improvements north, and northeast of the State House, have been perhaps equal to any other portion. The extensive building during the pressure of '40 and '41—the many substantial improvements now making in different parts of the city— the commodious tavern about to be opened by Mr. Latshaw between the American and the rail road—the ware-houses in contemplation in that quarter and other places, indicate the amount of capital Spring- field will employ, and the extent of trade it will ultimately command. Situated in the Sangamon valley—the seat of Government for a State which contains more fertile land than any other in the Union, can it be doubted by any who have witnessed the growth of other portions of the country, that Springfield will be one of the largest inland towns in the United States?

From the general pattern of the early forties there was no departure throughout the decade. The four sides of the square, and the adjacent blocks as well, filled up with busi- ness structures. Many of them were creditable buildings, but on the north side "Chicken Row" remained an eyesore. In some particulars, however, there was real improvement. The state house was completed, externally at least. On the east side of the square, immediately north of the State Bank Building, a court house, very similar in appearance, was

[10] Grimsley's was a four-story brick three doors west of the corner of Sixth and Adams. Jewett & Hitchcock's store was also near the southeast corner of the square. Grubb & Lewis had a three-story brick immediately south of the State Bank, which stood where the Marine Bank is now located.

erected.[11] In 1843 a market house was built in Sixth Street between Washington and Jefferson, the street being widened ten feet on either side to make room for the necessary passageways. At least a beginning was made in laying sidewalks. Many private residences, some of them elaborate, were constructed, and the citizens were making an effort to beautify their dwellings.

In building and beautification the people of Springfield undoubtedly made progress during the town's first decade as the state capital, but there was one feature of the environment which, if it changed at all, became worse. That was the mud. At its best the sticky black loam of central Illinois is bad enough, but the Springfield variety seems to have been the worst the state afforded. At least it was the subject of continual comment by travelers, editors, and the citizens themselves; jokes were made about it; and in the memories of old settlers it remained as vivid as the deep snow of 1831.

To the editors of the town the mud was a subject on which one could always work off a bad temper. In the winter of 1842 the editor of the *Register* asserted that in passing from the square to any part of the city it was necessary to wade through mud knee-deep. The legislators, he said, were sick of being mired, and were not minded to stand the nuisance much longer. Clean up, he warned, or risk the loss of the capital. Four years later a correspondent of the *Journal* revealed how much effect this and many similar exhortations had had. "Within a few rods of the public square," he wrote, "there is a descent of some fifteen feet, into a ravine; and yet we have ponds about, loathsome to the eye, and which, when hot weather comes upon us, will be sickening to the smell. The crossings of our streets are covered with mud, and even some of our sidewalks are rendered almost impassable by accumulations of the same article." On occasion

[11] The court house was commenced in the spring of 1845 and completed a year later.

there was resort to sarcasm, like the following: "We see no reason why the proposition which will soon go before our city authorities for sending for a quantity of wild rice—an aquatic plant—to be grown within the limits of the corporation, will not be a good speculation. It will grow in water from six inches to a foot deep—produces well and is a very nutritious article of food. A sufficient quantity could be raised in the State House yard to secure rations for all the State officers." The ink might just as well have been saved. At the end of the forties the mud was no less deep than it would have been had the editors completely ignored it.

Second only to the mud as a subject of public-spirited indignation was the hog nuisance. Hogs ranged at will through the streets, wallowed in the mud holes, disputed the narrow sidewalks with pedestrians, and rooted up the boards at frequent intervals. Comments such as this—" 'Chicken Row' was highly perfumed yesterday by opening the 'hog wallows' in front of the stores"—frequently appeared in the newspapers. Unlike the mud, however, the hogs had sturdy defenders. As scavengers they helped to keep the city clean; and to allow them to run loose was to enable the poor to raise their own meat. Counter arguments were that the hogs created more nuisances than they removed; that they were often found dead within the city limits; and that a dead hog was never known to have an owner. Nevertheless, whenever a hog ordinance was before the city council, the defenders of the poor and the porkers were found to have influence enough to prevent its passage. The most that was ever done was to require owners to place rings in the hogs' snouts on the theory that this would prevent the destruction of the sidewalks, but there was immediate and widespread complaint that even this mild requirement was ignored.

Hogs and mud were evidences that absence of civic pride

was widespread. There were other indications of slovenliness. Piles of manure were permitted to accumulate around the stables; privies were often neglected; and too frequently the gutters became dumping grounds for discarded clothing, trash and garbage. In the summers flies abounded, and with heat the stench from filth was sometimes sickening.

The plain truth is that from certain points of view Springfield was a very unlovely city. Abraham Lincoln often told a story which illustrated its uninviting character. One day a meek-looking man applied to Thompson Campbell who, as Secretary of State, had custody of the State House, for permission to deliver a series of lectures in the Hall of the House of Representatives.

"May I ask," said Campbell, "what is to be the subject of your lectures?"

"Certainly," was the solemn reply, "they are on the second coming of our Lord."

"It's no use," said Campbell, "if you will take my advice you will not waste your time in this city. It is my private opinion that if the Lord has been in Springfield *once*, he will not come the *second time*."

The crudities of the capital, however, faded as one became a participant in the activities of the town. The experience of Mrs. B. S. Edwards, who came to Springfield in the winter of 1839-40 as a bride, was typical. As the stage on which she and her husband had traveled from St. Louis lumbered slowly through the mud of the unlighted streets, she could think only of the forbidding aspect of her new home, and her heart was heavy at the prospect. At the American House a number of passengers were discharged. Then the driver headed for the home of her husband's brother Ninian, where the young couple were to stay. Within all was bright, cheerful and hospitable. In less than a week Mrs. Edwards was in the swing of a "legislative winter," and her forebodings were forgotten.

A connection with the Edwards family meant ready entrance to the select circle of Springfield's society. Patron and patroness were Ninian W. Edwards and his wife, Elizabeth Todd Edwards; and their home, on the site of the present Centennial Building, was the popular gathering place. With them lived Mary Todd, Mrs. Edwards' sister, who had left her Lexington home for the more congenial household of her brother-in-law. Nearby was the home of Lawrason Levering and his wife, and with them, during the winter of 1839-40, lived Levering's sister Mercy, who quickly became an intimate of her young neighbor from Kentucky. Relatives of the Todd-Edwards family were prominent—another Todd sister, Francis, who had married Dr. William Wallace; Elizabeth, the daughter of Dr. John Todd; John T. Stuart, a cousin of the Todd sisters; and his wife. Most constant attendants among the men were Joshua F. Speed, James C. Conkling, Dr. E. H. Merryman and Abraham Lincoln.

The yellow pages of a number of letters written by Mercy Levering, Mary Todd and James C. Conkling from 1840, when Miss Levering returned to her home in Baltimore, until late in the following year, when she came back to Springfield as Mrs. Conkling, furnish a series of pictures of social life among the elite of the town. First comes an account of a picnic in the summer of 1840, from the hand of James C. Conkling. "Two or three weeks since," he wrote, "Miss Rodney and Miss Thornton gave a pic-nic near Dr. Houghan's. They selected a most beautiful spot, where we assembled in the latter part of the afternoon. . . . 'Twas really a delightful scene. The branches of some of the tallest trees formed a canopy over our heads to screen us from the rays of a cloudless sun. A velvet lawn spread itself beneath our feet. The table was loaded with a profusion of delicacies which our ladies know how to prepare so well. The graces flew while daylight lasted and as the dim twilight gathered around us the Graces and the Muses both tripped it 'on the light fantastic toe.' . . ."

Winter comes, and with it lawyers, legislators and visitors. Mary Todd writes in the midst of the Christmas festivities:

"Mr. Edwards has a cousin from Alton spending the winter with us, a most interesting young lady, her fascinations, have drawn a concourse of beaux & company round us. . . . I know you would be pleased with Matilda Edwards, a lovelier girl I never saw. *Mr. Speed's* ever changing heart I suspect is about offering *its young* affections at her shrine, with some others. There is a considerable acquisition in our society of *marriageable gentlemen,* unfortunately only 'birds of passage.' *Mr. Webb,* a widower of modest merit, last winter, is our *principal lion,* dances attendance very frequently. We expect a very gay winter, evening before last my sister gave a most agreeable party, upwards of a hundred graced the festive scene."

"Summer in all its beauty has again come . . . ," wrote Mary Todd six months later. "The June Court is in session and many distinguished strangers grace the gay capital. We have an unusual number of agreeable visitors, some pleasant acquaintances of last winter, but in their midst the *winning widower is not. Rumor* says he with some others will attend the Supreme Court next month. . . . Mr. Speed, our former most constant guest has been in Kentucky for some weeks past, will be here next month, on a visit *perhaps,* as he has some idea of deserting Illinois. . . . The interesting gentleman, whom Mrs. Roberts gave you for a beau is now a resident of this place, Mr. Trumbull, is Secretary of State, in lieu of Judge Douglass, who has been rapidly promoted to office.—Now that your fortune is made, I feel much disposed in your absence, to lay in my *claims,* as he is talented & agreeable & sometimes *countenances* me.—"

Naturally, in a group of young people, weddings took place

frequently. "I had no idea I should be instrumental more than once again in changing the name of a lady," Conkling wrote his fiancée in the autumn of 1840. "But last evening Miss Todd and myself (standing partners you perceive), with the assistance of Parson Bergen in his usual dignified manner passed through the usual ceremonies of such an occasion. And about 10 o'clock we packed them in the stage and sent them off to Chicago." A month later he described another ceremony in which he had participated. "A week ago last Thursday evening," he wrote, "our friend Mr. C. departed from the state of celibacy in which he had long been lingering. I assisted in performing the last offices and consigned him with all due ceremony to the happiness of a matrimonial life. . . . The party was very small. Miss T. was the only lady present unconnected with the family. Her presence reminded me of other days and even she did not appear as merry and joyous as usual."

Of all Springfield weddings, however, the most famous was the one in which Miss Todd herself played the principal part.

During the summer and fall of 1840 it was apparent, to their intimates, that Abraham Lincoln and Mary Todd were taking more than casual pleasure in each other's company. Rumors of a prospective wedding went the rounds. And then, on New Year's Day, 1841, something happened between them. They ceased to see each other. To her friends Mary Todd seemed as gay and flirtatious as ever, but Lincoln was crushed. For a week or so he was too ill to attend the legislature regularly, and when he did recover he was dejected, morose, and inclined to shun his former friends.

The gossip was that Mary Todd had jilted him. "Poor L'.," wrote Conkling to Mercy Levering; "how are the mighty fallen! He was confined about a week, but though he now appears again he is reduced and emaciated in appearance and seems scarcely to possess strength enough to speak above a whisper. His case at present is truly deplorable but what prospect there may be for ultimate relief I cannot pretend to say. I doubt not but he can declare 'That loving is a painful thrill, And not to love more painful still' but would not like to intimate that he has experienced 'That surely 'tis the worst of pain To love and not be loved again.'" To which Miss Levering replied: "Poor A—I fear his is a blighted heart! perhaps if he was as persevering as Mr. W. he might finally be successful."

The winter wore off, and with it went much of Springfield's gaiety. "The Legislature has dispersed," wrote Conkling in early March. "Whether any persons regret it I cannot pretend to say. Miss Todd and her cousin Miss Edwards seemed to form the grand centre of attraction. Swarms of strangers who had little else to engage their attention hovered around them, to catch a *passing smile.* By the way," he added maliciously, "I do not think they were received, with even ordinary attention, if they did not obtain a *broad grin* or an *obstreporous laugh.*"

Lincoln remained an object of not-too-sympathetic commiseration. "And L," wrote Conkling, "poor hapless simple swain who loved most true but was not loved again—I suppose he will now endeavor to drown his cares among the intricacies and perplexities of the law. No more will the merry peal of laughter ascend *high in the air,* to greet his listening and delighted ears. He used to remind me sometimes of the pictures I formerly saw of old Father Jupiter, bending down from the clouds, to see what was going on below. And as an agreeable smile of satisfaction graced the countenance of the old heathen god, as he perceived the incense rising up—so the face of L. was occasionally distorted into a grin as he succeeded in eliciting applause from some of the fair votaries by whom he was surrounded. But alas! I fear his shrine will now be deserted and that he will withdraw himself from the society of us inferior mortals."

The gossips were now coupling Mary Todd's name with that of Edwin B. Webb, of Carmi. Although a widower with two children, and much older than Miss Todd, Webb paid her a strenuous courtship. Friends thought that he would succeed, but they were wrong. When Mercy Levering hinted at an engagement, she was quickly disillusioned. "In your friendly & confiding ear," her friend wrote, "allow me to whisper that my *heart can never be his*. . . . There being a slight difference of some eighteen or twenty summers in our years, would preclude all possibility of congeniality of feeling, without which I should never feel justifiable in resigning my happiness into the safe keeping of another, even should that other be, far too worthy for me, with his two *sweet little objections*."

Those in Springfield who were sure that Lincoln was a rejected suitor would have been surprised by a casual allusion in this same letter if they could have seen it. Lincoln, Miss Todd confessed sorrowfully, "deems me unworthy of notice, as I have not met *him* in the gay world for months. With the usual comfort of misery, *I* imagine that others were as seldom gladdened by his presence as myself, yet I would that the case were different, that he would once more resume his station in Society, that 'Richard should be himself again,' much, much happiness would it afford me."

The months wore on. Mary Todd succeeded in covering a wound with flashing but superficial gaiety, while Lincoln struggled with the tormenting doubts which had driven him to break the engagement on that "fatal first of January," 1841. Finally, in the late summer or autumn of 1842, Mrs. Simeon Francis brought the two unhappy lovers together. Reconciliation followed. Again Lincoln wrestled with the dark suspicion that he was incapable of love as he had imagined it. This time he conquered his fears. As a result, a marriage took place, with unexpected suddenness, on November 4, 1842, at the home of Ninian W. Edwards. Instead of a wedding trip, the bride and groom quietly moved to the Globe Tavern, where they secured board and room at $4.00 a week. Seven days after the wedding the young husband closed a letter to another lawyer with the remark: "Nothing new here, except my marrying, which, to me, is matter of profound wonder."

Lovers' quarrels and reconciliations, engagements and marriages furnished the material for many an evening's gossip among the select circle of Springfield's young people, but in the social life of the town as a whole they made no more than a ripple. Far more interesting, to townspeople and visitors alike, were the public social functions which followed each other at short intervals whenever the legislature and courts were in session.

Hardly had the first legislature assembled in Springfield when an invitation to a cotillion party, bearing among others the names of S. A. Douglass,[12] N. W. Edwards, J. F. Speed, J. Shields and A. Lincoln as managers, was issued. Rarely thereafter, throughout the forties, was there a winter when several similar functions did not take place.

"There was a ball here tonight," a woman guest at the American House recorded in her diary one December night in 1840, "and they made a dressing room of the ladies' parlor, and I sat there and viewed them all as they came in. A number of the ladies carried bundles in their arms and were accompanied by maids. The bundles, which were a mystery to me, were deposited on the bed, where the mystery soon developed, for the bundles began to kick and squeal, as hungry babies will. The mothers, after performing their maternal duties, wrapped the infants up again and left them with many charges to nursemaids not to mix them up. The ladies were handsomely dressed, but not in the latest style. They wore handsome gowns of silk and satin, made with low necks and short sleeves."

[12] As a young man, Douglas spelled his name with a double "s."

When Sidney Breese was elected to the United States Senate late in 1842 he celebrated the event by giving a large ball at the American House on New Year's Eve. A correspondent sent a description to the New York *Herald*, which the *Register* proudly reprinted. "Our United States Senator-elect," the reporter wrote, "gave a splendid blow-out at the American Hotel, on New Year's eve. . . . This was a delightful affair for a new city, and far beyond my expectations; the only draw-back was we had not ladies enough—there were 300 or 400 gents, and not more than 40 or 50 ladies, and half of them married or engaged. . . . Judge Breese was very polite and attentive, and tried to make everyone happy; in person he is a short, very thick set, dignified, gentlemanly looking man, about 45 years of age; he is a capable man for his office, and will fill it with honor to the State and himself. Judge Douglass, his opponent, was present, and took an active part in the dancing."

With Judge Breese's ball a new custom was inaugurated. Prior to that time the accepted accompaniment of a senatorial election was a dinner to the faithful in which wines and liquors flowed to the ultimate demoralization of the diners and the destruction of no small amount of china and glassware, but thereafter evening entertainments, or "levees," became the rule. Thus in 1844, James Semple gave a "brilliant party" at the American House; and two years later the levee at the state house in honor of Douglas' elevation to the Senate was "a perfect jam." In 1849 five hundred guests attended James Shields's party, at which the music was excellent and "the refreshments well got up."

But balls and levees were only one form of group entertainment. The construction of the Northern Cross Railroad offered possibilities for novelty and pleasure as well as commercial advantage. Hardly had the road been opened when a large party, accompanied by a band, went to Jacksonville, where they met with open-handed hospitality. (Among them was Mary Todd, who enjoyed the trip thoroughly. "God be praised for that," wrote Abraham Lincoln when he heard of her pleasure.) A few weeks later Jacksonville returned the visit, and two hundred guests sat down to "a sumptuous supper" at the American House.

The Northern Cross quickly went to ruin, but excursions in sleighs or carriages—to Rochester or New Berlin or Athens—continued. And when, at the end of the decade, the railroad was rebuilt and trains ran again, the old practice of community visiting was resumed, to continue more or less regularly until after the Civil War.

For the liberal-minded of the community—the element which attended the balls and dancing parties—the theater was often available. The Illinois Theatrical Company, which included in its membership young Joe Jefferson and his father, played to crowded houses in the weeks following the location of the state government at Springfield, and returned in the early winter for the session of the legislature. To this sojourn Jefferson attributed an incident which he recorded in his *Autobiography*. Stimulated by a religious revival, the opponents of the theater had induced the city council to place such a high license fee upon performances that it was practically prohibitory. The troupe was in despair, when a young lawyer who gave his name as Abraham Lincoln came to them and said he thought he could adjust the difficulty. As Jefferson told the story, Lincoln appeared before the councilmen and made a long speech, in which he not only traced the history of the drama from earliest times, but did it so tactfully and skillfully, and with so much good humor, that the city fathers readily yielded to his closing plea and removed the exorbitant tax. The story is doubtless apocryphae, for the minutes of the town council show that Lincoln was not present when the case was considered, but it has become firmly embedded in the folklore of Illinois.

The theater-goer in the early forties could hardly complain of not receiving his money's worth, at least in quantity. Performances customarily included a long tragedy and a shorter comedy, and often other attractions as well. Thus a company playing in 1842 offered the drama of "The Denouncer, or the Miser of Marseilles," songs by two of the actors, a dance by a third, and a performance of "The Weathercock" in conclusion. The price of tickets was fifty cents.

For some reason, however, the theater waned in popularity, although there were occasional professional performances throughout the decade. To take its place came the circus. There had been at least one circus performance in the early thirties, and in 1841 June, Titus, Angevine & Company's "Circus and Caravan" showed in Springfield for two days. It was not until the latter half of the decade, however, that circuses came thick and fast, at the rate of two or three a year. Thus in 1848 Welch, Delavan & Nathan's "National Circus" exhibited for two days, and within two weeks Raymond & Company's "Mammoth Menagerie" was in town. The next year saw the advent of Mabie's troupe and Crane & Company's "Great Oriental Circus," both playing two-day stands before large crowds.

All the traditional features of the circus were evident. There were parades through the streets, bands, menageries, gymnasts, tableaux and "spectacles"—all under canvas tents. Not even the rodomontade of the press agent was lacking. There was "Youthful Richard Rivers, whose professional path has literally been strewn with garlands"; Frank Pastor, "the most wonderful child in the world"; the "Three Prize Darkies," guaranteed "to move every ear with delight and every soul with ecstasy"; and W. H. Kemp, "the best clown in America." Even an ordinary parade offered a chance for involved exaggeration. Thus the advance agent promised that when "The Great Philadelphia Zoological Garden" exhibited in Springfield, the menagerie would be preceded "by the grand novel spectacle of an elegant Music Car, drawn by two noble Elephants, containing a superior band of music, with brass instruments, who will enliven the scene by executing some of the most popular pieces of music."

Press agents were always careful to emphasize the moral character of their performances. The people were assured that "the most fastidious" could listen to the jokes of Rockwell & Company's clown "without a blush." When the "Learned Pig," who could tell time, add and multiply, and play cards with anyone in the audience, was exhibited at the City Hotel, patrons were promised an entertainment "strictly moral and instructive." Even stronger claims were made for Raymond & Company's "Mammoth Menagerie." "The exhibition," said its advance notices, "serves to entertain, and instruct all in the wondrous works of the Supreme Being, and is particularly impressive on the minds of youth."

Such emphasis on moral values, coupled with the undercurrent of protest against theatrical performances, indicates the presence of a large element who must have found their chief recreation in soberer diversions. Of these there were many. Lectures on a wide variety of subjects were given frequently. Because of the lack of transportation facilities, the speakers were usually local men or visitors from nearby towns. Springfield ministers and doctors, and the professors of Illinois College at Jacksonville, spoke most frequently. The range of subjects indicates a lively intellectual curiosity. Scientific subjects had the greatest attraction. During almost any winter one could hear addresses on chemistry, astronomy, geology and electricity. Occasionally a mesmerist or phrenologist appeared. On these occasions a week of engagements, all well attended, was the rule.

Those interested in music had frequent opportunity to indulge their tastes. A band was formed in the thirties, and reorganized in 1839 under the direction of Jack Hough, the cabinetmaker. C. J. F. Clarke, an observant Yankee

RAYMOND & CO.'S
MAMMOTH MENAGERIE.
AND
HERR DRIESBACH,
With his collection of
Highly-Trained Lions, Tigers, Leopards, &c.

**Triumphal Entry of the New and Gorgeous
Roman Band Chariot!**
Containing the NEW YORK BRASS BAND, and
drawn by Ten Grey Horses, of the largest size.

This Stupendous work of art exhibits classical figures of colossal stature, in bold and vigorous sculpture
grouped with lordly animals of the forest. The panels
are adorned with approiriate painting, the whole
being surmounted by an immense Canopy, supported
by two Giraffes, and decorated with silken tapestry,
on the apex of which is perched an *American Eagle.*

Length of Chariot,   30 feet.
Height to summit of Canopy,   20 "
Weight .n full,   8000 lbs.

**Will be exhibited at Springfield on Tuesday,
August 22d, 1848; one day only, from 1 P. M. to
4 P. M.**

CIRCUS ADVERTISEMENT, 1848

"Here I Have Lived"

CONCERT

TO BE GIVEN BY THE

JUVENILE CHOIR,
Under the Direction of
M R. M U N S O N,

AT THE FIRST PRESBYTERIAN CHURCH,

On Thursday Evening February 4th, at ½ past 6 o'clock.

PROGRAMME.

PART FIRST.

1. The Children are Coming.
2. What is that Music I Hear?
3. The Cuckoo.
4. American War Song.
5. Brightly Speed the Hours.
6. The Haunted Spring.
7. This Bright and Frosty Morning.
8. The North Wind doth Blow.
9. United in a Joyous Band.
10. Light may her Heart be. (To my Mother.)
11. Gipsey's Wild Chant.
12. Where Shall We Go?

PART SECOND.

1. Oh, How Sweet when Day Light Closes.
2. Bób O'Linkum.
3. Awake! The Song of Merry Greeting.
4. The Pear Tree.
5. Float Away.
6. Beauties of Nature.
7. Oh! 'tis Sweet to Sing.
8. Never Look Sad.
9. Come Brothers, Tune the Lay.
10. The Sleigh Ride.
11. Good Night.

ADMITTANCE 25 cents. Tickets may be obtained at the Book Store and American House. Also at the Stores of E. R. Wiley and T. Alsop, SPRINGFIELD, February 4, 1847.

who lived in Menard County and wrote pungent letters to his family in the East, heard the members in action at Petersburg and commented that "they played very well *for a new country*." Singing societies were formed from time to time and gave occasional concerts. Now and then—more often as the town grew larger—professionals appeared. The Swiss Bell Ringers performed at the American House in the summer of 1846. A year later the Misses Browne gave a series of vocal and piano concerts in the Senate Chamber before audiences which listened with "breathless interest." The Augusta Family, negro singers, performed in a pavilion on the State House grounds in the summer of 1849, with city officers on hand to prevent an outbreak of race violence. Earlier in the year the Alleghenians, a mixed quartet, had given a series of concerts in the Senate Chamber. To these and similar entertainments the charges were low—ordinarily twenty-five cents. If the artists were competent, the people crowded to hear them, and often held them in town for several appearances instead of the one or two originally scheduled.

Supplementing social activities like these were public meetings of various kinds. A Fourth of July rarely passed without a public observance. Ordinarily the same pattern was followed—a parade, the reading of the Declaration of Independence, and an oration, by James C. Conkling or Abraham Lincoln or one of their fellow members of the bar, on the significance of the day. Occasions of national sorrow were elaborately observed. In honor of the death of William Henry Harrison the bells of the city were tolled at sunrise and minute guns were fired at two o'clock in the afternoon. This was the signal for the people to assemble at the Second Presbyterian Church, where a choir under the direction of John F. Rague sang hymns and Albert T. Bledsoe eulogized the dead President as "a scholar, a hero, a patriot and a statesman." When Andrew Jackson died a citizens' committee, which included Lincoln, John T. Stuart and Ninian W. Edwards, planned a public meeting at the State House where E. D. Baker, the Whig congressman-elect, spoke on the life and career of the great Democrat.

Occasionally a traveling celebrity stirred the town to excitement. The visit of Daniel Webster in 1837 was long remembered, but the arrival of Martin Van Buren, on June 17, 1842, aroused even more interest. The Springfield Band, the Sangamon Guards, and a large delegation of citizens on foot and in carriages, met the former President a mile from town as he came in on the Rochester road, and escorted him into the city. There the Springfield Artillery fired a salute of thirteen guns, after which Van Buren responded briefly to the welcoming address of David B. Campbell, the mayor. For the balance of the day the famous guest received callers at the American House. That evening a ball was given in his honor. The next day—Saturday—Van Buren visited the State House, and on Sunday he attended services at the Methodist and Second Presbyterian churches. On Monday he left for Jacksonville, having won the hearts of all except the most fanatical of his political opponents.

Another source of diversion available to all—at least during legislative sessions—was "the lobby." This was an institution which had its origin in the presence of numbers of male visitors interested in public questions and not averse to combining the discussion of them with a little horse play. Men with these purposes in mind found a most convenient meeting place in the lobby of the State House, and so the group which gathered there on idle evenings came to be known by that name.

An elected president—"Coke, Speaker"—was charged with preserving order (when the preservation of order seemed desirable), and with appointing suitable committees. The list of committees and committee appointments for the first of the Springfield lobbies, which has been preserved,

shows clearly the nature of this unique institution. A. W.
Calvary of Greene as chairman, with Messrs. Prickett of
Will, Buckmaster of Madison, Flood of Adams, Baker of
Randolph and Lockwood of Morgan, were charged with
formulating "rules for the government of the Lobby, the
preservation of order in the Halls, Ante-Chambers, Porches
and Dormitories; also measures to be adopted for the comfort and accommodation of loungers, loafers, and those
afflicted with yawning, gaping, stretching, ennui, and the
blue-devils." The committee on "feats of activity and
agility; foot racing, ground and lofty tumbling, and all exer-
cises of the 'Stadium,' the 'palestra' and the 'Campus Mar-
tius' " included Nathaniel Pope and Bowling Green—both
fat men. Doctor McCurdy of Fayette, Colonel May of
Sangamon and Major Miller of Morgan were appointed a
select committee, "fully authorized to enter into contracts
for supplying the House with wood and water, stone-coal
and peat; also pipes, tobacco and segars for fumigating on
the most approved Knickerbocker principles, and to audit
and settle all accounts therefor, and to draft and report to
this House a poetry bill for the payment and liquidation of
the same."

Most of the appointments, however, were of a serious
nature. There were committees on subjects of both political
and general interest. In the former class were "finance, and
the perfecting our present system of revenue"; and "the
Bank of Illinois, and the Bank of the State of Illinois." In
the latter class were committees on the history of the state,
with Thomas Ford, John Mason Peck and Cyrus Edwards
as members; on agriculture and the improvement of breeds
of domestic animals; on colleges, academies, common schools
and the interests of literature generally.

Meeting at frequent intervals, the lobby did much more
than entertain. Since many of the state's leading men
took part in the discussions, questions before the General

Assembly were often debated with a breadth of knowledge greater than that which the legislature alone afforded. For this reason, as well as because of its meeting place, it came to be known as the "Third House," and to exercise a real influence on the formal sessions of the state's lawmakers.

It was not the lobby, however, nor the balls and concerts and lectures of Springfield, which left the most lasting impression on the memories of those who frequented the capital during these years. Rather was it the simple, cordial hospitality of her citizens. When, as old men, the young lawyers of the forties recalled the early days of their practice, the welcome which they had always found in the homes of Ninian W. Edwards, his brother Benjamin S. Edwards, John T. Stuart, Nicholas H. Ridgely, Stephen T. Logan, James L. Lamb and Thomas Mather—to name but a few—was the one recollection which time had not dimmed. "The old-fashioned, generous hospitality of Springfield—hospitality proverbial to this day throughout the State," exclaimed Isaac N. Arnold of Chicago forty years later. And then, with the picture of Mrs. Lincoln, awaiting with clouded brain the end of her days in a darkened room, in his mind, he recalled the dinners and parties at which she had presided. "In her modest and simple home," he said, "everything orderly and refined, there was always, on the part of both host and hostess, a cordial and hearty Western welcome, which put every guest perfectly at ease. Mrs. Lincoln's table was famed for the excellence of many rare Kentucky dishes, and in season, it was loaded with venison, wild turkeys, prairie chickens, quail and other game, which was then abundant. Yet it was her genial manners, and ever-kind welcome, and Mr. Lincoln's wit and humor, anecdote, and unrivalled conversation, which formed the chief attraction."

"We read much of 'Merrie England,'" said Arnold, "but I doubt if there was ever anything more 'merrie' than Springfield in those days."

CHAPTER VI

Enlarging Interests

WHEN Springfield was a frontier village with a few hundred inhabitants whose energies were devoted almost entirely to wringing a living from a stubborn environment, breaks in the monotony of daily life came infrequently. But as its population grew, and men whose horizons extended beyond a mere existence became residents—in a word, as it attained maturity—currents of life to which it once would have been impervious aroused it to vigorous action and reaction.

Politics, for one thing, ceased to be a succession of petty quarrels and became a matter of real significance.

The leading politicians of their respective communities were frequently the members of the legislature and the lawyers who practised in the courts at Springfield. Naturally, the one city where they met face to face became a center of their activities. There the merits and weaknesses of prospective candidates could be carefully canvassed, combinations worked out, and party issues tested in the fire of debate. By 1839, moreover, party lines were pretty tightly drawn, and Whigs as well as Democrats were setting up central committees to operate the party machinery. Since residence in the capital made possible ready contact with men from all parts of the state, the central committees were composed almost entirely of Springfield men. Thus in a double sense the city became a political focal point.

Prominent in each party were a few leaders whom their opponents described as members of a "clique" or "junto." Guiding spirits of the Democrats were Stephen A. Douglas (until his removal from Springfield), John Calhoun, Virgil Hickox, and Weber and Walters of the *Register*. Among the Whigs, Stuart, Lincoln, Baker, Logan and A. G. Henry were supposed to dominate. To each group their rivals imputed not only autocratic power but also an unlimited capacity for chicanery. Highhandedness, selfishness and corruption were regularly and impartially charged by both sides.

In sober fact, opposing sets of politicians were merely trying to make political capital out of the central control which both parties were adopting. Naturally they exaggerated. Springfield men certainly exercised greater influence than their number warranted, but they cannot be said to have dominated the politics of the state. Party organization had not yet developed to such a degree as to make absolute control by any small group possible. Because of their native ability, ready contact with other leaders, and the strong newspapers with which they worked in close harmony, their influence was sometimes decisive, but their real dominance rarely extended beyond their own congressional district.

Moreover, while the newspapers devoted columns in each issue to political matters, it was only during the presidential campaigns that the rank and file of the voters became genuinely aroused. Then politics attained an emotional pitch of almost unbelievable intensity. Witness the log cabin and hard cider campaign of 1840—the rowdiest, noisiest presidential campaign in the history of the country.

Although the candidates—William Henry Harrison and Martin Van Buren—were not yet nominated, the campaign began in Illinois in October, 1839, when both parties held their state conventions in Springfield. From the beginning, orgies of speech-making characterized it. One of the first

took place in mid-November in the court room at Springfield.
Cyrus Walker of Macomb, a Whig elector, started off in the
afternoon, and Douglas for the Democrats followed. Lincoln, another electoral candidate, spoke in the evening. The
next night Douglas spoke again, and Lincoln followed. On
the third evening Edmund Wiley held forth for the Democrats and E. D. Baker concluded for the Whigs.[1]

Before the campaign was over such marathons of oratory became so common that the newspapers printed only
perfunctory accounts of them, but as one of the first, this
meeting attracted considerable attention. The *Register's*
comment is notable for the sharp shot the editor took at
Lincoln. Admitting that the first speech of the young Whig
lawyer was "truly ingenious," the editor accused him of an
"assumed clownishness . . . which does not become him,
and which does not truly belong to him. . . . Mr.
L[incoln]," he continued, "will sometimes make his language correspond with this *clownish* manner, and he can

[1] Perhaps it was this series of speeches which James C. Conkling had in
mind when he wrote the following letter to Mercy Levering on November 18,
1840: "I cannot but smile whenever I reflect upon the martyr-like patience
that you manifested upon the few occasions last winter and the deep interest
that some ladies exhibited in listening to some of those long and tedious
speeches that were inflicted upon us. Some of them I confess were highly
entertaining, but how gratifying it must have been to you when in the middle
of the evening some long winded double tongued fellow arose and expressing
a determination to make *a few brief* remarks commenced by drawing a
quire of paper out of his pocket, cutting up his speech into seventeen heads
with the prospect of flourishing half an hour on each. Then followed the
interesting story concerning the receipts and expenditures of the government
with illustrations about commerce and exchange—embezzlement and defalca-
tion exemplified in the persons of Price and Swartout, Boyd and Harris,
diversified by a beautiful episode upon agricultural interests and domestic
manufacturers and ornamented and embelished by the most exquisite caricatures of little Matty Van and Old Tip. Then succeeded a vast hetero-
genous mass of rant and nonsense, lighted up occasionally by a fitful blaze of
fancy, which appeared like an ignis fatuus in an ocean of fog and mist, and
the whole concluded by the most violent denunciation against the administration—by hurling anathemas against the rulers and scattering the fulminations
of political wrath among its adherents—by depicting in the most glowing
colors that awful and horrid state of oppression under which we exist and
by which we are just permitted to breathe and describing that paradisaical
happiness, peace and contentment we shall enjoy under the influence of
reform."

thus frequently raise a loud laugh among his Whig hearers; but this entire game of buffoonery convinces the mind of no man, and is utterly lost on the majority of his audience."

At short intervals other speaking tournaments were held, but it was not long before the campaign got beyond the stage of mere argument. By a blunder comparable only to the fatal "rum, romanism and rebellion" of a later day, some disgusted Democrat referred to Harrison as a log cabin and hard cider candidate. With a flash of genius the Whigs turned the derisive characterization into a rallying cry, and transformed Harrison, a pious, well-meaning mediocrity, into a hard-handed hero of the glorious days of the Revolution, a veritable god of the pioneers. Serious issues were forgotten—or ignored—as the Whigs turned the campaign into a carnival of emotion. Log cabins were erected everywhere, sober business men proclaimed unlimited faith in homespun and hard cider, and throats went hoarse in shouting such refrains as the following:

> Let Frenchmen drink claret and sweet muscadine,
> And Germans drink hock on the banks of the Rhine;
> But give me to quaff, with friends warm and true,
> A gourd of hard cider to old Tippecanoe.

> In the White House Van Buren may drink his champagne
> And have himself toasted from Georgia to Maine—
> But we in log cabins, with hearts warm and true
> Drink a gourd of hard cider to old Tippecanoe.

So far as Springfield was concerned, the high point of the campaign came on the 2nd, 3rd and 4th of June, when a gigantic Whig rally, officially entitled the "Young Men's Convention," was held there. Delegates began to arrive on Tuesday, June 2nd. Some, coming from places as far distant as two hundred miles, had been eight and ten days on the road. They carried their own camp equipment, slept on the

ground at night, and cooked their own food. They came in
wagons, on horseback, and in many cases in canoes mounted
on wheels. On arrival they were taken to the prairie north
of the residence of Elijah Iles, where a camp had been prepared for them and a pavilion erected for speaking. By
Tuesday night 5,000 people, representing the states of
Indiana, Iowa, Missouri and seventy counties in Illinois,
were on the grounds.

The convention organized on the following morning, and
then indulged in a parade. At the head of the procession
came two hundred and fifty veterans of the Revolution and
the War of 1812. Next came the out-of-state delegates, and
then the delegations from Illinois. First among these was
the Cook County contingent with a miniature brig, thirty
feet long and completely rigged, drawn by six white horses.
Fayette County had a log cabin which its delegates had
dragged all the way from Vandalia. The men from Cotton
Hill precinct of Sangamon County used twenty-six yoke of
oxen to pull their exhibit—a log cabin shaded by a large tree
in upright position, with the entire delegation, eighty in number, perched on the roof. Many groups brought canoes and
hard cider barrels; bands were plentiful, banners myriad.

Forming in line at the north end of Sixth Street, the delegates paraded to the prairie south of town, where they
marched, counter-marched and cheered themselves hoarse.
Having performed all the evolutions the marshals could think
of, they headed north again. At one o'clock the line reached
Dr. Houghan's park, north of the city, where an old style
barbecue was served to 15,000 people.

There was an almost unbelievable amount of speech-
making. Immediatly after the barbecue the orators commenced, and, with a short intermission for supper, followed
one another until midnight. The next day the same schedule
was followed. Even the *Sangamo Journal* commented in some
wonderment at the close attention given to the "flood of elo-

quence which was poured out by the different gentlemen called upon the stands."

The meeting came to an end on Thursday evening, June 4th. On the next morning the Chicago delegation, ready to start for home, marched to the *Journal* office, and there presented the brig to the Whigs of Springfield. E. D. Baker accepted the gift, and in turn presented the Chicagoans with a grey eagle. Baker's speech was characteristic, both of the man and the time. He described the eagle as young, "like our Republic, and as we now are, tied and manacled; and he requested that whilst our country continues to be misruled and misgoverned, and tied to the car of power, that this Eagle, the emblem bird of our Republic, might be likewise restrained of its liberty; but that, when they should hear the tidings in November of the election of the war-worn veteran of Tippecanoe to the Presidency, he then desired that the Eagle may be loosed from its fetters, and permitted to roam free as the breezes of heaven, and as the principles we advocate."

And Simeon Francis, reporting the incident, recorded in all seriousness that during most of Baker's speech the eagle appeared to droop and languish, but when the orator in a burst of eloquence described the flight of the bird upon its prospective release, it "reared its head, expanded its eyes, and gave a loud cry."

Emotional fervor characterized the campaign throughout its course. To the attempts of the Democrats to create some discussion of national issues, the Whigs replied with laudation of Harrison as a soldier and farmer, and with charges that Van Buren was a fop and an aristocrat. All over the state log cabins were erected. A week before the election the Whigs of Springfield raised a cabin on a lot a short distance south of the American House. There nightly meetings were held, speakers repeated the praises of the hero of Tippecanoe, and the audience shouted out the choruses of the songs which filled columns in nearly every issue of the *Journal*.

Even the women took an active part, although by common consent politics were normally the exclusive concern of the male. At the first meeting in the log cabin sixty women were present. James C. Conkling, writing to his fiancée of Mary Todd's return from a visit in Missouri, said that he first saw her at the *Journal* office, "where some fifteen or twenty ladies were collected together to listen to the Tippecanoe Singing Club. It has lately become quite a place of resort," he added, "particularly when it is expected there will be any speeches." After the election Miss Todd herself confessed: "This fall I became quite a *politician,* rather an unladylike profession, yet at such a *crisis,* whose heart could remain untouched while the energies of all were called in question?"

On more than one occasion during the campaign the strain on emotion came close to the breaking point. Once it actually snapped. Simeon Francis and the editors of the *Register* had become involved in an argument concerning Douglas's connection with *Old Hickory,* a Democratic campaign newspaper. In the course of the argument Francis overstepped what Douglas considered the bounds of endurance, whereupon Douglas set out to cane him. Francis himself described the encounter. Douglas's eyes "glared like live coals," he wrote, "his frame dilated into grand and gigantic proportions, and with a voice like seven-toned thunder he bellowed forth his ire; 'flashing and fiery, fierce and free' came his words . . . he got a stick bigger than himself—snatched by his irresistible energy from the unwilling hand of John Calhoun, he came up by a masterly flank movement—big words fell from his lips, his mighty hand raised the stick—it fell and we received the blow upon an unoffending apple, which was as we thought secure from the chances of war—in our left hand coat pocket."

The *Register's* version was somewhat different. "Mr. Francis seems to think it an honor to escape from a caning with his life," it commented, "and a friend of ours says the honor is enhanced from the fact that this is not the first de-

liverance of the same kind. Mr. Francis had applied scur-
rilous language to Mr. Douglass, which could be noticed in
no other way. Mr. Douglass, therefore, gave him a sound
caning, which Mr. Francis took with Abolition patience, and
is now praising God that he was neither killed nor scathed.
Mr. Francis was caned, however, and the infamy rests upon
him with becoming grace."

Eventually, amid charges of election frauds in contemplation and offers of bets on Harrison's success from the Whigs,
the campaign came to an end. But for all their exuberance,
the Whigs were forced to see the state go for Van Buren.
There was comfort, however, in the fact that the national result was a victory. The machine which Andrew Jackson had
perfected had its weak points after all. The Springfield
group, moreover, could take satisfaction in the two-thirds
majority which Sangamon County gave to Harrison. But it
was a satisfaction soon to be destroyed. In less than six
months the President was dead, and with John Tyler of
Virginia in the White House the great victory turned to
dust and ashes.

With the close of the national campaign, the people settled
down to four years of comparative quiet so far as politics
were concerned. Surfeited with the emotionalism of the past
six months, state and local issues aroused only a mild interest,
although there was much amusement when Abraham Lincoln
and Joseph Gillespie jumped from a window in December,
1840, in a fruitless attempt to prevent the adjournment of
the special session of the legislature which was then in progress. (The *Register* suggested that the State House be
raised another story so that even Lincoln, with his long
legs, would have to climb down the water spout.)

But politics were not the only subject capable of arousing
the 3,000 inhabitants of the capital to high excitement. In the
summer of 1841 the Fisher "murder" caused tension just as
strained, and much more dangerous, than that which had re-

sulted from the Harrison campaign. Several times mob action seemed likely.

Everything started on an afternoon in early June—the 2nd, to be exact—when four men left Myers's boarding house in Springfield for a walk about the town. Their names were Archibald, William and Henry Trailor, and Archibald Fisher. The Trailors were brothers who lived in different parts of the state—Archibald at Springfield, Henry at Clary's Grove, William in Warren County. Fisher was an odd-job carpenter who had been living recently with William Trailor. The four men left the boarding house together, but that evening only the three Trailors returned for supper. Fisher's absence was the cause of some comment among the other boarders, so the three brothers spent several hours in searching for him, but without success.

The next morning they searched again, but at noon Henry and William started for their respective homes. Some of Myers's boarders remonstrated, but on the whole no general notice was taken of the affair. Three or four days later Henry Trailor reappeared and, with his brother and several others, spent another day in ineffectual search, only to give up again and return to his home.

Hardly had Henry Trailor left for Clary's Grove when a letter came from a postmaster in Warren County. The writer stated that William Trailor was boasting that Fisher was dead and had willed him his money, amounting in all to $1,500. He added that Trailor's story seemed strange and his conduct unnatural, and asked for the truth of the matter. The letter was made public, and immediately intense excitement prevailed in Springfield. Under the direction of the mayor and attorney general, an intensive search for Fisher's body was commenced. Large searching parties were formed, the timber and prairies thoroughly combed, cellars and wells of all sorts looked into, and even fresh graves opened. After twenty-four hours of fruitless effort the search was given up,

and officers were sent to arrest the Trailors and bring them
to Springfield. Two days later Henry Trailor appeared, in
custody.

At once the mayor and attorney general set out to draw a
confession from the prisoner. For two days he steadily denied all knowledge of what had happened to Fisher, but on
the third day, protesting his own innocence, he made a confession. His story was a strange one. On the day when Fisher
and his brothers had started out to see the town, he said,
they had wandered out to the timber to the northwest of the
city. There, without his knowledge at the time, William and
Archibald had murdered Fisher, and had temporarily concealed his body. The next day, before separating for their
homes, they had told him what they had done, and had asked
his help in disposing of the body. He accompanied them to
the woods, and stood guard at some distance while they removed a dead body from a dense thicket, placed it in their
wagon and started in the direction of Hickox's mill pond on
Spring Creek. Half an hour later they returned, saying they
had put him in a safe place, whereupon Archibald returned
to Springfield and William and Henry started for their
homes.

Archibald Trailor had borne such an excellent reputation
in Springfield that until his brother made this disclosure he
had not even been arrested. Now he was seized and put in
jail, and there was no little talk of a hanging at the hands of
the people. No time was lost in examining the thicket where
the body was said to have been concealed. There buggy tracks
leading in the direction of the mill pond were found. Hundreds took part in dragging the pond, and when no body
was found, tore down the dam.

Before the water was completely drained, the officer who
had been sent for William Trailor arrived in Springfield with
his prisoner. With them was a certain Doctor Gilmore, also
from Warren County, who swore that Fisher was not only

alive, but living at his home. The entire population of Springfield was dumbfounded. But when the doctor's story was related to Henry Trailor, he reaffirmed his own version of what
had happened without the slightest deviation. The crowd
at once concluded that Gilmore was a confederate engaged in
a desperate attempt to secure the release of the prisoners,
and excitement once more rose to fever heat.

The next day William and Archibald Trailor were ar-
raigned before two justices of the peace on a charge of murder. Josiah Lamborn appeared for the prosecution; Logan,
Lincoln, and Baker for the defendants. Henry Trailor was
put on the stand and withstood a severe cross-examination
without becoming entangled in any way. Other witnesses cor-
roborated some of his statements. Doctor Gilmore was then
sworn as a witness. He stated that on the morning of William
Trailor's arrest Fisher appeared at his home, that he was in
feeble health and could give no rational account of his recent
movements, that he understood him to be subject to occasional
temporary derangements, and that he would have brought
him with him to Springfield had his physical condition permitted. The doctor's demeanor was so convincing that the
justices discharged the prisoners, in spite of the fact that as
the hearing ended Henry Trailor was still asserting that no
power on earth would ever reveal Fisher alive.

That evening Abraham Lincoln wrote an account of the
mystery to Joshua Speed in Kentucky, prefacing it with the
statement that "we have had the highest state of excitement
here for a week past that our community has ever witnessed;
and although the public feeling is somewhat allayed, the
curious affair which aroused it is very far from being even
yet cleared of mystery." After relating all the circumstances
of the case, Lincoln finished with a description of the consternation which the conclusion had caused. "When the doctor's story was first made public," he wrote, "it was amusing
to scan and contemplate the countenances and hear the re-

marks of those who had been actively in search for the dead body: some looked quizzical, some melancholy, and some furiously angry. Porter, who had been very active, swore he always knew the man was not dead, and that he had not stirred an inch to hunt for him; Langford, who had taken the lead in cutting down Hickox's mill-dam, and who wanted to hang Hickox for objecting, looked most awfully woebegone: he seemed the 'wictim of hunrequited hafection,' as represented in the comic almanac we used to laugh over; and Hart, the little drayman that hauled Molly home once, said it was too *damned* bad, to have so much trouble and no hanging after all."

A few days after the discharge of the Trailor brothers, Fisher himself appeared in Springfield. On June 22 the people of the capital assembled in public meeting and passed resolutions regretting that their fellow-citizen, Archibald Trailor, should ever have been accused of the crime, and asserting that their respect for him had been in no way diminished by the accusation. But it was an ineffectual restitution. For two years Archibald Trailor shunned society, and then died of no apparent ailment. His brother William had already preceded him in death. Henry lived a few years longer, a broken, deranged man. None of the principals ever referred to the episode, and the mystery remains as dark and perplexing as it was on the night when Lincoln related the facts to Joshua Speed.

In scarcely more than a year the citizens of Springfield were again in a turmoil. This time the basic cause was politics, complicated by Abraham Lincoln's propensity to let a sarcastic pen outrun his better judgment.

For the state of Illinois, the years following the panic of 1837 were a financial nightmare. Due to the heavy commitments of the internal improvement system, her obligations were huge. On the other hand, prices were low and taxes were hard to collect. To make matters worse, by 1842 the state banks—the State Bank at Springfield and the Bank of Illinois at Shawneetown—were not redeeming their paper in specie. Their notes, circulating in the state to the amount of several millions, passed at large discounts.

To protect the state from the payment of taxes in this depreciated currency, the State Auditor, acting under a law passed several years earlier, issued a proclamation ordering collectors to suspend the collection of the revenue, and under no circumstances to accept state bank paper at more than its current value. Since the bulk of the currency in circulation was state bank paper, the auditor's action, wise in itself, was intensely unpopular. The situation was a capital one for the Whigs, and the Springfield group—the "Junto"—lost no time in taking advantage of it.

The State Auditor was James Shields, a young Irishman who had made rapid strides in the Democratic party. Upon coming to Springfield in 1841 he had formed a partnership with James C. Conkling, who, though a Whig, had written his fiancée a description which discloses an attractive personality. "A young gentleman of fine talents with a considerable touch of Irish eloquence," he characterized Shields. "Pray don't let the appellation Paddy convey to you the idea that he is a great, brawny, double fisted, uncouth Irishman. Quite the reverse. A person might possibly detect the place of his nativity by his looks, but his tongue is smooth as oil. He is a warm Democrat, but as he is not a violent politician I think we can jog along very sociably." But Shields was also possessed of an effervescence of spirits and an excess of gallantry which made him a fine subject for ridicule, and the fun of chaffing him was all the keener because of his lack of a good sense of humor.

At the time the collection of the revenue was suspended the *Sangamo Journal* was publishing, under the heading of "Lost Townships," a series of letters containing vernacular statements of Whig doctrines. The third of these letters, dated

August 27, dealt with Shields and his proclamation. The author was supposed to be a widow named Rebecca, who was reporting to the editor her conversation with a farmer of the Lost Townships. To save his face the farmer, a Democrat, insisted that Shields was a Whig, and to prove his assertion described him as he had seen him at a social gathering in Springfield.

"I seed him when I was down in Springfield last winter," said the farmer. "They had a sort of a gatherin' there one night among the grandees, they called a fair. All the gals about town was there, and all the handsome widows and married women, finickin' about trying to look like gals, tied as tight in the middle, and puffed out at both ends, like bundles of fodder that hadn't been stacked yet, but wanted stackin' pretty bad. . . . They wouldn't let no Democrats in, for fear they'd disgust the ladies, or scare the little gals, or dirty the floor. I looked in at the window, and there was this same fellow Shields floatin' about on the air, without heft or earthly substance, just like a lock of cat fur where cats had been fighting.

"He was paying his money to this one, and that one, and t'other one, and sufferin' great loss because it wasn't silver instead of State paper; and the sweet distress he seemed to be in—his very features, in the ecstatic agony of his soul, spoke audibly and distinctly, 'Dear girls, it is distressing, but I cannot marry you all. Too well I know how much you suffer; but do, do remember, it is not my fault that I am so handsome and so interesting.' . . . He a Democrat! Fiddlesticks! I tell you Aunt 'Becca, he's a Whig, and no mistake: nobody but a Whig could make such a conceity dunce of himself."

His vanity touched, Shields demanded the name of the author from the editor. He was told that Abraham Lincoln had written the piece in question. Before he could demand an apology, however, Shields was called to Quincy, and by the time of his return, Lincoln had gone to Tremont for the fall session of the Tazewell court. Meanwhile, another "Lost Townships" letter had appeared in the *Journal*. This time Rebecca, having heard of Shields' anger at her previous communication, came forth not only with an apology but with an offer of marriage as well. "I know he's a fighting man, and would rather fight than eat," she admitted; "but isn't marryin' better than fightin', though it does sometimes run in to it?" If the Auditor should insist on combat, Rebecca gave him the privilege of choosing whether she should wear breeches or he petticoats, "for," she concluded, "I presume that change is sufficient to place us on an equality." The letter was crudely done, but it served to rub salt in wounds already smarting.

Finding Lincoln absent when he got back to Springfield, Shields took John D. Whitesides and started after him. Meanwhile E. H. Merryman and William Butler, learning their purpose, set out for Tremont, passed Shields and Whitesides during the night, and succeeded in warning Lincoln before his pursuers arrived. He said that he was opposed to duelling, and would avoid it if he could without degradation, but if that were impossible, he would fight.

A few hours later Shields and Whitesides reached Tremont. Whitesides called on Lincoln at once, and presented a note from the Auditor demanding a full retraction of all offensive allusions. There followed an interchange of correspondence in the best manner of the code, even to meticulous references to "Captain" Lincoln, which finally ended with a challenge and its acceptance. Thereupon all except Shields started for Springfield.

Arriving there, they found the town in great excitement. To avoid arrest, Lincoln determined to leave early the following morning. Before leaving he instructed Merryman, his second, to offer his full apology to Shields if the latter would withdraw his first communication and substitute another "without menace or dictation." In case of a refusal, the weapons were to be cavalry broadswords of the largest size and the place a spot within three miles of Alton on the Missouri side of the river. The next morning the seconds met, but failed to compose the difficulty. Merryman, whose arrest was also threatened, then left for Jacksonville to meet Lincoln, procure broadswords and proceed to the dueling place.

The parties met as agreed. On the dueling ground friends patched up the quarrel, and the principals returned to Springfield in reasonable harmony.

But the matter was far from ended. Whitesides published in the *Register* an account of the affair which Merryman resented, and he in turn published his version in the *Journal*. One thing led to another until the challenges could hardly be kept track of. On October 5, nearly two weeks after the peaceful conclusion of his own escapade, Lincoln described the uproar to his friend Speed.

You have heard of my duel with Shields, and I have now to inform you that the dueling business still rages in this city. Day before yesterday Shields challenged Butler, who accepted, and proposed fighting next morning at sunrise in Bob Allen's meadow, one hundred yards' distance, with rifles. To this Whitesides, Shields's second, said "No" because of the law. Thus ended duel No. 2. Yesterday Whitesides chose to consider himself insulted by Dr. Merryman, so sent him a kind of quasi-challenge inviting him to meet him at the Planter's House in St. Louis, on the next Friday, to settle their difficulty. Merryman made me his friend, and sent Whitesides a note, inquiring to know if he meant his note as a challenge, and if so, that he would, according to the law in such case made and provided, prescribe the terms of the meeting. Whitesides returned for answer that if Merryman would meet him at the Planter's House as desired, he would challenge him. Merryman replied in a note that he denied Whiteside's right to dictate time and place, but that he (Merryman) would waive the question of time, and meet him at Louisiana, Missouri. Upon my presenting his note to Whitesides and stating verbally its contents, he declined receiving it, saying he had business in St. Louis, and it was as near as Louisiana. Merryman then directed me to notify Whitesides that he should publish the correspondence between them, with such comments as he thought fit. This I did. Thus it stood at bed-time last night. This morning Whitesides, by his friend Shields, is praying for a new trial, on the ground that he was mistaken in Merryman's proposition to meet him at Louisiana, Missouri, thinking it was the State of Louisiana. This Merryman hoots at, and is preparing his publication; while the town is in a ferment, and a street fight somewhat anticipated.[2]

Fortunately, the dueling fever finally abated without serious consequences. But it was never forgotten, and lives in prairie lore in such tales as that which has Lincoln, when informed that as the challenged party he would have the choice of weapons, reply, "How about cow-dung at five paces?" In sober fact, however, it was to be a source of mortification to Lincoln throughout his life. He soon refused to discuss it, even with close friends, and as time went on, the mere mention of his "duel" aroused his acute displeasure, and was certain to bring a sharp rebuff to the rash gossiper.

While the dueling excitement was running its course the people of Springfield were becoming interested in a problem that was to distract the state for more than four years.

In 1838 the Mormons, after having been expelled from Ohio and then Missouri, took refuge in Illinois. There, at Nauvoo in Hancock County, they soon built a flourishing settlement. Politicians of both parties, anxious to curry favor, enabled them to obtain charters of such liberality that they became practically independent of higher authority. Gradually the goodwill which had originally greeted them turned to distrust. By participating en masse in politics they aroused ac-

---

[2] The manner in which many writers have handled this episode of Lincoln's life leads one to suspect that they were ignorant of the fact that in 1842 dueling was still a prevalent practice. To cite a few examples: in 1838 William Graves killed Jonathan Cilley in a duel near Washington; in 1841 August Belmont, the American agent of the Rothschilds, fought Edward Heyward at Elkton, Maryland, and was wounded in the thigh; and on June 25, 1842, James Watson Webb, editor of the New York *Courier and Enquirer*, received a minor wound in a duel with Thomas F. Marshall fought near Wilmington, Delaware.

tive antagonism. During the summer of 1842, throughout the contest for state offices, rumors of all sorts were in circulation. Numerous thefts and robberies were charged against them, and many believed that they planned to overthrow the government when their strength should be great enough. The Whigs, angered by the Mormons' recent support of the Democratic party, eagerly gave circulation to such gossip. In Springfield the *Sangamo Journal* filled its columns with anti-Mormon tirades.

A few months later Springfield found itself, for a few days, the focus of the Mormon question. Since 1840 attempts had been made to extradite the Mormon leaders to Missouri, to stand trial there for alleged participation in an attempt to assassinate the governor of that state. Finally, in December, 1842, Governor Ford issued a warrant for the arrest of Joseph Smith, the Mormon leader. Smith retained Justin Butterfield as counsel, and Butterfield sued out a writ of habeas corpus from Judge Pope of the United States District Court. At the hearing Butterfield coined a pun so famous that it still lives in the legal lore of Illinois.

Because of the parties involved, the case had aroused great interest. Present were Smith and his twelve Apostles, as well as many of the leading men of the state. The court room was so crowded that several ladies who were present—among them Mrs. Lincoln and one of Pope's daughters—were seated on either side of the judge. Amid a deep silence Butterfield, in long blue coat with brass buttons and buff-colored waistcoat, rose slowly to his feet. Pausing until he had surveyed the row of fashionably dressed women before him, he spoke:

"May it please the court:

"I appear before you today under circumstances most novel and peculiar. I am to address the Pope (bowing to the judge) surrounded by angels (with a very low bow), in the presence of the holy Apostles, on behalf of the Prophet of the Lord!"

Pope discharged the Mormon leader, but as time went on feeling against the strange sect became ever more intense. Smith himself aggravated conditions by the idiotic act of announcing his candidacy for the Presidency of the United States in 1844. Soon afterward discord developed in the Mormon church, and an opposition group established a newspaper of its own. Smith's followers countered by demolishing the press. Excitement mounted. Wild rumors spread—that Smith had been crowned and anointed king of the Mormons; that he had created a select band of followers named Danites who were sworn to obey his every command, murder and treason not excepted; that the whole church was a community of murderers, thieves and outlaws; that counterfeiting was being carried on on a large scale at Nauvoo; that polygamy was being practised widely.

Violence seemed so near that the governor was asked to call out the militia. He preferred instead to make a personal investigation, and proceeded to Nauvoo. While he was there a mob murdered Joseph Smith and his brother Hyrum in the jail at Carthage. Disorder continued until fall, when Ford ordered Brig. Gen. John J. Hardin, Cols. E. D. Baker and E. H. Merryman of Springfield, and Col. William Weatherford, to raise 500 volunteers and restore order in Hancock County. Among those who offered their services were the military companies of Springfield. No resistance was offered, but John Norris, of the Springfield Cadets, was shot accidentally, and died within a short time. By early October order prevailed, and the Springfield men returned to their homes.

Peace, however, had not yet come to the distracted community. In the fall of 1845 disorder in Hancock County once more reached the danger point, and once again Hardin with a force of several hundred militiamen established himself at Carthage. This time he induced the Mormons to agree to leave the county in the spring. Warm weather came, and the exodus started. By the middle of May it was estimated that 16,000 Mormons had crossed the Mississippi. But perhaps a thousand remained in Nauvoo, and by their presence inflamed their neighbors to a final outbreak.

By autumn Nauvoo was a besieged city. Outside was a force of several hundred men, armed with muskets, rifles and small cannon; inside were the remnant of the Mormons and many non-members of the sect who had purchased the property of the departed faithful. Several skirmishes took place, but there were few casualties. Finally the Mormons were induced to yield, whereupon their enemies entered the town and expelled not only them but also the non-Mormons who had joined them in their resistance.

To protect the latter in their property rights Ford called for volunteers. For months the people of Springfield—and Illinois in general—had been indifferent to affairs in Hancock County, believing that the wisest course was to let the inhabitants fight out their difficulties; but conditions finally became so notorious that George R. Weber, editor of the *Register* and major of militia, raised 120 men in and around Springfield and proceeded to Nauvoo, where the force encamped in the shadow of the temple. Although the anti-Mormons resented their presence bitterly nothing happened, and after two weeks all except fifty men under Captain Connelley of Springfield were withdrawn. Winter came, and ice and snow prevented further disorder. By spring practically all the Mormons had gone. In their absence passions quickly cooled. The "Mormon War" was over.

While Springfield and Springfield men had been drawn into the Mormon troubles repeatedly, other events had frequently crowded them out of the town's attention. One such distraction was the presidential campaign of 1844.

With the feverish Harrison campaign fresh in memory, both parties made heroic efforts to re-create the emotional intensity which the Whigs had achieved in 1840. In Springfield the chief reliance was placed on huge flagpoles instead of the log cabins of four years earlier. Late in July the Democrats erected a hickory pole one hundred feet in height, and unfurled a banner made by the Democratic ladies of the town. David B. Campbell made the address of the day, and the Springfield Artillery paraded and fired a salute of thirty-two guns.

At once the Whigs made plans for a party rally which would show up the Democratic gathering as a puny effort. August 3rd was the date set. Handbills were sent out over the county, and a large crowd gathered to see an ash pole, many feet longer than the hickory pole of their rivals, put into place. The task seemed to be successfully accomplished when two workmen, John Brodie and William Conant, attempted to move one of the derricks with which the pole had been lifted. Suddenly a guy rope snapped. For an instant the pole wavered, and then crashed to the ground. Brodie was killed instantly and Conant was seriously injured. The balance of the program was abandoned, but that evening a considerable group gathered in "impressive silence" at the home of J. A. Corneau, where E. D. Baker and John J. Hardin of Jacksonville made brief addresses.

Among the Whigs were a few hotheads who charged the Democrats with responsibility for the accident. At first no one paid any attention to their insinuations, but events of the next week or two convinced the scatter-brained that there was truth behind the charge. One by one, the workmen who had been hired to erect the Whig pole fell ill. All of them, it was found, had drunk at the public well. For several days rumors circulated that the well had been poisoned by the Democrats. Finally a farmer who lived near Rochester came forward with an explanation. A week or two earlier, he said, he had watched a small boy place a package on top of the pump. A moment later it fell in. Both he and the boy had tried to recover it, but without success. It had contained fly salve for horses! Thus the mystery was solved, and the Democrats vindicated.

After waiting two weeks the Whigs made a second attempt to raise an ash pole, and this time there were no casualties. Truly their rivals were overshadowed, for the pole, in six sections, measured 214½ feet. A week later an American flag and a Clay banner, made by the Whig ladies of Springfield, were unfurled with elaborate ceremonies. Speechmaking, interspersed with songs by the Clay glee club, lasted all afternoon; and in the evening the city was illuminated with bonfires and displays of fireworks.

For the most part, however, no unusual enthusiasm marked the campaign. The personal popularity of Henry Clay was great, but the Democrats enjoyed the advantages of larger numbers, superior organization and popular issues. As a result, they carried Illinois for James K. Polk by a comfortable majority. Three weeks after the election the party gathered in Springfield for a celebration. One hundred guns boomed a prelude to a torch light parade through the principal streets. At the head of the procession was a dead raccoon, suspended neck-down from a gallows, while above it crowed a live rooster. The homes of prominent Democrats were illuminated, and in windows all over town shown transparencies with appropriate mottoes.

One reason for the success of the Democrats was the position of the party on two issues in which the people of Illinois were deeply interested—the annexation of Texas, and the northern ("54-40 or fight") boundary of Oregon.

For several years the people of Springfield had had a lively interest in conditions in Texas and Oregon. Periodically, public meetings gave opportunity for the expression of opinion. In February, 1843, two large meetings, held in the State House on successive nights, passed resolutions affirming that the United States had an unquestioned right to the whole of Oregon Territory, that it should take immediate steps to occupy it and establish a territorial government, and that consent to the surrender of any part of the territory should never be given. A year later the Texas question was dealt with no less emphatically. A call for a public meeting, sent out over the signatures of 123 citizens, posed the question in these words: "The people of Texas, our brothers by birth, the friends of liberty by education, appeal to our sympathies for protection; and ask to attach themselves to this great Republic, that they may become with us one people, united in interest and communion, as we are already by our devotion to human liberty and the rights of man . . . Shall they ask in vain?" The meeting passed resolutions in favor of immediate annexation.

In the beginning the tendency of the Whigs had been to oppose extreme measures in both Oregon and Texas. Thus at the Oregon meeting in 1843 Usher F. Linder of Charleston and E. D. Baker took "the British side of the question," to quote their opponents; and at the Texas meeting fourteen months later Baker and Lincoln opposed annexation. The campaign of 1844, however, showed the party the futility of opposition. The result was apparent at a large Oregon meeting held in June, 1845, at which Hardin and Baker, as well as Douglas and John Calhoun, assented to resolutions affirming the "indisputable" title of the United States as far as 54°40′, calling for the military occupation of the disputed territory, and proclaiming that "we are ready, willing and anxious, if necessary, to maintain the American title to the whole country by an appeal to arms."

Therefore it was to no apathetic community that news of war with Mexico came in mid-May, 1846. On the 25th of that month Governor Ford issued his proclamation calling for 3,000 volunteers. On the same day John J. Hardin, Brigadier General of Illinois militia, let it be known that he had enrolled his own name—the first Illinoisan to offer himself—and called for volunteers from his brigade. Five days later a rally was held in Springfield. The military companies paraded the streets, and then, with as many citizens as could crowd in, gathered in the Hall of the House. The Governor, E. H. Merryman, Lincoln and others stirred the crowd with speeches on the necessity of sustaining national honor and national rights. By nightfall seventy men had volunteered.

Throughout Illinois the war fever flamed. In a few days the three regiments which had been assigned to the state were filled, and volunteers by the thousand were being turned away. Disappointed at not receiving a command, E. D. Baker, in Washington as the Representative of the Springfield district, got authority from the President to raise a fourth regiment and hurried home to recruit it. On June 6, at a public meeting held in the state house, eighty men enlisted. In less than three weeks the ranks of the regiment were full.

For two weeks the Fourth Illinois, as Baker's regiment was designated, was encamped on the prairie at the southern limit of Springfield. Included were two local companies under Captains H. E. Roberts and Achilles Morris. The town was war-mad. Crowds gathered to watch the recruits stumble through the manual of arms, and ladies sewed on flags for the "brave hearts who were so nobly responding to the call of their country." When the regiment struck its tents on June 27 and started for the concentration camp at Alton, the sighs of friends and tears of parents were lost in the cheers of the entire population. War was a glorious adventure.

After two weeks at Alton, the Fourth Regiment was transferred to Jefferson Barracks at St. Louis, to train there until transports should be available. The people of the river city were favorably impressed. "The regiment is handsomely uniformed," said the *Missouri Democrat*, "in blue roundabouts and pantaloons, with glazed oil-cloth caps, and in the equipment of the United States infantry they make as handsome a display as has at any time been seen in our streets."

Late in July the men were put on transports for New

Orleans, whence they reshipped for the Rio Grande, which they reached on August 15th. With the exception of an overland march to reinforce Taylor at Monterey, where they arrived too late to be of any use, the men of the Fourth Illinois remained at various camps on the San Juan and Rio Grande for nearly four months.

Before many weeks the young enthusiasts from Illinois learned that war was far from the romantic excursion they had imagined. Even before the regiment left St. Louis, William Walters, who left the office of the *Illinois State Register* to volunteer, fell ill, and later died, but death did not begin to take toll in earnest until the Rio Grande was reached. There, at one time or another, nearly every man in the regiment was sick. Unhealthy climate, poor food and water, forced marches and an almost complete ignorance of sanitary precautions combined to prostrate the troops. By late October, 1846, the regiment which had gaily marched out of Springfield with 770 men had been reduced to 530. Sixty had died, and more than a hundred had been confined to hospitals or sent home, too emaciated for service. Only 400 were fit for duty. Before the Fourth Regiment left Matamoras for Tampico in mid-December nearly one hundred had died, and men said that the dead march had been played so often that even the birds knew its strains.

When the regiment was ordered south the prospect of battle was welcome. After a month and a half in Tampico, transports took the men to Vera Cruz. There, in the action which finally reduced the defenses and opened the way to Mexico City, Capt. H. E. Roberts won the distinction of being the first American to disembark, and the entire regiment bore itself creditably.

Meanwhile, Springfield had been thrown into excitement by the news of the Battle of Buena Vista. The first reports had reached the city late in March, but at that time the outcome of the engagement was unknown. On April 1 the American victory was proclaimed, and there was great rejoicing. But there was also sorrow, for the death of John J. Hardin was announced. Although a resident of Jacksonville, Hardin had been a familiar, popular figure in the capital. A few days after the news of his death was received, the citizens of Springfield met at the court house. Judge Treat was called to the chair, and Abraham Lincoln explained the purpose of the meeting and offered resolutions expressing sorrow at the death of Hardin and those who had fallen with him.

Six weeks after the Battle of Buena Vista the news of Cerro Gordo reached Springfield. This time anxiety was intense, for sons and brothers were involved. First reports were disquieting. Victory was proclaimed, but Baker was said to have lost forty-five killed and wounded in only a portion of his regiment, and Shields, commanding a brigade, was reported fatally wounded. For days the town was tense with fear. The mails were slow, and several weeks elapsed before the casualties were entirely reported. Then it was known that Shields would recover, and that only a few Springfield men had lost their lives. Battle was hardly more dangerous than camp life in Mexico.

With anxiety over the fate of friends and relatives was mixed pride in the performance of the Illinois troops. The citizens thrilled to an account of the battle, which James H. Merryman of Springfield's Company A wrote to his father. On the evening of April 17th Shields's brigade, which included both the Third and Fourth Illinois, had got into position on a height overlooking the enemy's works. "We were up at break of day," Merryman wrote;

—a bright Sunday morning. I looked around me;—the scene was grand and imposing: the east just tinged with the rays of the rising sun; lofty mountains just visible in the distance, and Orizaba appearing above all. . . . The side of the hill glistened with bayonets. There lay the Illinois boys, eager for the fight, and anxiously await-

ing that day which should bring them fame and glory. . . . The
order was given to move. On we went for two hundred yards, when
everything that the Mexicans could bring to bear was fired, and
great was the noise of six and four pounders, grape and cannister,
ball and buckshot, whistling through the air. For six hundred yards
we were exposed to the fire of the largest battery, called Tower Hill.
Finally we got under cover of the chapparal of an opposite hill.
Several were wounded, and Lieut. Cowardin killed by this fire. On
we went towards the Jalapa road. . . .

We pushed on through the chapparal until coming upon a small
plain. A heavy fire in our front announced to us the fact of there
being a battery there. We were a good deal astonished, I assure
you; and rather discouraged when we saw our brave general carried
to the rear, severely wounded. But the voice of our brave and gallant
Colonel, who was second in command, restored our equilibrium. He
made his dispositions. His orders were obeyed,—and the extreme left
of the enemy's position was carried by the 4th Illinois volunteers, with
the loss of 46 men killed and wounded.

It was a glorious sight to see the enemy *bamas*. We captured
six pieces of cannon, Santa Anna's carriage, *his wooden leg,* and
18,000 in specie. . . .

We pushed on in pursuit of the enemy with our brigade and
two pieces of artillery. We overtook them. Four or five squadrons
of lancers charged towards us, and 40 men of our regiment re-
pulsed them. Three times they tried it, but it was NO GO. On they
went at a gallop. Gen. Twiggs led the pursuit and 'swore terribly.'
He shouted, "Huzza, my Illinois bloodhounds, pursue them, d—n 'em,
after 'em boys, and be d—d to them!" We overtook them again,
eight miles from the battle ground, at El Encero, Santa Anna's
hacienda, fired upon them with the artillery, and gave up the pursuit.

Before the end of the Mexico City campaign the Third and
Fourth Illinois were sent back to New Orleans and there discharged. In small parties they trickled home. By the Fourth
of July all the survivors had returned, so the day was made
the occasion of a citizens' tribute to them. Headed by the
Springfield Brass Band, Captain Fisher's Springfield Infantry
and Captain Smith's Decatur Infantry, the veterans in
weatherbeaten uniforms, with Baker at their head, marched

to the grove east of town,[3] where a bountiful dinner was served. Several thousand heard James Barrett read the Declaration of Independence, W. I. Ferguson's oration of the day, and Baker's response. In the evening the volunteers were the guests of honor at a piano concert which the Misses Browne gave in the Hall of Representatives. Afterward the floor was cleared and there was dancing until half-past eleven.

Ten days later many Springfield citizens, and the members of the constitutional convention then in session, traveled to Jacksonville to attend the funeral of John J. Hardin. For Springfield, these solemn rites concluded the war. Later a number of her residents enlisted in a company of Mounted Rifles, but saw no active service. No enthusiasm greeted their departure, and their return went unnoticed.

On the heels of the Mexican War, and colored by it in almost every particular, came the political campaign of 1848.

In Springfield, interest centered in the contest for Lincoln's seat in Congress. Although at the outbreak of the war Lincoln had joined the other politicians in making speeches about national honor, in Congress he had followed his party in denouncing the conflict as unnecessary and unjust. In particular, he had introduced a series of shrewdly worded resolutions demanding of President Polk the exact spot on which first blood was shed, thus attempting to pin the responsibility for the conflict on the United States. To the people of his district, this was a close approach to treason. They had gone into the war with enthusiasm, they were proud of the record of their soldiers, and they wanted no one to tell them that they had been in the wrong. All over the district resolutions denouncing Lincoln and his "spot" interrogatories were adopted. In derision the Democrats nicknamed him "Spotty" Lincoln.

This record alone was a heavy load for Stephen T. Logan, the Whig candidate, to carry, and by remaining in Wash-

[3] Bergen Park.

ington instead of returning to defend himself, Lincoln did not make it any lighter. But when an active opponent who had served gallantly in the field—Maj. Thomas L. Harris of Petersburg—was added to his troubles, Logan's doom was made certain. At the August election the district, heretofore safely Whig, went emphatically for Harris. The Democrats rejoiced boisterously. When the returns indicated the result cannon boomed and bonfires blazed, bands paraded the streets of Springfield, and far into the night orators congratulated the party on its victory.

But war service was a two-edged sword. When the Whigs selected Taylor, with the fame of his conquests still fresh, to oppose Cass, it cut in another direction. In November came the turn of the Whigs to rejoice.

In Springfield they did it lustily, for Whig victories in presidential elections were rare occurrences. November 21st was the day selected for formal jubilation. In the afternoon a national salute was fired. At nightfall the homes and stores of the faithful were illuminated. Two hours later the lights were put out in order that the torchlight procession might appear to better advantage. At nine o'clock, when the parade disbanded at the square, bonfires, rockets, and fireworks blazed all over town. "There was much joy, much congratulation," the *Journal* observed smugly, "—much expression of high hopes of the future of the country under the new administration."

The outbreak of war with Mexico had forced the Polk administration to a compromise on the question of the Oregon boundary. To the people of Illinois this was pusillanimity—but their resentment at the nation's failure to back up its claims did not deter them from taking eager advantage of the territory to which the title of the United States had been confirmed. Even before the settlement of the boundary question an epidemic of Oregon emigration had set in. Hardly an issue of a newspaper appeared without its notice of the formation of an Oregon company. Articles on the history and geography of the Northwest were read eagerly, and letters from emigrants were frequently published.

Springfield and Sangamon County were not immune to the prevailing fever. Beginning in 1845, each spring saw the departure of expeditions. Notices like the following were typical: "Several families will leave Sangamon County this spring, for Oregon and California. Among them are some of our best citizens." For months afterward the progress of the expedition, its hardships and hopes, would be described in letters received by friends and relatives.

With the discovery of gold in California in 1848, the rate of emigration speeded up sharply. In the spring of 1849 parties left Springfield for the gold fields every few days, and it was estimated that the total exodus from Sangamon County was not less than 150. So far as possible, the Springfield papers kept track of the emigrants and printed the letters they wrote home, together with many columns of advice to emigrants.

From Springfield, the favorite route to both Oregon and California was overland by way of Independence, Missouri. Hardships were a matter of course, and were accepted stoically, but the disasters which befell one Sangamon County organization were so horrible that its story has become the epitome of the tragedies of the overland trail.

In the early spring of 1846 a notice, signed "G. Donner and Others," appeared in the *Sangamo Journal*. "Who wants to go to California without costing them anything?" the first sentence read. The services of eight young men of good character who were able to drive ox-teams were solicited.

The party was quickly made up. With the families of James F. Reed and George Donner as nuclei, thirty-four persons left Springfield on April 14, 1846. Other groups joined them as they moved westward. One month after departure they were on the Kansas River a hundred miles west of Independence in a company which totalled more than three hundred men, women and children. Soon afterward, however, the majority of the emigrants, whose destination was Oregon, selected a northern route, while the Reeds and Donners, with a smaller number, pushed on for California.

Traveling slowly up the valley of the Platte they reached Fort Laramie without mishap, and then crossed the Rocky Mountains to Fort Bridger in safety. Here they made a fatal mistake. By this time it was early autumn. Instead of following a longer but well established route to the north of the Great Salt Lake, they chose a much shorter but far more dangerous trail due west past the lake's southern tip. Hardships came in quick succession. Cattle and horses strayed and were stolen, lack of water caused great suffering, and—worst of all—winter was fast approaching and provisions were running short.

On the cut-off which the party had taken there were no settlements or stations. Obviously, the only thing to do was to send one or two men forward to Sutter's in California for provisions, leaving the main body of emigrants to follow as best they could. After severe hardships the emissaries reached Sutter's ranch, secured food supplies, and started back. But by this time heavy snows had fallen and the mountain trails were impassable. Repeated attempts to break through failed. The stark fact was that relief was impossible before spring.

Meanwhile, snow-bound, the emigrants prepared to make the best of an apparently hopeless situation. Throwing hasty shelters together, they began to parcel out the scanty supply of food. Soon it was gone. Then the cattle which remained were killed, and then the dogs. Finally only hides remained—hides and the bodies of those who were dying almost daily. When spring came, and relief arrived, the fleshless bones of those who had starved to death were found in the cabins of more than one half-demented survivor.

The miracle was that any lived through the four months of horror. Yet forty persons out of seventy-two finally reached California; and James F. Reed was able to write back to Gershom Keyes in Springfield: "The disasters of the company to which I belonged, should not deter any person from coming who wishes to try his fortune."

California—Oregon—Mexico: the words alone are indicative of the far-flowing currents of life which the years of the forties swept into Springfield. Before the decade closed, however, the world impinged from even more directions upon the little prairie capital.

For one thing, there was an eddy of French social philosophy. In Paris, Charles Fourier was propounding the "science of social unity." Man and his environment, Fourier believed, were out of harmony. And since God made man and man made the environment, the environment must be changed. To do this so that human desires—which, in Fourier's belief, were all good—would have free play, cooperation was necessary. Families must pool their property in a sort of joint-stock enterprise, live in a common dwelling, and apportion necessary work in such a way as to give each individual the greatest opportunity for the use of his own talents and at the same time hold drudgery to a minimum. Happiness would be the certain reward.

Expounded in the United States by Arthur Brisbane, with the enthusiastic support of Horace Greeley, Fourier's doctrines led to the formation of more than thirty communities, or "phalanxes," as they were called. Lick Creek in Sangamon County—now Loami—was the scene of one of these experiments.

Early in 1845 a group led by the Rev. Theophilus Sweet became converted to Fourierism and decided to form the Sangamon Association. A preliminary organization was adopted, stock was taken and paid for by contributions of land, labor and sometimes money, and work was commenced on a communal dwelling. Before the Association actually started to function, however, a merger was made with a group of Ohio Fourierists who called themselves the Integral Phalanx. Taking this name, the two organizations joined forces and set out to realize the dreams of the master on the Illinois prairies.

The experiment lasted little more than a year. In the beginning all went well, but before many months had passed discontent was evident. Women who were accustomed to an abundance of butter and eggs and milk began to chafe at the restrictions of the community commissary. Men who worked hard discovered that there were not a few who preferred to do nothing—and succeeded in realizing their desire. Others, who had invested property, saw those who had contributed only labor enjoying the same comforts that they were accorded. "The shareholders kept losing," said one member, "and those who came in with nothing were getting along very well."

Early in 1846 the president, John S. Williams of Cincinnati, resigned. Later in the year others withdrew. Finally the survivors confessed failure, and decided upon dissolution. The end of the Integral Phalanx was reached in a Springfield courtroom on an April day in 1848 when the judge, on the petition of Stephen T. Logan, ordered the property to be re-conveyed to the original grantors.

In Springfield the prevailing attitude towards this attempt at realizing the millennium was one of skepticism. Yet the attempt itself was only an exaggerated expression of an idealism discernible in so many forms that it almost characterizes the period. With the majority, however, it took form most frequently in a lively sympathy with peoples who were aspiring to political rather than economic democracy. The people of Springfield were always willing to applaud the prospect of Irish liberty, and Kossuth and the aspirations of the Hungarians stirred them to high enthusiasm.

At the very end of the decade came an unusual opportunity to give practical expression to their sympathy with the downtrodden.

The story starts on the island of Madeira in 1838, when a Scotsman named Robert Reid Kalley, on his way to China as a Presbyterian missionary, became so ill that he had to land and await recovery in the port of Funchal. Within a few hours he seems to have determined that the Far East offered no better field for conversions than that which he found around him. At any rate he stayed; and during the next few years, with the aid of others, succeeded in establishing a militant Protestant congregation. Naturally, this result was not altogether welcome to the resident Roman Catholic hierarchy. Opposition, passive at first, became more and more determined, and at last broke out in violence. Finally, in the midst of serious rioting, pastor and flock—now numbering more than a thousand—took refuge on shipboard.

Several hundred of the exiles quickly found refuge in Trinidad, where the planters were badly in need of laborers. But for the refugees the location proved unfortunate. Sickness was wide-spread, and many found difficulty in making a living. Their leaders determined on removal.

In the United States the plight of the Portuguese had received wide publicity. The American Protestant Society, with headquarters in New York, became actively interested in their predicament, and sent a representative to Trinidad to investigate their condition. As a result of his visit, arrangements were made with the American Hemp Company for the transport of the exiles to the United States and their settlement in Illinois at Island Grove, midway between Jacksonville and Springfield. On the strength of this prospect, most of the exiles started from Trinidad to New York. And then the American Hemp Company failed to make good its engagement. As a result, in the spring of 1849 the New York churchmen found themselves with several hundred homeless

Portuguese on their hands, with more soon to arrive from Trinidad.

At this point the people of Jacksonville, with fine philanthropy, took the initiative. A telegram was sent offering asylum and a livelihood in that city to those already in New York, and suggesting that those to come later could be cared for in Springfield. To this proposal Springfield gave hearty agreement. But before it could be acted upon cholera made its appearance in the Middle West and threw Morgan and Sangamon counties into almost hysterical apprehension. The refugees were warned to wait until the danger had passed.

By autumn, when the cholera was on the wane, the first of the Portuguese started westward. A Springfield committee, headed by Simeon Francis, made plans to receive them. However, the arrival, on November 13, 1849, of 130 persons, found preparations far from complete. The committee hastily procured four vacant houses, but the furnishings available consisted of a few chairs, three tables, three water buckets, two bedsteads, a limited amount of bedding, and a few cups and saucers. An appeal for furniture, clothing and provisions met a generous response. For days Francis, James A. Barrett, the Rev. Albert Hale of the Second Presbyterian Church, and other kindly men and women devoted themselves to the strangers. Gradually places were found for them, and they were absorbed into the community.

At the same time that the first contingent of Portuguese reached Springfield, a similar group arrived in Jacksonville. For several years small parties made their way to both cities. By 1855 there were 350 in Springfield. In spite of the fact that nearly half the number were recent arrivals, thirty families had built homes of their own, and nearly all were prosperous and happy. On the prairies of Illinois, three thousand miles from home, they had finally found contentment.

CHAPTER VII

Making a Living

JUBILATION over the acceleration of business which followed the location of the state offices in Springfield did not blind the people to basic economic realities. There was still the problem of transportation and the farmers' surplus. However, even here there seemed to be reason for optimism. The Internal Improvement System had collapsed in the panic of 1837, but one railroad was under construction, and part of it at least would be finished. That was the Northern Cross, originally planned to extend from Quincy to the Indiana line. It was obvious that funds would be exhausted long before these termini were reached, but its completion from the Illinois River to Springfield appeared to be a certainty.

Surveys for the Northern Cross had started in November, 1837. Six months later the first rail was put in place at Meredosia. By the summer of 1839 the track had been laid for twelve miles east of the Illinois River, and grading was in progress in the neighborhood of Springfield. On January 1, 1840, the road was finished as far as Jacksonville, but more than a year elapsed before the extension to Springfield was completed. The first train ran into the new capital on February 15, 1842.

To the optimists of the Sangamo country—and in 1842 almost everyone could be called by that name—the Northern Cross seemed to carry a definite promise of prosperity. "The road passes for sixty miles through the richest portion of Illinois," the *Journal* observed, "and the vast surplus produce of the counties of Morgan, Sangamon, Logan, Christian, DeWitt, Macon, and a considerable portion of Shelby, will seek a market over the lines of this road. In addition to this all the merchandise for the supply of these counties will be brought in on the road. The facilities for cheap and expeditious travelling to the thousands who visit and pass through this city annually, will furnish also a large item of income."

At first the fulfillment of this promise seemed likely. Springfield merchants loaded quantities of flour and pork on the cars for the New Orleans market, and passengers, excited by the prospect of reaching Jacksonville in two hours and ten minutes, flocked to the trains. In one day 205 barrels of flour and thirty passengers left Springfield for Meredosia. In comparison with stage and wagon rates, tariffs were low. Passengers were charged $2.50 for the entire trip, while the freight on a barrel of flour to the Illinois River was only twenty cents. "We think our citizens ought to hold a celebration on account of the opening of the road," said the editor of the *Register*.

But disillusionment came quickly. In less than two months there was open complaint that the facilities of the road were too limited to move the crops of the tributary country. It was estimated that unless equipment were greatly increased, three months would be required to move the surplus stored in Springfield alone. Moreover, as soon as the first excitement wore off, sober heads realized that at best the Northern Cross could be no more than a very shaky bridge across Springfield's economic slough of despond. New Orleans was the market for the Sangamon country. But in the spring New Orleans was flooded with the produce of the lower Ohio and upper Mississippi valleys, and prices became so low that the farmer often received almost nothing. To be sure of a quick sale at a good price, flour and hogs had to reach the city on the Gulf in advance of the spring torrent of farm products. But this was possible only when the shipper had ready access to the Mississippi which, below St. Louis, was rarely blocked with ice. What good could come of a railroad to the Illinois River, likely to be ice-blocked during the most important months of the shipper's year? Was a surplus any less a surplus in the warehouses of Meredosia than in those of Springfield?

By the summer of 1842 unrest among the farmers was proof of the failure of the Northern Cross as a solution of the transportation problem. In communications to the newspapers farmers were pointing to the difference between the price of wheat in Springfield and other cities. With thirty-three cents a bushel being paid in Springfield, wheat was quoted in Philadelphia and New York at from $1.00 to $1.25, yet the cost of transportation was only fifty cents. Dark looks were cast in the direction of the merchants. "Many of the farmers in advance of the harvest go in debt to the merchants," said the *Register,* "giving their obligations to discharge those debts with wheat at the Springfield prices. The merchants having thus bound the farmers, hands and feet, fix the Springfield prices at the very lowest notch. . . . The merchant buys the farmer's wheat—he employs the farmer to haul it to Alton or Chicago, and of course makes a profit. If the farmer had hauled it to Alton or Chicago without selling to the merchant here, the profit would be his. . . . Wheat is now selling for one-third more in St. Louis than in this city, and the mechanic in Springfield has to pay the merchant more for flour than it is sold for at St. Louis."

In August, the farmers of the county met in Springfield to discuss remedies. Some favored the organization of a county society to market their wheat; others preferred neighborhood groups for the same purpose. In the end, however, the participants contented themselves with adopting resolutions blaming most of their troubles on the absence of good money; asserting that if the merchants attempted to make an exorbitant profit at their expense it would be their duty to organize and market their product themselves; and calling on the more prosperous among them to hold back crops so that the needy could dispose of theirs at better prices. Needless to say, neither merchants, farmers, nor the price of wheat responded to the appeal.

As time went on, the failure of the Northern Cross became glaringly apparent. Its physical equipment was primitive. In building the road ties had been laid on mud sills without ballast. Spiked to the ties were oak "stringers," on which narrow strap iron rails one-half inch thick were fastened. The ends of the strap iron were mitred so that each rail would take the weight of the wheel before it had left the preceding rail, but this precaution failed, after a time, to prevent the ends from curling. Sometimes the ends curved higher than the wheel center, and became what were known as "snake heads." Underrun by the wheels, they shot up through the flimsy cars, and sometimes through an unfortunate passenger or member of the train crew.

The passenger coaches were short, stubby, and similar in appearence to an old-fashioned omnibus. Smooth benches extending lengthwise along the car served for seats. Lacking divisions or handholds, any sudden lurch was likely to precipitate the passenger half the length of the car, or hurl him in a heap on the floor. No conveniences of any sort were provided.

Uncertainty, however, rather than discomfort and danger, was the railroad's greatest defect. The two engines were wood-burners, with an amazing consumption capacity for their small size. Not infrequently the passengers had to pitch in and saw to make up a deficiency at one of the wood stations. Water was another problem. Tanks were far apart, and too often the supply ran out between them. Then the passengers had to trudge back and forth, each with two buckets, between the stalled train and the nearest well—sometimes miles away—until the tank was filled. In the winter other difficulties arose. Water was conveyed from tender to boiler by a leather hose which froze in cold weather. When this happened the crew had to build a fire under it to thaw it out. If the leather cracked under the heat, as it was likely to do, the train was hopelessly stalled, and the passengers were compelled to wait for long, cold hours until the other engine made its appearance.

The financial history of the Northern Cross shows the rapid rate of its disintegration vividly. The state of Illinois accepted it from the contractors on May 13, 1842, and immediately leased it to private operators at an annual rental of $10,300. Two months later the lessees surrendered their lease. S. M. Tinsley & Co. were then persuaded to lease it at the rate of $6,000 in par funds and $4,000 in depreciated state indebtedness per year. At the end of twelve months they cancelled their lease. In April, 1844, the road was offered for sale, but when no purchaser could be found, it was rented to C. Ludlum and W. D. Baxter for $160 per month. But by this time the locomotives, far away from repair shops, had become so decrepit that they could barely crawl. Finally they were abandoned altogether, and mules, hitched tandem fashion, pulled the occasional load of freight that was offered.

One result of the collapse of the railroad was an attempt to conquer prairie distances without benefit of track and ties. When James Semple of Alton completed a term in the United States Senate in the spring of 1847 he set to work on a steam-propelled conveyance which could be operated on the flat prairies of Illinois. Using parts from one of the discarded Northern Cross engines as a nucleus, he constructed what he called a "Prairie Car." Measuring forty feet in length and twenty feet in width, the frame was strong enough to accommodate fifty passengers and to sustain the weight of a steam engine which applied power to wheels six feet in diameter and nearly that wide. In the center was a tall mast with a large canvas sail which was to be used when the wind was in the right direction.

After a number of short trial trips, Semple announced that the Prairie Car would make a distance run from Springfield to Alton. At the appointed time so many would-be passengers were clinging to the framework that lots had to be drawn to determine who would make the trip. Finally, in a cloud of smoke, the contrivance started. At first all went well. Then, near Chatham, something broke, the car stalled, and to complete the disappointment a brisk shower broke. The trip was abandoned and the crowd trudged back to Springfield, wet and disillusioned. Semple continued his efforts for several years, but never came nearer to success than on this first attempt at a long distance run.

Another result of the failure of the Northern Cross was that Springfield had to depend entirely on stages for passenger travel and mails. Here the years had brought some improvement. More trips were scheduled, fares were lower, better stages were in use, and the bridging of many streams saved time and reduced the hazards of travel. In 1842 Frink & Walker advertised departures for Peoria and thence via Peru, Ottawa, Joliet and Lockport to Chicago daily except Sunday at four A. M. The fare to Peoria was $4.00; to Chicago $12.00; and passengers were promised a through trip in three days "without riding nights." Every Tuesday, Thursday and Saturday stages left for Burlington by way of Peoria, Knoxville and Oquawka; and for Galena via Peoria and Dixon's Ferry. The fare to the former destination was $9.00; to the latter $13.00. Passengers were promised "first rate Troy built coaches" with four horses, and if notice were given the night before, travelers would be picked up at their homes.

In the summer stage coach travel was often a source of

keen pleasure. In the days of railroads Isaac N. Arnold recalled the agreeable aspects of some of the trips he had made from Chicago to attend the summer sessions of the United States courts at Springfield—"a four-in-hand with splendid horses, the best of Troy coaches, good company, the exhiliration of great speed over an elastic road, much of it a turf of grass, often crushing under our wheels the most beautiful wild flowers, every grove fragrant with blossoms, framed in the richest green, our roads not fenced in by narrow lanes, but with freedom to choose our route; here and there a picturesque log cabin covered with vines; the boys and girls on their way to the log schools, and the lusty farmer digging his fortune out of the rich earth . . ."

But even in the summer, when conditions were best, travel often became both uncomfortable and hazardous. "Sometimes," said Arnold, "a torrent of rain would in a few hours so swell the streams that the log bridges and banks would be entirely submerged, and a stream which a few hours before was nearly dry, became a foaming torrent. Fording, at such times, was never agreeable, and sometimes a little dangerous."

In the winter travel by any means was likely to be a nightmare. Roads were still mere tracks across the prairies, which became quagmires in the winter rains and snows. Even the mails, which were given precedence, came through at unpredictable times. As late as 1849, during a spell of bad weather, six days were required to bring one small mail from St. Louis. At times like this passenger travel was a succession of dangers. Coaches mired or overturned, ran off bridges submerged by swollen streams, or plunged into flooded creeks only to find out—too late—that the bridge had washed out. Discomfort and vexation were certain concomitants of winter travel, with injury and even death never beyond possibility.

That a growing community would be content with such

means of transportation was not to be expected. Even before the Northern Cross had stopped running there was
sporadic agitation for more and better railroad facilities.
This time a connection with Alton, by means of a road which
would join the old line at New Berlin, was the goal. In the
main the argument, as always, was economic. Under the most
favorable conditions, said the *Journal* in 1845, it cost 15 cents
to transport a bushel of wheat from Sangamon County to
St. Louis. If a railroad were built from Jacksonville and
Springfield to Alton, the cost could be reduced to 8 cents a
bushel. James N. Brown of New Berlin, a leading advocate
of the road, estimated that the farmers of Sangamon County
lost from $1.50 to $2.00 on every hog they drove to Alton,
while the cost of shipping by rail would not exceed 50 cents.

The *Register* tried to reinforce the economic argument
with the threat that unless steps were taken to improve transportation facilities, Springfield might expect a determined
effort to remove the capital to Peoria. The people, said the
editor, "having waded thro' miles and miles of low wet
prairie, at times almost impassable, in going to the seat of
government for years, . . . begin to desire its location
where it will be more easy of access, and more acceptable to
the vast body of the people of the State." The only way to
prevent Alton from joining the disgruntled element was to
take the initiative in building a railroad to that city.

But Springfield and Sangamon County were apathetic.
Only ten years had elapsed since the Internal Improvement
System had promised a solution for the transportation problem of the entire state—and all the promise had finally
amounted to was a few mules drawing an occasional flatcar
over rusty strap iron rails. The people were quite willing to
agree that the only obstacle to prosperity in central Illinois
was the lack of transportation facilities; that northern Illinois, with no greater natural advantages, was attracting
a disproportionate share of settlers because of its superior

accessibility—but if railroads were to be built, they preferred to have someone else put up the money.

Indifference, however, failed to stifle the enthusiasts. Early in 1847 a charter for the Springfield and Alton railroad was secured from the legislature. In May subscription books were opened in Springfield, public meetings were held, and influential citizens wrote open letters to the newspapers urging the people to subscribe. Abraham Lincoln and nine others, in a letter bearing almost conclusive evidences of Lincoln's style, estimated the annual cost of transportation between St. Louis and Springfield at $132,000, and predicted that the construction of the railroad would decrease the cost of goods purchased, increase the price of goods sold, and enhance the value of real property.

In the midst of this agitation—on April 26, 1847, to be exact—the old Northern Cross was put up for sale at public auction in accordance with a law passed at the last session of the legislature. Nicholas H. Ridgely and Thomas Mather decided that it was a likely speculation. Ridgely started the bidding with an offer of $10,000. There it hung, with no other bids, while the auctioneer called "Going . . . going . . ." at interminable length.

Meanwhile, in a barber shop across from the court house, Col. P. C. Johnson, the only citizen of Springfield who described himself as a capitalist, heard the crying of the sale. When he learned of the property being offered, he jumped out of the chair and hurried over, arriving just in time to bid $10,100. Ridgely immediately countered with $11,100, to which Johnson promptly added another $100. Thus the bidding went until Ridgely stepped over to his rival.

"Who are you bidding for, Colonel?" he asked. "Yourself or some other party?"

"For parties in St. Louis, who have agreed to pay me a commission," was the answer.

"Would you not as soon receive a commission from Springfield as St. Louis?" Ridgely asked with studied carelessness.

"Certainly, that is satisfactory," the Colonel replied and walked away.

The road was quickly struck off to Ridgely for $21,100. The next day Johnson called, passed the time of day, and silently received a silently proffered check for $1,000.

In a short time Ridgely and Mather disposed of the Northern Cross to a group of Eastern capitalists who felt that the time was finally ripe for railroad building in Illinois. They set to work at once. During the winter of 1847-48 piles of new ties began to accumulate along the right of way, and with spring construction work began in earnest. By mid-summer new track had been laid from Naples to a point near Jacksonville, one engine was in transit and two others had been ordered, a number of freight cars had already been received, and passenger cars were under construction at Cincinnati. Even the skeptics were convinced that the road would be in operation within a few months.

Once more rosy forecasts were the order of the day. "A number of new houses are going up," commented the *Journal*, "and many of the old ones are refitting; and our building mechanics find full employment. The expectation is general that Springfield is about to become a place of considerable importance for produce operations. A great benefit will also result to the country from the Rail Road, by opening a cheap means of communication with the Illinois river, and giving us access, with the aid of the Canal, to the great lake markets."

If this prediction were to come true—and there seemed every likelihood that it would—profound changes in the economic structure of Springfield and Sangamon County were in prospect. That being the case, the nature of that structure, as it was on the eve of change, becomes of interest.

In comparing the economy of the forties with that of the preceding decade, one is struck by similarities much more than by points of difference. Town and country were almost as closely interdependent as they had been ten and fifteen years earlier. The farmer still traded a large part of his crop to local merchants in return for the commodities with which he could not supply himself. That part of his surplus which he either could not or would not dispose of in this way he drove, in the form of hogs, to market at Beardstown or Alton. However, the cost of this sort of transportation was heavy, and only a small profit resulted.

These basic factors in the agricultural scheme had several important results. With no more than a small profit possible under the most favorable conditions, there was no incentive to bring land under cultivation. In 1839 Simeon Francis stated that most of the desirable land in the neighborhood of Springfield had already been entered, but six years later Solon Robinson, the agriculturist, noted that there was an abundance of uncultivated land "within gun shot of the capital." According to the census of 1850, not much more than half the acreage of Sangamon County was being farmed.

Similarly, there was no incentive to intensive cultivation. Farm methods had changed little from earlier years. The cast iron plow had come into fairly common use, but it did not scour readily in the black prairie loam, and many farmers preferred its wooden predecessor. Grain was still sown by hand and cut for the most part with cradles. Fertilizing was unheard of, and manure was considered an embarrassment rather than a source of increased yields. Rotation of crops, said Robinson, "is corn, weeds, hogs, mud and corn."

Because corn could be turned into hogs, and hogs could be driven to market, and because soil conditions and climate were favorable, nearly every farmer put most of his acreage in this one crop. "Our soil, our climate, and the habits of our people are all highly favorable to the production of corn," the *Illinois Journal* commented in 1849. "This great staple is produced with us, with less labor and attention than anywhere else; the quantity raised is incredible. . . . The raising of corn is the favorite pursuit of our farmers, and the many attempts that have been made with us to divert a portion of our agricultural industry into other channels have found little success." The census of 1850 provided statistical proof of this statement. In round figures, it reported an annual yield of 100,000 bushels of wheat; 350,000 bushels of rye and oats; and 3,300,000 bushels of corn in Sangamon County. Morgan County, with a yield of 2,700,000 bushels, was the only other county whose corn production exceeded the two million mark.

Although corn far outranked all other crops in importance, there was another agricultural product in which Sangamon stood at the head of the counties of the state. That was wool. With a yield of 120,000 pounds in 1850, Sangamon surpassed Fulton, its nearest rival, by nearly 40,000 pounds. Being light in weight, wool could be transported at relatively low cost, and Springfield merchants had encouraged the farmers of the neighborhood to grow it. More effective, probably, as a stimulus, was the woolen factory in Springfield, which offered an accessible market.

Springfield's industry was determined by the type of agriculture practised in the Sangamon country. Manufacturing was of relatively small importance, and the character of such as there was derived directly from the neighboring farms. In addition to the wool carding and manufacturing establishment, there were flour mills, pork packing establishments, and distilleries and breweries. Two foundries and two brickyards were the only industries in the town which did not have an obvious relation to the surrounding country. Actually, the chief product of one of the foundries was a cast iron plow, so that in reality there were only three manufacturing establishments whose dependence upon agriculture was not complete.

Most important among Springfield industries was pork

packing. In 1845 it was estimated that $60,000 was employed annually in this business, while the capital required for all other manufacturing totalled only $150,000. Pork, cut up, pickled in brine and packed in barrels, was easier to transport than hogs on the hoof. The industry developed at an early date. In 1843 it was said that between 7,000 and 8,000 hogs were killed and packed in the capital, and a factory for making lard-oil—a by-product—was in operation. Still, the industry grew slowly. By 1849 the packing of 15,000 hogs was reported, but it was estimated that 120,000 had been raised in the Springfield district during the preceding winter, and that 52,000 had been killed at Beardstown.

In manufacturing, machinery played an unimportant part. Pork packing and brick making required hand labor, but many more men found occupation in such long-established crafts as cabinet making, cordwaining, carriage and wagon making, boot and shoe making, tailoring, tanning and coopering. In addition there were chair makers, harness and trunk makers, hatters, tin-, copper-, and blacksmiths, watchmakers, and representatives of all the building trades. It is probably safe to say that exclusive of textiles, which were mainly imported, the majority of the manufactured articles which a typical resident of Springfield bought in any year from 1840 to 1850 were made by hand within the limits of the city.

Many of the craftsmen sold their products direct to the consumers, and therefore were merchants as well as manufacturers. Many more, however, devoted themselves entirely to the business of buying and selling. Merchandising was, in fact, the most important occupation of the town, employing more than three times as much capital annually as the manufacturing establishments.

Specialization had made its appearance in the years which had passed since Elijah Iles had been able to supply all the settlers' needs from one small log store. A directory of Springfield business men published in the summer of 1849 lists a number of establishments confining themselves in the main to certain types of goods. Thus Corneau & Diller, and D. & I. P. Spear, dealt in drugs; P. C. Canedy and Birchall & Owen sold not only drugs but books and stationery as well. E. B. Pease & Co. confined themselves to hardware, cutlery and iron, but they were the only firm in Springfield which dealt exclusively in those commodities. There were three bakers and confectioners, three clothing dealers, two jewelers, two butchers and one milliner. Listed also were three livery stables and one bath house. (Concerning the latter the directory commented: "The practice of bathing, has always been regarded as a great security and promoter of health, and it certainly is of comfort and cleanliness.")

Moreover, there was the public market on North Sixth Street where, on certain days of the week, the farmers sold their produce direct to the townspeople. Prices and the commodities offered differed from time to time, but those which follow—for January 1, 1846—are representative:

Beef, fore quarter	$1.50
Beef, hind quarter	$2.50
Pork, per pound	3¢— 4¢
Veal, per pound	2¢— 3¢
Venison, saddle	$1.00 —$1.50
Chickens, each	6¢— 8¢
Ducks, each	10¢
Turkeys, each	25¢—60¢
Prairie chickens	6¢
Quail, per dozen	25¢—37½¢
Corn meal, per bushel	25¢
Buckwheat flour, per pound	2¢
Potatoes, per bushel	25¢
Green apples, per bushel	$1.25
Butter, per pound	12¢
Cheese, per pound	8¢
Lard, per pound	8¢
Tallow, per pound	7¢
Eggs, per dozen	20¢

But for the most part, business remained unspecialized. Thus, in 1849, there were twenty-five establishments dealing in dry goods, groceries and general merchandise. Some of these firms conducted both wholesale and retail businesses, and all of them were buyers and exporters of farm products. (The pork packers were simply merchants who chose this method of disposing of the farmers' substitute for ready cash.) Butter, bacon, feathers, lard, beeswax and eggs were readily accepted in exchange for "store goods." In addition, home manufactured articles such as jeans, flannels, linsey-woolseys, socks, mittens, rag carpets, tow linen and straw hats were offered and received.

The prevalence of exchange, rather than payment in money, led to long credits. Merchants would advance goods to honest farmers whether the latter had produce to balance the account or not. Finally there would be a reckoning, generally either at Christmas or "hog killing time." Total advances would be set off against total credits, and the balance either made up in cash or carried forward as a debit or credit in the next year's account.

The practice was full of hazard for the storekeeper, for he could never know what the produce he accepted in the early fall would be worth when he got it to market the following spring. But cash transactions were hardly less uncertain. In place of a national currency of known value, there were bank-notes issued by hundreds of institutions of all degrees of solvency. If the merchant were to survive, he had to know the approximate value of each issue. With the adoption of the constitution of 1847, which prohibited banking in Illinois, the monetary situation became even worse, for then the banks of issue were all at a distance, and reliable information regarding their condition was harder than ever to secure.

In spite of these drawbacks many Springfield merchants had built up substantial businesses. Conspicuous among them were a number of pioneer merchants—John Williams, who

had clerked for Elijah Iles, William P. Grimsley, Eliphalet
B. Hawley and Jacob Loose, Joseph and Edward R. Thayer,
B. C. Webster, S. M. Tinsley, S. B. Opdycke, James L. Lamb
and Charles R. Hurst. In the forefront, however, stood a
relative newcomer. After four years of experience in Beardstown and Naples, Jacob Bunn had established a business in
Springfield in 1840. His success was phenomenal. "We
have heard it said that his business will reach one hundred
thousand dollars the present year," the *Journal* commented
with awe in 1849. Visitors to the capital were so deeply impressed that sometimes they expressed their admiration in
print. "There is nothing you can name," wrote the editor of
the Charleston *Globe,* "belonging to his line of business, that
he has not on hand, and that too in quantities to suit any of
our purchasers." Bunn's wholesale advertisement, offering
400 sacks of coffee, 200 hogsheads of New Orleans sugar,
100 barrels of "crushed, loaf, and clarified sugar," 200 barrels of molasses, and 5,000 barrels of salt, shows that the
editor was not writing in idle flattery.

Bunn and the other merchants of Springfield looked forward to a substantial increase in business when the railroad
would go into operation. Their hopes were not disappointed.
The first train ran the length of the Sangamon and Morgan
—that was the new name—on July 23, 1849. A week before
that date corn in any quantity had been available in Springfield at 15¢ per bushel; a week afterward it was scarce at
25¢. The price of wheat and flour made a corresponding
advance. Salt was typical of imported articles. In 1848 the
price in Springfield had been $3.50 per barrel; three weeks
after the Sangamon and Morgan was finished it had dropped
to $2.25. The railroad was a success.

The success of one undertaking gave encouragement to
the proponents of another. Stock subscriptions to the Alton
and Sangamon were coming more easily, and the construction of the road now appeared to be a certainty. All over

Illinois, in fact, railroads were being projected. The isolation of Springfield—and every other sizable town in the state for that matter—was near an end.

The effect was to be profound. In the last years of the decade a discerning observer might have noticed an accumulation of signs that fundamental changes were imminent. For some time ready made clothing, and boots and shoes, had been available in Springfield. Quantity-made furniture was being offered for sale. With cheap transportation, permitting the importation of manufactured articles unencumbered with prohibitive freight charges, an enormous increase in the sale of such articles was certain to take place. The handcrafts were bound to suffer. But for quantity production greater opportunities were opening. Already enterprising men were turning to steam. Four of the town's five flour and lumber mills, and all the distilleries, were using it; and John Hutchinson had just installed an engine in his cabinet making shop. All that was needed to ring in the machine age was the development of coal mining, which was still confined to outcrops on hillsides and creek and river banks.

Agriculture, likewise, was on the verge of change. John Deere had perfected the steel plow, and his factory at Moline was turning out thousands annually. Cyrus McCormick's reaper was fast winning acceptance. The basic tools of quantity production were ready for the farmer whenever their use would be profitable, and that time would be reached as soon as his crops could be carried quickly and cheaply to distant markets. Farming in the Sangamon country was about to emerge from a subsistence to a commercial basis.

Springfield, considered as a community, was not to be unaffected by forces of such potency. As we have seen, her central position in the life of the state was due in the main to her isolation. Now that isolation was being destroyed. With railroads running, legislators could return to their homes more often, and lawyers would not need to remain for the entire length of court terms. The telegraph, already in use, diminished still further the necessity for long attendance. Moreover, other cities had developed as the years had passed. Chicago, hardly more than a village in 1839, counted 30,000 inhabitants in 1850 as against 4,500 for the capital. Already the United States courts were sitting there as well as at the seat of government, and since the adoption of the constitution of 1847 the supreme court was meeting also at Mt. Vernon and Ottawa. In a word, men came to the capital less often, and stayed for shorter periods, than they had formerly been obliged to do. As a result, Springfield slipped from her throne. The state offices would continue to give her an importance beyond that which her size alone could have won for her, but she would no longer be the center of life in Illinois. Her regal age was over.

CHAPTER VIII

Civic Spirit Develops

"THE most important event to Springfield was the completion of the Alton and Sangamon Railroad, now the Chicago, Alton and St. Louis Railroad. The completion of that road breathed into us a new life, and, lately, the extension of the Great Western Railroad's connections to Toledo, has been of incalculable benefit to our city." Thus wrote James H. Matheny in 1858.

By its original charter, the Alton and Sangamon was to run through Waverly in Morgan County and join with the Sangamon and Morgan at New Berlin. But when residents of Morgan County failed to subscribe for a single share of its stock, and New Berlin took only two shares, Springfield interests began to urge the adoption of a direct route north from Carlinville. Their argument was given point by the fact that the new road, already under construction at its southern terminus, was being built with tracks twelve inches wider than those on the Sangamon and Morgan. The advocates of the direct route took their case to the legislature, and at the session of 1851 received the charter amendment they desired. A few weeks later authority to extend the road northward was also granted.

By mid-summer of 1851, a year after work had commenced, ten miles of track had been laid, more than a third of the right of way between Alton and Springfield had been graded, and the entire distance was under contract. Completion of the road to Springfield by January 1, 1852 was confidently predicted. Actually, it was September 9th of that year when the first train from the river city ran into the capital, to be greeted with a national salute and the cheers of hundreds of citizens. A month later 400 excursionists formally celebrated the opening of a rail connection between the two cities. Leaving St. Louis on the steamer *Cornelia* at 6:00 A.M., the party reached Springfield at 2:00 in the afternoon. Two hours later, after a complimentary dinner served in the road's new machine shops, the party departed, to reach home at midnight. "It was a glorious sight—the careening of the passenger train over our prairies!" one of Springfield's editors exulted. "The railroads of Illinois will hasten our state to her brilliant destiny!"

Work on the railroad north of Springfield continued steadily. On October 15, 1853, the tracks to Bloomington were finished, and two days later the first cars ran through. Early in the following year a connection with Chicago was established. Devious though it was—travelers changed to the Illinois Central at Bloomington and to the Rock Island at La Salle—an all-rail route to the metropolis was hailed joyfully, and a large party from Springfield, made up of members of the legislature as well as townspeople, eagerly accepted the invitation of Chicago citizens for a triumphal visit. Within a few months the direct route was finished. On July 26, 1854, the last spike was hammered home, and four days later the first train ran from Alton to the city on the lake. In little more than a year the southern extension, from Alton to St. Louis, was completed.

Meanwhile the Sangamon and Morgan—or the Great Western, as it was now called—was extending its tracks also. By the fall of 1853 trains were running as far east as Mechanicsburg, where stage connections for Urbana, Danville, and Lafayette, Indiana, could be made. Steadily the road was extended eastward, with the result that the con-

nection with Toledo, which Matheny looked upon as one of
Springfield's red-letter days, was made in late November,
1856.

It was soon apparent, however, that to lay tracks was
easier than to run trains over them—easier, that is, than to
run them safely. Accidents happened with appalling fre-
quency. Typical of the first years of operation was the
record for a few weeks in the fall of 1853. On October 13, a
short distance south of Lincoln, two cows were struck.
The locomotive and baggage car were derailed, two firemen
were killed, and the engineer had both arms broken. On
November 1 a train from Alton struck a cow north of Carlinville. The fireman was killed instantly, the wood passer
fatally injured, and the engineer's legs were both broken.
In consequence of this accident, section masters were ordered
to run over their sections in hand cars an hour before train
time and drive the stock to a safe distance. Two days after
this order was issued a wood train from Springfield to Lick

VIEW IN WASHINGTON STREET, SPRINGFIELD, ILLINOIS.

From *Ballou's Pictorial Drawing-Room Companion,* November 15, 1856

Creek ran into a cow. One man was killed, several were injured, and four cars filled with wood were shattered.

Snow was another source of trouble. A heavy fall in January, 1855, paralyzed traffic to and from Springfield for nearly two weeks. The storm commenced on the 20th. On the 24th the first train to reach town in four days limped in from the south, having been marooned on the prairies all that time. Not until the 28th did a train from Bloomington force its way into the capital, and several more days passed before regular traffic was resumed.

In the minds of the people, however, troubles of this sort, and even a life now and then, were a small price to pay for the benefits the railroads conferred. For one thing, Springfield was growing rapidly. Between 1840 and 1848, a gain of 1300—from 2600 to 3900—had been registered.[1] In the next two years, during which the Sangamon and Morgan went into operation, the population jumped to 5100. By 1855 it had mounted to 7250, and in 1860 it stood at 9400. Thus a gain of nearly 5000 was recorded in the decade of the 50's, as against 2500 in the preceding ten year period. Even more striking was the increase in property valuation, which rose from slightly less than $1,000,000 in 1847 to $2,365,000 in 1853, and to $4,400,000 in 1858.

The individual citizen, however, was not so likely to be impressed with figures such as these as by the tangible evidences of progress which came within his own observation. He was not slow to draw inferences from the fact that outside the town virgin prairie was being broken as never before, while within the city new businesses were being established in rapid succession—William Pierce's broom factory, John Cook's soap and candle establishment, Hoyt's woolen mill, Huntington and Campbell's planing mill, the car factories and repair shops of both railroads, and several new

[1] The figures are given in closest hundreds.

brickyards. Moreover, each day presented undeniable evidence of brisk business in the teams which lined the State House yard. On a single circuit of the square on an April Saturday in 1854 an observer counted 140 teams and as many saddle horses, with large numbers of both teams and horses hitched in side streets and alleys. Retail trade on a fair Saturday was estimated at $15,000; on any week day the estimate was half that amount. Annually, about two and a quarter million dollars changed hands in Springfield.

The railroads were welcome to the credit. Simeon Francis expressed the general attitude when he contrasted conditions in 1853, when he was writing, with 1843. Then one got to market in wagons; now, he said, two railroads run into Springfield. Instead of $1.25 per hundred, beef brings $7.00; corn sells at 20c instead of 6c; potatoes at 50c instead of 8c; and butter at 25c instead of 5c. Ten years ago, he continued, improved farms in Sangamon County sold for from $3.00 to $8.00 an acre; now they bring from $15.00 to $30.00. The laborer who then received $10.00 per month now gets $20.00. On the other hand, manufactured and imported commodities have gone down in price. "In those times," he concluded, "few of our farmers, indeed of our citizens, could indulge in such luxuries as coffee, sugar, tea, or a broadcloth coat—and now the amount that was required to buy either a suit of clothes or a dress, will pay for clothing a family of girls."

Nor did a recurrence of the cholera, absent from Springfield for nearly two decades, have any serious effect upon the growth of the town. In the summer of 1850 cholera symptoms accompanied several sudden deaths, but when no epidemic developed the physicians denied the presence of the dread disease. During the following summer, however, several clear cases appeared and a number of deaths resulted. In 1852 and 1853 Springfield escaped, but in 1854 a mild epidemic developed. Throughout the summer cases were reported almost daily, and on one September day ten cases, several of them fatal, came to the attention of the authorities. With cool weather the disease abated. During the following year an occasional individual was stricken, but by 1856 the cholera had disappeared entirely.

Even the panic of 1853 failed to retard Springfield's progress materially. Local business men were mainly concerned with the effect of widespread bank failures on the pork market, which was stagnant, with hogs selling for $4.25 instead of $5.50 as they had brought the preceding year. But wheat was worth $1.00 at Alton and $1.05 in St. Louis— a good price, though slightly lower than that of the last year or two. When the panic finally struck Springfield directly, as it did when the Mechanics and Farmers Bank closed on November 22, 1854, the result was not disastrous, for the people were quickly convinced that the bank was basically sound, and that its depositors would ultimately be paid in full.

From such embarrassment as the panic did cause, recovery was rapid. By the early winter of 1855 hogs were selling at $6.00, although it was generally recognized that that price was too high to last. Wheat was quoted at $1.50 in Springfield, and produce prices were the highest on record. By the following summer, business had advanced beyond the pre-panic level. In one week in May, 1856, the Chicago and Alton[2] alone delivered 125 carloads of lumber to Springfield, while during June daily lumber shipments varied between fifteen and twenty cars. Large quantities of lime, coal and general merchandise were received and forwarded every day. Construction was in full swing and, as always when that is the case, the town hummed with activity.

No better time can be found for taking a sort of industrial and commercial survey of Springfield than this year

[2]The corporate name of this railroad changed so frequently that I shall refer to it by the name by which it is best known in Illinois.

of 1856. One panic had been successfully withstood, and no signs of another which was soon to follow were apparent. The railroads had been in operation long enough for their effect to be manifest. What changes had they brought about?

In the first place, it is apparent that the export of farm products had taken an enormous leap, and constituted the foremost business of the town. In 1856 the Great Western shipped 450,000 bushels of wheat and 90,000 bushels of corn from Springfield, and it was estimated that equal quantities were exported on the Chicago and Alton. In addition, local mills, six in number, ground 500,000 bushels of wheat into 100,000 barrels of flour. Trade in cattle and hogs, shipped live to Eastern markets, had become a business large enough to bring $1,500,000 to the city annually. Pork packing had also grown in importance, though less rapidly than the trade in live animals. Still, from 25,000 to 30,000 hogs were killed and packed each year. The export of wool, in spite of the increased quantities which were manufactured locally, reached 200,000 pounds, with a value of $100,000, in 1856.

One result of the increase in exported produce was the development of specialization. Formerly the grain exporters and pork packers had been the leading merchants, forced in this way to dispose of the produce they had taken in exchange for goods. Now the business was in the hands of men who devoted their entire time to it. Post and Brother, and L. S. Warner, were the town's grain dealers, with Elijah Iles, still a pioneer, the owner of the first—and largest—elevator. Pork packing had become the exclusive concern of James L. Lamb and Jacoby and Company. Cattle and hogs, and much of the grain as well, were purchased direct from the farmers by buyers from Chicago, St. Louis, and other large cities.

Another result, which was partly cause as well, was the stimulation of intensive agriculture. At last the farmer had a market for all that he could raise. How quickly he took advantage of the opportunity may be seen from the fact that Springfield's three farm implement dealers—B. F. Fox, G. L. Huntington and T. W. S. Kidd—disposed of 270 reapers in the year 1856 alone.

In the second place, manufacturing had received a notable impetus. In 1856 Armstrong's woolen mill was employing twenty workmen and using 75,000 pounds of wool in the manufacture of cloth, flannels, blankets and yarn; and a second, though smaller, establishment had commenced business. In addition, E. R. Wiley employed twenty men and sixty-five women in making ready-made clothing. At G. S. Manning's carriage and wagon shop fifteen men found work. Besides the railroad car shops, three foundries employed an average of twenty men each the year around. Brickyards had increased to seven in number, with a yearly output of 6,000,-000 bricks, in the manufacture of which seventy-five men were needed. The flour mills and pork packers gave work to many more.

The craftsmen had not been displaced, however. J. H. Adams and J. H. Force, hatters, still made a third of the hats they sold, and the seven shoe dealers of the town employed fifty shoemakers. J. A. Hough and other furniture men still made a good part of the beds and bureaus they sold. In many other shops at least part of the goods offered for sale were made by hand on the premises.

In fact, business in Springfield during the 50's was remarkable more for increases in volume than for structural changes, though structural changes were evident. That the value of sales increased mightily is plain. In 1856 twenty-three dealers in dry goods—in other words, general stores—were credited with an aggregate business of $800,000. Six wholesale merchants added another $300,000. Dealers in country produce did business amounting to $120,000. The hardware and stove trade, divided among seven firms, totalled $215,000. Four jewelry stores enjoyed an aggregate volume amounting to

$100,000. In fact, in the year 1856 the total sales of Springfield merchants—exclusive of grain and flour, cattle, hogs and packed pork—approximated $3,000,000 according to the best estimate which can be made. Not only was this a neat sum in itself, but it represented a gain of three quarters of a million over 1854, and an enormous advance over the days before rail transportation.

One reason for the increase, and at the same time a significant indication of industrial and commercial growth, was the development of banks. In 1835 the State Bank of Illinois had been established at Springfield, but in the crash of 1837 it had been forced to suspend specie payments. Thereafter it was in constant trouble, with the result that in 1839, by act of the legislature, it was forbidden to accept new business, and in 1843 it was ordered to liquidate within five years.

By that date the entire state was without a banking system. The Democratic party was in control, and hostility to banks of any sort was a cardinal article of Democratic faith. Framed under the party's influence, the constitution of 1847 required every bank charter granted by the legislature to be submitted to popular vote for ratification. The effect was a practical prohibition.

Still, the need for the services which banks performed— the safeguarding, loan and transfer of money—was so great that ways were being found to get around the legal obstacles. Merchants with strong boxes kept money for their customers, more often as a personal favor than as a business transaction. Men of substance frequently invested in loans, but the legal rate was high—ten per cent—and the demand so great that higher rates were often demanded and paid. Naturally, only those in pressing need of money borrowed, with the result that progress was much slower than it would have been had credit been generally available at reasonable rates.

What this situation meant to Springfield was clearly set forth by the editor of the *Illinois Journal* early in 1850.

"Some of our business men," he wrote, "have sufficient capital, at all times, to sustain their credit and take up their liabilities, without difficulty. To others of less means, it would often be a convenience if loans of money could be obtained to make operations perfectly safe, and of general and individual benefit, if they could be had. Even to all classes, at times, when accounts cannot be collected—and there are such times—moderate and short loans would enable business men to carry on their business more pleasantly and successfully. To the mechanics of this city, those doing prudent and profitable business, small loans, occasionally, would be of great advantage. There are many of them—young men of good habits, known industry and business tact—who, with a small loan and the means they have on hand, would erect for themselves dwellings, and thus make themselves more comfortable—stimulate them to greater industry, and render them permanent and valuable citizens. . . . What we want is capital here that can be borrowed, at all times, on good security, and which may tend to encourage and stimulate industry, and to enable those to get along and make money and render themselves useful to society, who were not 'born with gold spoons in their mouths'."

Developments of the next year or two proved the editor's case. On January 1, 1851, Jacob Bunn who, with John Williams, had been carrying the main burden of such unofficial banking as Springfield had enjoyed, opened a private banking house on the southeast corner of Fifth and Adams streets. A few weeks later the Springfield Marine and Fire Insurance Company secured from the legislature a charter which enabled it to perform all the functions of a bank except that of issuing currency. By spring the company had effected the purchase of the old State Bank Building on the east side of the square—"the most chaste, beautiful and substantial building west of the Allegheny Mountains," it was called—and early in July the doors were opened for business. Late that year the legislature yielded to realities and authorized the formation of banks under certain restrictions, with the result that two more banks—Clark's Exchange and the Mechanics and Farmers—were organized in the following year.

The banks were quickly put to the test. As has been noted, the depression following the panic of 1853 was too much for the Mechanics and Farmers Bank. Clark's Exchange Bank also liquidated, but Nicholas H. Ridgely, its guiding spirit, at once set up a private banking house of his own. Thus, by the end of 1854, Springfield found itself with the banking system which was to serve it without change until the Civil War, when the First National Bank was organized in accordance with the National Bank Act.

Hardly had recovery been made from the panic of 1853 before a more severe crash—that of 1857—shook the country. Springfield was affected, of course, but the town kept its courage. Said the *Journal,* in October of that year: "In the midst of the failures, which are occurring throughout the country, it is peculiarly gratifying to be able to announce that Springfield yet stands erect and firm. Not a failure has yet occurred among our merchants and business men, and none are contemplated. The pressure has been pretty severe upon some of them, owing to their inability to obtain Eastern exchange, but they have nobly outrode the storm. . . .

"At present we are in the midst of hard times; money is scarce and dear, sales of real estate are perhaps less frequent, and trade may be somewhat less brisk than usual; but Springfield yet stands prosperous and unshaken. With a continuance of the same forebearance, which has thus far been practiced, relief will soon return; credit and confidence will be fully restored and the abundant resources of our citizens will again be made available."

These were brave words, for the prospect seemed black. Beef cattle were selling at $2.00 per hundred and wheat was 65c. Money seemed to be almost non-existent. The best barometer, however, was pork. In the winter of 1856 the packers had paid $5.00 per 100 on an average. On December 1, 1857, the price ranged from $3.00 to $3.25. Even so, the packers were not buying, and such sales as took place were made to drovers for live shipment. However, by the middle of the month there was noticeable improvement. The price had advanced to $3.75—$4.00 and the packing houses had commenced operations. When the season closed the total pack was only 2,500 less than that of the preceding year, although the price had remained at a much lower level.

As always, hard times focussed attention on the cost of living, and there was much discussion of that perennially vital subject. One participant climbed down from the realm of generalities and published an itemized account of the cost of maintaining a family of three adults and four children, clothing excluded. It follows:

Rent per year	$120
Meats	72
Flour	30
Tea and coffee	31
Butter	40
Milk	18
Wood	66
Potatoes	12
Sugar	12
Molasses	3
	$404

In view of the fact that in the prosperous year 1856 a weekly wage of $10.00 was considered good pay for a workman, the standard of living for Springfield's masses could hardly have been impressively high.

Because of its greater severity, recovery from the panic of 1857 was slower than from that of 1853. Trade stagnated throughout 1858, although the pork market reacted sharply from the low point of the previous season. Hogs opened at

$4.50 and mounted to $5.50, while the total pack numbered 37,000—a gain of nearly fifty per cent. The reason, however, was to be found in a short grain crop rather than in general recovery. In the summer of 1859 it was said that more dwellings were for rent in Springfield than had been vacant for many years. Still, the business men had survived two years of hard times without serious failures, trade was fair and the prospect seemed better. The end of the depression was in sight.

With all its ups and downs, it had been a prosperous decade. Of this Springfield gave many proofs. As early as 1851 three-story bricks began to appear among the wooden shacks on the north side of the square which made up Chicken Row. The real boom in building, however, commenced two or three years later. In the spring of 1854 so many new buildings were erected on the north side of Washington Street west of the square that the locality was dignified with the name of "Commercial Row." In May, 1855, when a bad fire destroyed part of the west side of the square, contracts for the erection of three-story brick buildings were let at once. At the same time R. F. Ruth and Mrs. Catherine Latham were planning buildings for the square's south side, Stephen T. Logan was erecting two buildings on the corner of Washington and Sixth streets, and S. B. Fisher had a store room under construction on Washington Street west of Sixth. In the fall of 1856 it was reported that forty new store rooms had been built since May 1, and that each one had been rented upon completion. Two years later Jacob Bunn erected one of the show buildings of the town on the corner of Fifth and Adams streets[3]—Bunn's Bank Building. By 1860 the appearance of Springfield's business section had been transformed.

Prominent among downtown improvements were public

[3] Where the First National Bank Building now stands. Bunn's grocery establishment stood on the southeast corner of the same intersection.

halls—Masonic Hall, at the corner of Fifth and Monroe streets, completed in 1853; Metropolitan Hall, on Third Street between Washington and Jefferson; Cook's Hall on the east side of the square. When Metropolitan Hall was finished in 1855 its seating capacity of 1,200 was the largest in the state, but three years later it was forced to yield, in popular favor at least, to the hall which John Cook built on the second floor of the building which he erected south of the Marine and Fire Insurance Company. In Cook's opinion the distinctive features of this auditorium—its size, its gallery, the gas lights—could be adequately represented only by the name of "Illiopolitan Hall," but this was too much for Central Illinois, and so it quickly came to be known by its owner's plain but familiar name.

Even more conspicuous were the new hotels. In 1854 Joel Johnson made a large addition to his City Hotel on West Washington Street.[4] The next year he sold the property to John W. Chenery, who had been managing the American House. The new proprietor improved the front of the building, added an ornamental doorway, rearranged the interior, bought new furniture and bestowed his own name upon it. When the Chenery House opened for business, each of its 130 rooms was lighted with gas and equipped with a bell for summoning servants—the latest improvements in public comforts. The next year—1856—J. D. Freeman built the St. Nicholas.[5] "From the Revere House in Boston, to the St. Charles Hotel of New Orleans, you can find no better accommodation," wrote a traveler who enjoyed its facilities in January, 1857, soon after the opening.

New dwellings matched the new structures of the business section. Residences sprang up by the hundreds. Three hun-

[4] Where the Illinois Hotel now stands. The Chenery House can be seen at the extreme right in the picture on p. 164.

[5] As originally constructed, the St. Nicholas was 60 by 100 feet in dimension, and five stories high.

dred were built in 1854. Early in the following year it was estimated that tenants for two hundred more houses could readily be found. During 1856 nearly four hundred dwellings were constructed. (Included in a list of improvements for that year was the following: "Addition to house on Eighth street, for A. Lincoln. Cost $1,300; Hannan & Ragsdale, Architects and builders.") Half a million dollars went into new buildings that year in Springfield, and the next two years saw the expenditure of equal sums.

While most of the new dwellings were modest homes, some were elaborate. "Almost palaces of homes have been reared since you were here," Mrs. Lincoln wrote to her sister in the fall of 1857, "hundreds of houses have been going up this season and some of them very elegant." On South Sixth Street were a group which the townspeople, in mingled pride and envy, dubbed "Aristocracy Hill." First among them was the substantial home of Jacob Bunn. Next to the south came the "castle cottage" of G. W. Chatterton, described as "Gothic, or Elizabethan, carried out with fanciful extension"—the "extension" apparently consisting of a tower, embattlements, ornamented spires and composition chimney flues! Isaac R. Diller's new home across the street belonged to the group, as did a number of new dwellings south of the Town Branch.

West of Aristocracy Hill the new Governor's Mansion, completed in 1856, was a fine structure, but the show places of the town were the home of Joel A. Matteson and the Cottage Garden of N. H. Ridgely. A resident of Joliet at the time of his election as governor in 1852, Matteson became heavily interested in the Chicago and Alton Railroad and decided to reside in Springfield upon the expiration of his term. In 1856 he purchased a large lot on the corner of Fourth and Jackson streets and began the construction of a home which, when finished the following year, completely dwarfed the nearby Governor's Mansion. "The whole place

THE NORTH AND EAST SIDES OF THE SQUARE, 1860

THE SOUTH AND WEST SIDES OF THE SQUARE, 1860

has cost, he says, $100,000," Mrs. Lincoln observed, "but he is now worth a million."[6] Ridgely's Cottage Garden,[7] in which were combined the esthetic values of flowers and shrubs and demonstrations of the practical utility of the osage orange and fruit grafting, was one of the city's proudest boasts and the subject of praise from all who saw it.

Residential and commercial improvements, prosperity, a growing population—out of these developed a quality unknown in Springfield before 1850: a civic spirit.

In the spring of 1853 a visitor—the editor of the Rockford *Forum*—had a number of unlovely things to say about the capital. "Springfield presents neither a pleasant nor cheerful appearance," he wrote, "nor does it give any demonstrations of great enterprise, either public or private. There does not appear to be much taste or neatness in the arrangement of things, either of a private or public character, especially of a public, judging from streets, alleys, sidewalks, etc. . . . As to city improvements, it is horrible to think of them. Just think of a city containing seven or eight thousand inhabitants, with all the boasted wealth of this city, and so favorably patronized too, without a single good sidewalk in it, or even a public lamp to light a street!"

A few years earlier words like these would have drawn indignant rebuttals from the local editors, but now—and the fact is indicative of the changing mood of the town—there was only acquiescence. Streets and sidewalks were both bad, the *Journal* admitted, and it was time something was done about them.

For once the city fathers agreed. The Chicago and Mississippi Railroad had already eased the way by putting down planking on Fourth Street between Washington and Jefferson and building a board sidewalk in front of its station.

[6] The Matteson house, then occupied by R. E. Goodell, a son-in-law, burned to the ground in 1873, but the coachman's house at the rear of the lot escaped the fire and may still be seen.
[7] A tract east of Thirteenth Street and north of Washington.

Before the end of the year the councilmen decided to plank the streets around the square. Work commenced in September, but 1854 was well advanced before the job was finished. Once started, however, the movement continued. Every year more planks went down, with the result that by the end of the decade most of the downtown streets were finally out of the mud, if not free from it.

At the same time the beginnings of a system of street lighting were taking shape. Lamp posts—for oil lamps—were erected at the corners of the square in January, 1853. A year later the city council gave the Springfield Gas Company permission to lay pipes in the streets and alleys on condition that it would have a plant in operation by May, 1855, and that it would furnish light at the rate of $25.00 per year for each lamp. The company turned gas into the mains four months earlier than it had promised. Almost at once every store around the square was lighted with the new fuel. (Day after day notices appeared in the papers cautioning the user to turn off the gas, and *not* to blow it out.) Within a short time the pipes were extended to the residence districts, and Springfield's opulent citizens—or "the quality" as the phrase then went—parted forever with candles and lard oil.

Meanwhile, the legislature had been infected with the improvement mania and had made provision for the beautification of the State House yard. Unadorned, often littered with refuse, the grounds had been an eyesore for many years. Now (in 1854) a wrought iron fence was erected, the enclosure was planted with trees and shrubs and gravel walks were laid.

The result was to spur the local authorities to further action. On May 1, 1855—noteworthy in the annals of Springfield for the grand concert of Madame De Vries, M. Labarthe's May party and an eclipse of the moon—the old market house was torn down.

In its day the market house had been a thing of beauty and a point of pride. But times had changed, few farmers used it, and neglect had made of it a nuisance. Finally it became so bad that outspoken visitors made it the object of their choicest vituperation. Why do the people of Springfield let "that miserable abortion of a Market House" stand in the middle of one of the principal streets,[8] and right in the face of the Capital! a disgusted St. Louisan exclaimed. "Tear it down—take it—hide it—hide it—it is a blot on the face of the City!"

"Go over to the ravine in the south part of the city—buy a block of ground and build a capacious Market House thereon," this outspoken visitor advised. The city council followed the suggestion, although not for some years after the old structure had been demolished. But in the summer of 1860 the contract was let for a new building on the corner of Fourth and Monroe streets, and work began at once. Built of brick, 40 by 140 feet in size, space was provided for the sale of meat, fruit and vegetables, and the basement was fitted up for a public eating room.

Still another public improvement was occupying the attention of the council. That was the matter of a suitable burial place. Early in Springfield's history Elijah Iles had donated four acres of ground west of the town [9] for a graveyard, and somewhat later John Hutchinson laid out six acres a short distance farther west [10] for the same purpose. Together, the two cemeteries sufficed for thirty-five years. But by the 50s it was clear that further provision had to be made. Moved to action by Charles H. Lanphier, one of its members, the council purchased a small tract of land north of the city in 1855. The next year an additional purchase was made, and the name "Oak Ridge," suggested by Mayor John Cook,

[8] Sixth Street.
[9] The site of the old Senior High School, at Spring and Adams Streets.
[10] Where the Senior High School now stands.

adopted. Although further burials were prohibited in the old city graveyard, Hutchinson's Cemetery was still in use, and little was done at Oak Ridge except to enclose the grounds with a common post and board fence. Nevertheless, the land was in possession of the city and dedicated to burial purposes, and one more notable project merely awaited the future for its fulfillment.

Meanwhile, an effort was being made to solve the perennial mud problem by other means than street planking. Originally the little streams which emptied into the Town Branch had provided fairly effective drainage, but because of the growth of the city an artificial substitute had become a necessity. Where the Branch and its tributaries intersected streets culverts were built, and sewers[11] and drains were laid on the principal downtown thoroughfares. By the end of the decade quagmires had been eliminated, although mud still found a way to ooze between the planking and make wet weather miserable for the fastidious for many years to come.

With the Town Branch itself, nothing was attempted. Once the groves through which the little stream meandered had been a favorite place of resort; now the slaughter houses threw their offal into it and at times it became a crimson stench. The citizens held their noses, shut their eyes and swore.

The hogs were another insoluble problem. Agitation over the question of the confinement or non-confinement of the porcine population never ceased. Early in the 50s the council ordered the hogs shut up. Shortly afterward, at one session in 1853, it repealed the ordinance and then immediately reversed itself and repealed the repealer. "Much talk and considerable feeling has been manifested by a portion of our citizens immediately interested, and distinctions have been drawn of Hog and Anti-Hogites," one of the papers re-

[11] Not, of course, sanitary sewers. These had to await the installation of a public water system.

ported. A year later the old ordinance providing for confinement was again revived. And so it went, with whichever side was momentarily most vociferous in possession of the legal badge of victory. Meanwhile, regardless of the law, the hogs continued to root up sidewalks, wallow in the mud, and bedaub fences and houses with slime.

Hand in hand with physical improvement went progress in the services the city rendered its inhabitants. In 1854 five policemen were added to the one law officer who had served the city for many years, and six years later the force was put in uniform. The officers grumbled loudly because the uniforms were to be purchased at their own expense, but the council refused to yield, and the order stood.

Of greater interest, both practically and socially, was the creation of an organization for fire protection. For years there had been a town fire warden, and fire hooks, ladders, and buckets were supposed to be available at all hours in the market house. But when the outbuildings of the City Hotel caught fire one night in the summer of 1850 every hook was found to be broken and not a single fire ladder could even be located. Only the hardest kind of work on the part of the townspeople saved the hotel itself. Other fires followed every few months—the Sangamon & Morgan station in 1852; Johnson's Old Tavern, four stores in Chicken Row, and Chatterton's jewelry store on the west side of the square in 1853; the City Mill and the Chicago & Mississippi car shops in 1854. Not until more than half the block on the west side of the square burned on the night of May 11, 1855, did the city take action. Prodded by the most disastrous fire in the town's history, the council requested the mayor to call on the citizens with a subscription paper for raising the money for two fire engines and other apparatus. The citizens, scared, subscribed enough for one engine. Nine months passed before it was delivered, and then the council refused to accept it. Another year went by. Finally, early in 1857, the council ordered an engine in Boston and provided for a building to house it.

Late in May, 1857, when the delivery of the engine was expected momentarily, Fire Company No. 1 was organized. Three weeks afterward the engine was received, and the newly formed company, "gaily dressed in their handsome uniforms," drew it through the streets behind Burt's band and then formed at the northwest corner of the square for their first trial. Six months later a second engine was received, and Sangamo Fire Company No. 2 was formed forthwith. The first company—the Pioneers as they were now called—celebrated by hanging a bell atop their engine house. Fire engines and bell were too much of a temptation to the boys of the town, and a rash of false alarms broke out, not to subside until the novelty wore off. But the urge to be a fireman was too strong for such discouragements, and two more companies made their appearance in a short time—Hook and Ladder Company No. 1, and Young America Hose Company No. 1.

To property owners the fire companies were a valuable asset, but it is doubtful if the young men who joined them were motivated as much by a desire to render a civic service as by anticipation of the social pleasures they afforded. Following the precedent of the military companies, visits were exchanged with similar organizations in nearby towns. Typical was an exchange of visits which took place on Independence Day, 1858. Since the holiday fell on a Sunday, the Springfield companies were invited to Jacksonville on Saturday, July 3rd. The program—a parade, barbecue, balloon ascension and fireworks—took up the entire day. On Monday the Jacksonville companies returned the visit. The Pioneers entertained one company of visitors at the St. Nicholas, where Abraham Lincoln, a guest of honor, offered the toast: "The Pioneer Fire Company—May they extinguish all the bad flames, but keep the flame of patriotism ever burning brightly in the hearts of the ladies;" while the Sangamo Company fêted the Jacksonville Rescue Company at the United States Hotel, and that evening gave a ball in their honor at Concert Hall. Balls, incidentally, seem to have been a part of the fireman's regular routine, for each company gave several every year. With frequent parades, they added to the gayety of the town.

With the formation of fire companies the city began to realize, as it had never done before, the lack of a public water supply. In 1857 eight cisterns were dug in the business section. Even so, it was generally recognized that this was inadequate provision. So $3,000 was appropriated by the council for an artesian well, contingent upon the popular sub-scription of a similar sum. The money was soon raised, and drilling was begun on Washington Street near Eleventh, then the eastern limit of the city. The work continued intermit-tently, and unsuccessfully, for two years. Finally, when a depth of 1100 feet had been reached, the project was aban-doned, with the city and its inhabitants wiser in the ways of water underground and poorer by $10,000.

Thus the last of the improvements of Springfield's pros-perous decade ended in failure. Nevertheless, in ten years the town had made more progress than in all its previous history. Crudities in plenty remained, but substantial buildings faced a tree-planted square, fine homes sheltered many of the in-habitants, the mud at least was not quite so bad as it had been, and a civic spirit had come into existence and been made manifest in many ways. In comparison with older places, the prairie capital on which the eyes of the nation were soon to focus might still be a country town; but in com-parison with itself of other days, it had become a shining city.

CHAPTER IX

Social and Cultural Growth

NO less important than the impetus which the railroads gave to Springfield's commercial prosperity and physical improvement were their effects upon the social life of the town.

One result of quick, cheap and comparatively comfortable travel was the formation of numerous organizations—professional, educational, social—on a statewide scale. The convention—a seemingly necessary element in the life of all such bodies—was now, as never before, an easy matter. Centrally located, and having especial prestige because of its possession of the state government, Springfield quickly became a favorite gathering place. One of the first influential groups to be organized there was the Illinois State Medical Society, formed in the rooms of the State Library on June 4, 1850. With the completion of the railroad between Alton and Chicago, and the construction of lines elsewhere in the state, the number of conventions multiplied manyfold. Typical of many years were the first two weeks of January, 1855, when the legislature, the State Agricultural Society, the State Educational Convention, the State Colonization Society and the Illinois Maine Law Alliance were all scheduled to meet.

One of these organizations was already responsible for what soon came to be a fixed feature of Illinois life—the state fair. In the summer of 1851 the Sangamon County Agricultural Society was formed. Eighteen months later this body took the lead in organizing a larger group, the Illinois State Agricultural Society. One of the goals of the new organization was an annual, state-wide exhibition at which farmers could show their best products, learn what others were doing, and profit by the comparison. The grounds of the old Farmers' and Mechanics' Association west of Springfield [1] were available. The state society had some money, the legislature made a small appropriation, and the citizens of Springfield pledged enough to erect suitable buildings. With the way thus cleared, the exhibition was set for the middle of September, 1853.

Many weeks were spent in preparation. Around the grounds a high plank fence was erected, stables were built along the east and south sides, and a long shed for the display of fruits and handiwork was constructed at the western limits. Pens for hogs and sheep were knocked together, wells were sunk and chain pumps put in place. The central part of the grounds was reserved for heavy machinery. In town an energetic clean-up was inaugurated. When the urge to self-improvement manifested itself criticism was rarely mild, and now, with the good opinion of thousands of visitors as the prize, the editors were eloquent on the subject of the city's shortcomings. "The brick bats, trash, old hats, old boots and shoes and scraps of leather, rags, bones, manure, and many other things which grace some of our streets, in front of our doors, and are found in our alleys, should be hauled off, and hog holes filled up, and other nuisances abated," one of the papers urged. If only these things were done, a long step would be taken to correct the reputation for mud and filth for which Springfield was notorious.

To house thousands of visitors, the people realized, would be a hard problem. To meet it spare rooms were prepared and attics were cleaned and fitted with furniture. But the

[1] The area now bounded by Douglas and Lincoln avenues, and Washington and Governor streets.

event turned out to be even worse than the expectation. On the night of September 11—the opening day—400 were registered at both the American House and the City Hotel, smaller taverns were similarly crowded, and hundreds of men and women who were unable to find accommodations anywhere slept in chairs and on the floors. On later nights the jam was even worse. Estimates of the number of visitors varied from 10,000 to 20,000. In only one particular were accurate figures available: a statistically-minded enquirer who made the rounds of the butcher shops learned that in four days 47,950 pounds of meat had been disposed of, and this was not counting the small sales of one butcher who had the colossal misfortune to be ill during most of the fair, nor the vast quantities of pork and poultry which the farmers sold direct to the townspeople.

The fair itself was a great success. There were big displays of mowers and reapers, threshing machines, plows, harrows and other implements. Cattle and horses in plenty, and fair numbers of sheep, swine and poultry were exhibited. The fruit department was well supplied, and "Floral Hall" presented "a tasteful appearance." A profusion of needlework, patchwork, dry goods and clothing was in evidence. At nights Herr Alexander, the wizard, delighted crowds at Clinton Hall, and Pell's "Varieties" offered juggling, bear wrestling and banjo playing in a pavilion south of the American House. Interest continued unabated, and on the last day Professor Jonathan Baldwin Turner, the state's foremost exponent of industrial education, spoke on "The Millennium of Labor" to a large audience.

"The Fair is over and gone," the editor of the *Journal* wrote a few days later. "Its doings have become a 'fixed fact' in the records of our state.—There it will stand, a starting point for future reference and comparison. Its influence no one can foresee or determine." A fixed fact it was, but not in the history of Springfield. The following year the second state fair, better attended even than the first, was held in the same place, but in 1855 Chicago carried off the prize, in 1856 it went to Alton, and thereafter a different city was chosen each year.[2] In its place, the farmers of Sangamon County organized a county fair. At first it suffered from comparison with the statewide exhibition, but it soon grew to creditable proportions and became an annual Springfield event.

In addition to facilitating such gatherings as fairs and conventions, the greater ease and convenience of travel resulted in a large increase in the number of musicians, lecturers and entertainers who visited the capital. The Newhall Family, the Robinson Family, the Columbians, the Alleghenians—these came as before, but more frequently, while outstanding artists like Ole Bull and Adelina Patti appeared for the first time.[3] In January, 1853, Ralph Waldo Emerson gave three lectures in the State House. In 1854 Bayard Taylor spoke in the Baptist Church on "The Arabs"—"unquestionably the most delightful and popular lecture ever given to a Springfield audience," one of the papers commented. The following year he returned for three lectures on "Japan," "India," and "The Philosophy of Travel."

(Taylor arrived in a driving rain and found the town a quagmire. Wisely he kept his impressions to himself until he published the first volume of *At Home and Abroad* in 1859. There, in addition to a few remarks about the mud, he wrote: "I must do Springfield the justice to say that it has its sunshiny side, when the mud dries up with magical rapidity and its level streets become fair to look upon. The clouds cleared away on the morning after my arrival, and when my friend, Captain Diller, took me to the cupola of

[2]Until 1894, when Springfield was selected as the permanent location.

[3]Paul Julien and Patti appeared at Metropolitan Hall on November 3, 1855, and played a return engagement on the 12th; and Ole Bull, with Patti, Schreiber, and Roth gave a concert in the same place on August 18, 1856.

the State House and showed me the wide ring of cultivated prairie, dotted with groves of hickory, sugar-maple, and oak, which inspheres the capital of Suckerdom, I confessed that it was a sight to be proud of. The young green of the woods and the promising wheatfields melted away gradually into blue, and the fronts of distant farm-houses shown in the morning sun like the sails of vessels in the offing. The wet soil of the cornfields resembled patches of black velvet—recalling to my mind the dark, prolific loam of the Nile Valley.")

After Emerson and Taylor, the leading lecturers of the country followed in quick succession—Horace Greeley ("Reform and Reformers") and Henry Ward Beecher ("Conservatism and Progression") in 1855, Theodore Parker ("The Progressive Development of Mankind") in 1856, and Parke Benjamin ("Hard Times") in 1857. Prices were low—usually 25¢—and large crowds attended. But the biggest crowd of all was a tribute to notoriety rather than intellect. Springfield disapproved when Lola Montez—dancer, actress, and onetime mistress of the King of Bavaria—lectured on "Fashion" in the spring of 1860, but curiosity overcame scruples and Cook's Hall was packed.

Circuses continued their visits to Springfield, but none of them aroused such excitement as the organization which set up its big tent on the east side of the square on October 3, 1853—P. T. Barnum's "Grand Colossal Museum and Menagerie." Barnum's name was already a household word—too much so, it would seem, from the wail of disappointment which arose the next day. Tom Thumb was all that he was claimed to be, but the balance of the show was a fraud. The main tent contained "a few old shells, bones, stuffed skins, Indian relics, and a mummy. Next, a load of miserable caricatures, in wax . . . Then eight or ten carriages of animals . . ." In the side shows scattered around the square were ballet performers at an admission charge of

10¢; the Happy Family—"a small dirty coop of monkeys, dogs, possums, woodchucks, squirrels, a California tiger cat" and a hurdy gurdy to provide music—at 10¢; the "Great scotch Giant and Giantess" at 15¢; and a live alligator and California bear paired together for a dime. On the streets girls in Swiss peasant costumes ground music boxes and took dimes from the country boys.

No sooner was a large hall available than theatrical performances, unknown in Springfield for a number of years, were resumed. In February and March, 1855, a traveling stock company played in Metropolitan Hall to good crowds. The following year the Varieties Theater played two engagements in the same place. Early in 1857, during the "gay season," the great actor Charles Walter Couldock played for several weeks. A crowded house, "composed of the beauty and chivalry of the State," rewarded him when he gave a benefit performance of "Richelieu" on the last night of the season.

But even though their number had increased notably, visitors did not monopolize the provision of Springfield's amusements. Bands and other musical organizations of local people flourished. The Germans of the city formed a theater group and fitted up Carpenter's Hall for productions. Even local lecturers drew good audiences—so good, in fact, that Abraham Lincoln was induced to give his lecture on "Discoveries and Inventions" on two separate occasions.

Moreover, local organizations of one kind or another were multiplying rapidly. The exhibits of the Springfield Horticultural Society, first given in 1849, became annual events attended by hundreds, many of whom came from nearby towns. Each year after 1856 the Typographical Association held a "Franklin Festival," with dinner, toasts and dancing, on the birthday of the great printer-philosopher. The New England Society celebrated annually the landing of the Pilgrims at Plymouth Rock. In 1859 the admirers of Robert Burns, with Abraham Lincoln prominent among them, commemorated the centenary of the Scotch poet's birth with a dinner at Concert Hall at which a large number of "mysterious-looking bottles" circulated freely. Every year citizens' suppers were held at the State House, with the proceeds dedicated to the relief of the poor.

In addition, the citizens themselves found time for frequent dinners, parties and calls. Social activity started in earnest at Christmas. All day the streets were thronged with ladies purchasing gifts—much of the buying was done on the day itself—while the youngsters devoted themselves to setting off firecrackers and other explosives until every excitable horse in town had run away or been stabled.

New Year's Day was devoted to calling. "The observance of the day," commented one of the newspapers in 1857, "consists in making the annual New Year's call of compliments and congratulation. . . . In no Western town is there usually such an interchange of visiting as in Springfield and no where are they enjoyed with more zest. All the city and his wife are expected to make it a holiday and nobody is compelled to work except the cook."

Everyone kept open house. Girls gauged their popularity by the number of cards they had collected by the end of the day, so when absence or illness prevented them from receiving, ribboned baskets for cards were hung on doorknobs. Often callers came as early as nine o'clock in the morning. When a young man started at this hour, and received liberal potions of eggnog at most of the homes he visited, it is not surprising that by late afternoon he found walking a difficult occupation. Everyone served escalloped oysters, chicken salad, coffee, ice cream, cake and candy, and how digestions ever survived the ordeal is one of the mysteries of the century.

Immediately after the New Year, court sessions, and in odd years the legislature, drew many visitors and furnished additional reasons for social activity. Typical of the city's hospitality was the public invitation which Governor Matteson issued in 1853, asking members of the legislature, judges of the supreme court, strangers in the city and ladies to call at the executive residence on any Thursday evening during the legislative session between the hours of eight and eleven. In other Springfield homes—those of Jacob Bunn, Ninian and Benjamin Edwards, James L. Lamb, George Pasfield, Stephen T. Logan, John T. Stuart, Nicholas H. Ridgely and George L. Huntington, to mention but a few—"strangers," as they were called, were no less welcome. The diary of Orville H. Browning, who was a regular visitor in the city, reflects the hospitality which prevailed. "Went to Judge Treats to supper with the Supreme Judges, and Grimshaw & McChesney," he recorded on January 26, 1859. Two days later he attended a party at the Dubois home,[4] and the next day he took tea with the Rev. John H. Brown, pastor of the First Presbyterian Church. On February 2 he was present at "a large party" at Lincoln's, and the next day he was again a supper guest of the Browns. On February 9th he had supper at the home of John T. Stuart. The next evening there was a levee at Governor Bissell's—"a great crowd present, and a pleasant party." And so it went.

The Matteson administration was a particularly gay time. The Governor's family was popular and entertained lavishly. When the new mansion was completed in January, 1856, the Mattesons opened it with one of the largest parties the town had ever known, and thereafter it became a center of social life. Not, however, to the exclusion of other homes. "Within the last three weeks," Mrs. Lincoln wrote to her sister in February of the following year, "there has been a party almost every night and some two or three grand fetes are coming off this week. I may perhaps surprise you when I mention that I am recovering from the slight fatigue

[4]Where the Sacred Heart convent now stands.

of a very large and I really believe a very handsome entertainment, or at least our friends flatter us by saying so.
About five hundred were invited, yet owing to an unlucky
rain three hundred only favored us by their presence and
the same evening in Jacksonville, Colonel Warren gave a
bridal party to his son who married Miss Birchall of this
place which occasion robbed us of some of our friends. . . ."

"The inhabitants of this city," wrote John Reynolds in
1854, "enjoy the social pleasures and happiness arising out
of an intelligent and refined society, to a considerable extent,
and often indulge in the facinations [sic] and attractions
of tasty and elegant convivial parties. The streets of this
city are spacious and beautiful, which afford the gay and
fashionable citizens, *in good weather,* a delightful prome-
nade, which is much enjoyed by both sexes, *arm in arm,* or
separately. The citizens are celebrated for their hospitality
and urbanity of manners. They enjoy great pleasure in extending to strangers and others, the refined and elegant
civilities that are due from one to another in a polished and
accomplished society." The Ex-Governor was a notorious
flatterer who rarely spoke ill of anyone—at least in print—
but everything indicates that in this case he wrote without
his customary exaggeration.

But in spite of the keen enjoyment which the people of
Springfield found in social activities, the prevailing tone of
society was one of moral and intellectual seriousness. Early
in 1856 a number of citizens agitated the formation of a
library association. Within a week $700 was subscribed, an
organization was perfected, and officers were elected—T. J.
Carter as president, William H. Herndon and Thomas
Mather secretaries, and Jacob Bunn, treasurer. In May the
old rooms of the United States Court [5] were fitted up, and

---

[5] On the second floor of the building still standing on the southwest corner
of Sixth and Adams streets. When Stephen T. Logan's building at Sixth and
Washington was completed in 1855, the U. S. Court removed to that location.

a considerable number of books were made available to the subscribers. Sometime earlier an organization—a forerunner of the Y. M. C. A.—to promote "the mental and religious improvement of young men" had been formed. Another group, under the name of the City Lyceum, was meeting at regular intervals to discuss such subjects as "Ought capital punishment to be abolished?" and "Is it expedient to adopt the Maine liquor law in Illinois?"

The latter question recalls the great wave of temperance agitation which swept over the country in the fifties, with strong eddies disturbing the even course of Springfield's life.

At an early date in the town's history there were protests from those who objected to the sale of intoxicating liquors. A curious entry in the record book of the county commissioners' court for 1835—four years before Springfield was incorporated—reads as follows: "Whereas Petitions having been presented to this Court Signed by many respectable Citizens of Sangamon County praying the court to withhold Tavern licens or Grocery licens and the court having also had before them and now on file the written opinion of the Gentlemen of the Bar of this place The court thinks the matter of importance but makes no further decision thereon till the next term of this court." Nothing came of the petitions, but the Washingtonian movement of a few years later made itself felt. Beginning in Baltimore in 1840, when a number of habitual drinkers pledged themselves to total abstinence and determined to persuade others to do likewise, the movement spread rapidly. In mid-December, 1841, a delegation from Alton organized the First Springfield Washington Temperance Society. By the last day of the month the membership numbered 350, and six months afterward it was said that there were 700 Washingtonians in Springfield and 2,000 in Sangamon County. Prominent among them was Abraham Lincoln, who delivered the address at the first gala meeting—on Washington's Birthday, 1842—and antagonized many of the righteous citizens by stating his conviction that "such of us as have never fallen victims have been spared more by the absence of appetite than from any mental or moral superiority over those who have."

But the Washingtonian movement was too emotional to endure. Taking its place in the agitation against alcoholic liquor came the Sons of Temperance. This organization was founded in 1845 as a secret order whose members were pledged to temperance. Spreading slowly at first, by 1848 it was active enough in Springfield to hold demonstrations on Washington's Birthday and the Fourth of July, and nearly every year thereafter these days were occasions for parades in full regalia and public meetings devoted to the evils of strong drink.

The Sons of Temperance and its junior order, the Cadets of Temperance, with other organizations like the Roman Catholic Total Abstinence Society, were symptomatic of a widespread feeling among thoughtful people that the evils of intoxicants were exceeding tolerable limits. Many citizens, moreover, were becoming impatient with persuasion as a means to sobriety. In 1850 public opinion forced a popular vote on the question of whether licenses should be granted to taverns within the city limits, and the result was a three-to-one majority in the negative. Thus the retail sale of liquor was prohibited, although the purchase of intoxicants in quantities, for consumption at home, was still permitted. But the result was disappointing. Almost at once the complaint was made that license or no license, grog shops were operating as they always had. Although plenty of evidence was brought forward to prove the contention, the authorities refused to act. In the end, all efforts to keep the taverns closed were given up.

Over the country, however, a movement for downright prohibition was gaining momentum. In 1851 the Maine legislature passed a prohibitory law, and other New England states quickly followed the example. Opponents of liquor pressed hard for the adoption of similar legislation everywhere. In January, 1853, the Illinois State Temperance Convention met in Springfield and memorialized the legislature to pass a "Maine law." The legislature refused, but the agitation, which continued in the form of temperance lectures, temperance suppers and temperance meetings, had its fruit in May, 1854, when the people of the capital, by a vote of 468 to 391, decided to prevent the sale of spirituous, vinous or malt liquor in any quantity within the limits of the town.

The prohibition ordinance went into effect on August 1, 1854. By August 5th an establishment on the Peoria road outside the city limits was selling liquor at a rapid rate. Immediately there was hot debate on the practicability of the measure which had been adopted. *"Time* and *a fair trial* is necessary to the ascertainment of the efficacy of every law, and particularly of those of a reformatory character . . . ," said the defenders of the ordinance. "The total prohibition of the traffic in liquors as a beverage is the only hope for the suppression of intemperance. All other measures have failed." But the people of the city were inclined to doubt. On June 4, 1855, when a Maine law which the legislature had adopted subject to popular approval was put to a vote, Springfield cast 735 votes against it and only 631 in its favor. The result forecast the doom of the local prohibitory ordinance. On November 6, when a vote was taken on the question, the count was 450 for repeal and 322 for continuance. As soon as the result was known a procession formed, paraded the streets behind a band, and by the light of burning tar barrels held a jollification meeting on the square.

Other social evils as well as intemperance drew the attention of reformers. In 1859 it was said that there were no less than twenty gambling houses in Springfield, some of which were fitted up as elaborately as the glittering establishments of St. Louis and New Orleans. In one night during that year a local citizen was reported to have won over $5,000 at a single sitting. Houses of ill fame were numerous. "Why is it that the keepers . . . are protected when the order-loving part of the community undertake to rid their vicinity of those evils?" the reforming citizens asked. "Why is it that our police do not endeavor to break up those houses, in order to preserve peace and quiet in neighborhoods, benefit the youth and maintain the good name of our city?" But publicity aroused no response, and nothing was done.

In an age of organizations and moral fervor, it was natural that fraternal orders should flourish. Very early in Springfield's history the Masonic order had made its appearance. The first lodge, Sangamo Lodge No. 29, obtained a charter from the Grand Lodge of Missouri in 1822, but was later disbanded. Another lodge was organized in 1839, and rechartered the following year as Springfield Lodge No. 4. Among its early members were Samuel H. Treat, James Shields and Stephen A. Douglas. In 1840, also, the first Odd Fellows lodge—Sangamon Lodge No. 6—was organized with thirty-five members. The decade preceding the Civil War saw the expansion of both orders. New Masonic lodges were organized in 1849 and 1860, while the growing importance of the Germans as an element in Springfield's population was emphasized in 1855, when Teutonia Lodge No. 166 of the Odd Fellows was formed.

Meanwhile, the religious organizations of the city had expanded and multiplied. The Presbyterian Church, first house of worship to be erected in the town, soon became too small. A revival in 1840 led to a decision to build a new church. Subscriptions to the amount of $15,000 were secured, and in the fall of 1843 the building was completed. Two years later an organ was installed, to the consternation of the more conservative members. Meanwhile, the Second

Presbyterian Church was flourishing. With the influx of the Portuguese, a Portuguese Presbyterian Church was organized in 1849. In the same year dissention arose in the First Presbyterian Church over the resignation of Doctor Bergen, and the Third Presbyterian Church was organized. Two years later their church building, designed by George I. Barnett of St. Louis, the architect of the State Bank Building, was finished. But the number of Presbyterian churches was not yet complete, for in 1858 a division took place among the Portuguese, and the Second Portuguese Presbyterian Church came into existence.

Methodism, which antedated Presbyterianism, seemed to have greater cohesive powers, for the only duplication in congregations took place when the German members of the sect organized the German Methodist Church and erected a church building on the corner of Sixth and Mason streets in 1856. Like the Presbyterians, the Methodists had quickly outgrown their original church. Unlike them, however, they had been unable at once to raise funds for the construction of a new edifice. Nevertheless, in 1842 the building had been enlarged by the addition of transepts. By 1850 the Methodist society was the largest religious organization in the city, and a new and larger church was a necessity. Springfield was more prosperous than it had been ten years earlier, but even so the task of raising funds was a hard one. By the summer of 1851 the main part of a new structure had been completed, but all the money was gone. Public appeals for funds were made, but it was not until 1854 that the church was finally finished and dedicated.

In 1834 the Baptists had erected a small frame church on the southwest corner of Seventh and Adams streets. The society grew, and a new building became desirable, but a campaign for subscriptions fell far short of the necessary amount. Refusing to give up, the pastor, G. S. Bailey, set out in 1847 to raise money in the East. Seven months later he returned with $700. The congregation took heart, local subscriptions increased, and a church building was started. By the spring of 1850 the Baptists, too, had a new church.

The erection of one church building led inevitably to another. At the same time that the Baptists were planning a new edifice, the Episcopalians were completing a church to replace the small wooden structure which had served them since organization. On June 28, 1848, the new building was dedicated by the venerable Bishop Philander Chase, assisted by clergymen from Jacksonville and Rock Island. A few years later the Campbellites, or Disciples of Christ, as they were coming to be called, erected a brick building on the northeast corner of Sixth and Jefferson streets.

As time went on, new denominations supplemented those which had been organized early in Springfield's history. After occasional preaching by itinerant ministers, the Lutherans of the town had organized in 1841 under the leadership of the Rev. Francis Springer. Not until 1859, however, did they have a church building of their own. Meanwhile, their German-speaking brethren had formed Trinity Evangelical Lutheran Church, and were holding services in a small frame meeting-house on Third Street near Washington. By 1850, also, a Universalist society was holding meetings twice a month. Seven years later it had grown to such an extent that it undertook the construction of a church building of its own on the corner of Fifth and Cook streets.

By this time, the Roman Catholic Church had become established. For the first two decades of Springfield's existence only a handful of communicants resided in the town. In 1840 the Rev. George Hamilton reported to his Bishop that there were only nine Catholic families in the capital, and two other families in which the women were Catholics. Altogether they were too poor to afford a church. In fact, the priest had difficulty in finding even a room for services. During the preceding summer he had reported that there

was only one suitable vacant room in town, and since that
had been built for a theater, and would doubtless be used
for that purpose again, he did not think it becoming that it
should be devoted, even temporarily, to Divine worship.

However, the number of communicants increased steadily,
and in mid-August, 1842, the *Sangamo Journal* noted the
presence in Springfield of Bishop Kendrick of St. Louis and
two attending priests, come for the purpose of dedicating
"the neat Catholic Church, situate in the east part of the
city."[6] Henceforth, the paper stated, Springfield would have
a resident priest. As time went on the congregation outgrew
the small structure. In 1855 the northeast corner lot at the
corner of Monroe and Seventh streets was secured, and in
the following year the construction of the Church of the
Immaculate Conception was commenced. Before it was completed the first sisters of the Ursuline Order, five in number,
arrived in Springfield and opened a school in a residence on
North Sixth Street. The following year—1858—they
secured a larger building at the corner of Sixth and Mason
streets, where they conducted a parochial school and an
academy until the close of the Civil War. Thus, by the end
of the fifties, both the Roman Catholic Church, and one of
the teaching orders which have played so large a part in
the education of its children, were firmly established in
Springfield.

Although it antedated the church in the days when the
town was a cluster of log cabins, the school lagged behind
in its development. During the first decade there was only
one school in the town, though it was held in various places
and conducted by a number of schoolmasters. Two schools,
each with an enrollment of about sixty pupils, supplied all
educational facilities until the late thirties, when several

[6]Probably the church of St. John the Baptist, located on the south side of
Adams Street between Eighth and Ninth, although the official publication,
The Diocese of Springfield in Illinois, gives the year 1848 as the date of
erection.

smaller institutions—if they can be dignified by that name—
were organized. All were conducted by individuals as they
saw fit, without supervision and without standards of any
sort. Each family paid tuition for each child. Too often the
children of the poorer residents attended only long enough
to learn the rudiments of reading and writing, and there
were many who never attended at all.

In 1839 the Springfield Academy, newly incorporated,
opened in a new building on South Fourth Street. For fifteen
years this institution, together with the Springfield Female
Seminary which the Rev. J. F. Brooks conducted, and the
Mechanics' Institute, bore the brunt of the educational burden, although there were always a number of smaller
schools. The schedule of opening dates for the fall of 1850
listed, in addition to the two just mentioned, the Parochial
School of the First Presbyterian Church, the Rev. E. Miller's
Classical School, and the Springfield Young Ladies' Institute, which held classes in the rooms of the Baptist Church.
In this school tuition charges, doubtless the same as in the
others, were as follows: for each child, per quarter, in the
first class of the primary department, $2.50; for the second
class of the primary department, $3.00; for the advanced
departments, $4.00, $5.00 and $6.00. Thus a family with
three children in school would be forced to pay in the
neighborhood of $100 a year for tuition alone.

With the growth of social consciousness which characterized the ten years preceding the Civil War, the advocates
of a free, tax-supported school system became vocal. Many
families with small incomes, they pointed out, found it ex-
tremely difficult, if not impossible, to give their children the
simplest kind of educational opportunities. Other cities in
the state—Chicago, Galena, Joliet—had established free
school systems: must the capital forever lag behind?

The citizens answered in the negative in 1854. Plans for
organizing the system were made at once, but not until the

METHODIST EPISCOPAL

GERMAN LUTHERAN

FIRST BAPTIST

ROMAN CATHOLIC

FIRST PRESBYTERIAN

ST. PAUL'S EPISCOPAL

REPRESENTATIVE CHURCHES, 1860

(From a lithograph owned by
J. S. Sutton, Springfield, Ill.)

THE COURT HOUSE (LEFT) AND MARINE AND FIRE INSURANCE CO. IN THE 1850's.
(EAST SIDE SQUARE.)

THE GOVERNOR'S MANSION, 1860

(From a lithograph owned by
J. S. Sutton, Springfield, Ill.)

spring of 1856, when the first and third ward[7] buildings were finished, were classes inaugurated. At the same time facilities for pupils residing in the other two wards were provided in the basements of the Baptist and First Presbyterian churches. Two years later the second and fourth ward buildings were completed. Meanwhile a high school had been organized, and in 1859 a separate school for colored children was established.

With the appointment of a superintendent—S. M. Cutcheon of Ypsilanti, Michigan—in 1858, the organization was completed. But to secure satisfactory attendance was a different matter. In 1857 there were slightly more than 1,000 children enrolled in the public schools with an additional 300 in private schools, but it was estimated that nearly twice that many inhabitants of Springfield were under twenty-one years of age. Two years later, in his first annual report, Superintendent Cutcheon was able to make available exact figures, thanks to a city census taken in 1858. While there were 2,045 children between the ages of five and fifteen in the city, the number enrolled in the public schools was 1,293 with 250 in private institutions. Of 1,143 boys and girls over fifteen and under twenty-one, only 117 were attending public and 200 private schools. Thus 500 children under fifteen years of age, and more than 800 youths between fifteen and twenty-one, were not enrolled in any school. Moreover, the daily attendance—there being no compulsion —was often only half of the enrollment.

Still, the town was proud of its schools, and much attention was paid to the public examinations with which each term concluded. For a solid week self-conscious pupils declaimed Webster's Address to the Survivors of Bunker Hill, Patrick Henry's Speech on the War of American Inde-

[7]The northeast quarter of the city constituted the first ward, the northwest quarter the second, the southwest quarter the third, and the southeast quarter the fourth.

pendence, and such "pieces" as "The Gambler's Wife" and "Mother, Home and Heaven," while the prominent citizens of the board of visitors looked important and fathers and mothers alternated between pride and trepidation. On such occasions the public school system was an unqualified success.

At the same time that the public schools were being organized, an institution of higher learning was taking root. In 1851 the citizens, under the leadership of John T. Stuart, had bestirred themselves to secure for Springfield the academy and college which the Lutheran Church was planning to establish. When the children of Pascal P. Enos, one of the town's original proprietors, donated ten acres of ground in the northeastern part of the city, and others made subscriptions towards the construction of buildings and the establishment of scholarships, the location was assured.

In April, 1852, the institution, under the name of the Illinois State University,[8] admitted its first students. Until its own building, which was commenced at once, was ready for occupancy, classes were held in the Mechanics Union at the corner of Third and Washington streets. During the first year seventy-nine students enrolled in the preparatory department and three were admitted to the freshman class of the college. Tuition charges were $30.00 for a forty-week year in the college and $25.00 in the academy, unless one wished to undertake the "learned languages and more advanced sciences," in which case an additional fee was collected. Most of the students were from Springfield, and the few who came from outside the city provided their own room and board. The college urged them to club together, and assured prospective students that on the basis of the first year's experience, the entire cost of living for a thrifty student would not vary greatly from seventy-five cents a week.

[8] Not to be confused with the University of Illinois. The Illinois State University, never tax-supported, functioned under its original title until 1874, when its name was changed to Concordia College, and it became a theological seminary.

In five years the college was fairly well established. An "elegant four story edifice," with the first story of cut stone and the balance of brick, provided class-room facilities for 119 students, thirty-three of whom were taking college courses. Four professors, all ministers, a principal of the grammar school and a steward made up the faculty. The curriculum was exclusively classical. The freshman started with Latin and Greek grammar, Livy, Xenophon, algebra and universal history, and the senior wound up on Terence or Plautus, Sophocles, the evidences of Christianity, mineralogy and geology, and a general review. Studies in the Greek Testament, and "English Composition and Declamation," were continued throughout the entire four years. In the college catalogs it all looked very academic and imposing, but local youths like Robert Lincoln and Clinton Conkling, and John Hay, who came from Pittsfield to enter, learned to their disappointment that the combined efforts of four ministers, sincere though they might be, still fell short of the august requirements of Harvard and Yale and Brown.

The important fact, however, was not that the college failed to live quite up to its promises, but that the college existed at all. So it was with the public schools. Enrollment might be poor, and attendance even poorer, but at least a free school system had been established, and the only direction it could move—given a typical American city—was forward. And the same could be said with justice of the other cultural and religious and moral activities which the people had undertaken. Perfection might still be far distant, just as the streets were not yet free from mud, but what had been achieved was impressive.

CHAPTER X

Lincoln Emerges

FROM the beginning of Springfield's history the shadow of human slavery had rested upon it. Many of the town's first inhabitants were from the South, and some of them held slaves in their new home through the device of long-term indentures. On the other hand, there were Yankee residents even from the very outset. Naturally, the convention struggle of 1824 aroused the little hamlet no less deeply than the older communities. The murder of Lovejoy in 1837 stirred passions in Springfield, as elsewhere in Illinois. The Mexican War, with its potential extension of the institution, and the Wilmot proviso, devised to block that extension, found both opponents and protagonists in the prairie capital. Influential citizens were active members of the colonization society, which sought to palliate the scourge of slavery by purchasing slaves, emancipating them, and "colonizing" them in Liberia. Only now and then was the shadow deep black and clearly defined. Much of the time it was so faint as to be barely perceptible. But it was never wholly absent.

Therefore it was unavoidable that the bitter slavery controversy of 1850, which threatened for a time to wreck the Union, should have reverberations in Springfield. Trouble was precipitated by the request of California and New Mexico, territories acquired through the Mexican War, and Utah, for admission to the Union. Since California and New

Mexico had already excluded slavery in their constitutions, and since Utah was expected to do so, bitter opposition to the prospect of losing most of the new territory developed in the South. In Congress passions flamed in the representatives of both North and South, secession was freely threatened, and for a time disruption of the Union seemed possible, if not likely.

But tremendous efforts to effect a compromise finally succeeded. California was admitted as a free state; Texas, involved in a boundary dispute, was appeased by a grant of $10,000,000; and provision was made for the admission of New Mexico and Utah at a later date with or without slavery as they themselves should decide. To pacify the South a much more stringent fugitive slave law was passed, and to soothe the anti-slavery sentiment of the North the slave trade—but not slavery—was forbidden in the District of Columbia.

Originally these measures, which constitute the famous Compromise of 1850, had been referred to a committee of thirteen, headed by Henry Clay. From this committee came an "omnibus bill" providing for the admission of California, the settlement of the boundary of Texas, and the organization of New Mexico and Utah as territories. On this the opposition combined, and for a time the bill seemed likely to be the rock on which the country would go to pieces.

While tension was at its highest, the people of Springfield gave voice to their own feelings. On June 13 the newspapers published a call for a meeting of citizens favorable to the solution proposed by the committee of thirteen, to be held in the court house on Saturday evening, June 15th. Included among the eighty-three signers were men prominent in both parties—Democrats like Governor A. C. French, Mason Brayman, John Calhoun and Nicholas H. Ridgely; and Whigs like John Williams, John T. Stuart, Robert Irwin, and James H. Matheny—but the names of Abraham Lincoln, Stephen T. Logan and William H. Herndon were absent.

On Saturday night the court house was crowded. John Moore, of Bloomington, the state treasurer, was called to the chair, and care was taken to apportion the other offices of the meeting among representatives of both parties. Strong resolutions endorsing the proposed compromise, and asserting that it was favored by an "overwhelming majority" of the people of Illinois, were introduced and passed. Judging from the editorials which appeared in both newspapers, not only at this time but throughout the controversy, the meeting and its action accurately represented Springfield's attitude.

Before a final vote was taken on the omnibus bill, added solemnity was given to the national crisis by the death of President Taylor. When the news reached Springfield on July 10 the merchants closed their stores and business ceased for the balance of the day. Three days later, minute guns were fired and bells tolled from two o'clock in the afternoon until four—the hours of the President's funeral. Two weeks later, in congress, the proposal of the committee of thirteen came to a vote, and met defeat. Then, under the leadership of Douglas, the measures were taken up separately and passed. By the end of the summer compromise had been effected, the sections were at peace, and slavery— so it was said—would never again be a disturbing factor in the nation's life.

Nevertheless, it was a ghost which could not be completely exorcised. Officially dead, the issue could not be kept out of the congressional campaign of 1850, for Thomas L. Harris of Petersburg, the Democratic candidate, kept charging the Whigs with responsibility for the crisis through which the country had just passed; and Richard Yates, his Whig opponent, felt impelled to assert repeatedly that while he was against the extension of slavery to the territories, he was not an abolitionist. But the people were tired of the agitation. When James Shields came to Springfield in late October, fresh from Washington, he held a large audience for two and a half hours while he described the adoption of the compromise measures. When he concluded, the meeting not only endorsed the compromise, but gave its especial approval to the fugitive slave law, which had aroused a fury of opposition in the North, by resolving that it "imposes no duty upon the citizen inconsistent with the constitution of the United States, and that its execution will be acquiesced in by every good citizen; and that we will, in all the several relations we bear to the country, cordially and heartily aid in its execution."

So far as one can judge from the presidential campaign of 1852, slavery really was a dead issue in national politics. In Springfield the campaign started in June. Early in the month the telegraph brought news of the nomination of Franklin Pierce by the Democratic National Convention. Local party men were disappointed. For weeks the *Illinois State Register* had carried the name of Stephen A. Douglas at its masthead, and now a nonentity was presented as a candidate. A ratification meeting was announced, postponed, and finally held in the State House. The usual speeches were made, but no great enthusiasm could be generated for a candidate of whom the rank and file of the party had never even heard.

In the nomination of Winfield Scott two weeks later the Whigs were not much more fortunate. Military fame had turned the trick for Taylor, but the Mexican War was already fading into the past, and Scott lacked Taylor's personal appeal. Nevertheless, the Whigs too held their ratification meeting, and organized, not too hopefully, to overcome the ingrained Democratic proclivities of the state.

The news of Scott's nomination was less than a week old when the wires brought a bulletin which touched the towns-

people deeply. Henry Clay was dead. The idol of his party
for decades, Clay had won the respect of all lovers of the
nation by the battle he had fought for the Union in 1850.
On the evening of the day news of his death was received,
party friend and party foe met at the State House, where
Abraham Lincoln, as chairman, appointed a committee to
make arrangements for a suitable memorial service. One
week later—on July 6th—the first of seventy-six minute
guns (one for each year of Clay's life) was fired at eleven
o'clock in the morning, the stores were closed and business
was suspended. With the last gun a procession formed, with
the Odd Fellows, the Temple of Honor, and—ironically—
the Sons of Temperance and Cadets of Temperance at its
head! At the Episcopal Church the Rev. Charles Dresser
read the service for the dead. The meeting then adjourned
to the State House, where Lincoln spoke in eulogy of the
dead Kentuckian.

By mid-summer the faithful of both parties had organized
clubs which met at frequent intervals to shout the virtues
of their standard-bearers, but the people remained apathetic.
The only real enthusiasm of the campaign was manifested
when Douglas visited the city late in October. Then, in spite
of a driving rain, crowds surged around the railroad station, waiting to escort him to the State House where, from
the south portico, he responded to James W. Barrett's address of welcome. The next day, when he spoke in the Hall
of the House of Representatives, the room was packed,
and hundreds crowded the stairways and the rotunda in an
effort to catch the booming bass of "the favorite son of
Illinois." It was easy to see whom the Democrats really
wanted. Nevertheless, a few days later they dutifully went
to the polls and helped to swell the majority which made
Franklin Pierce President of the United States.

The first year of the new administration passed unevent-
fully. And then, on January 4, 1854, Douglas, as chairman

of the Senate Committee on Territories, reported a bill to organize the territory of Nebraska. Disregarding the fact that by the Compromise of 1820—the Missouri Compromise—slavery had been prohibited in the region from which the new territory was to be formed, the bill left all questions pertaining to slavery in the hands of the inhabitants. An immediate uproar followed. Amendments were proposed, rejected and adopted, until on February 6 the bill emerged in final form. By that time the slavery provision had crystallized into a declaration that the restriction provided by the Missouri Compromise was "inconsistent" with the Compromise of 1850, and therefore "inoperative and void," and that it was "the true intent and meaning" of the act "not to legislate slavery into any Territory or State, nor to exclude it therefrom, but to leave the people thereof perfectly free to form and regulate their domestic institutions in their own way, subject only to the Constitution of the United States." Four months were to elapse before the fate of the legislation was determined, but one fact was apparent at once—the problem of slavery was again before the American people, more ominously than ever.

Springfield's reaction was immediate, though not vociferous. Twelve days after Douglas's report the *Journal* deplored the introduction of the bill, and declared its opposition to any molestation of the compromise measures. As the debate progressed, it gave its support consistently, though in moderate terms, to the Anti-Nebraska bloc which quickly formed. Moreover, if Abraham Lincoln was correctly informed, the Democrats were hardly less disturbed than the Whigs by what was taking place in Washington. A month after the introduction of the original Nebraska bill, the Illinois legislature met in special session. "Of the one hundred members composing the two branches of that body," Lincoln wrote in 1855, "about seventy were Democrats. These latter held a caucus, in which the Nebraska bill was

talked of, if not formally discussed. It was thereby discovered that just three and no more, were in favor of the
measure. In a day or two Douglas's orders came on to have
resolutions passed approving the bill; and they were passed
by large majorities!!!"

However this may have been, the Democrats, once lined
up, remained solidly behind the measure. When, after months
of uncertainty, news of its passage reached Springfield on
May 23, the Springfield Artillery brought out their field
piece and fired a national salute, and then 113 guns for each
vote which it had received. "The booming cannon announced
a moral victory more glorious than can be achieved upon
the bloody fields of Europe, should her present wars last a
century," proclaimed the *Register*. But the cleavage which
the bill had wrought, not only in Springfield but throughout
the North, was evident from the *Journal's* comment: "The
old 'Nebraska swivel' was pulled out last night, and pounded
away one hundred and thirteen times to the number of the
'band of traitors' that have just enacted the great lie of
'popular sovereignty' over the heads of the American people."

With the Nebraska Bill on the statute books, both friend
and enemy awaited the fall congressional campaign, when
it was certain to be the paramount issue. But before that
campaign commenced, an incident took place in Springfield
which illustrated the intensity of the emotions which the
slavery question had by this time aroused.

In the course of an Illinois speaking tour, Cassius M.
Clay of Kentucky, widely known as an abolitionist, came to
the Illinois capital on July 10. The secretary of state refused
to allow him to speak in the rotunda of the State House,
where his meeting was to have been held, so a stand was
hastily erected in the Mather grove.[1] There a large crowd,
many of whom, like Lincoln, lay prone on the grass, listened

[1] Where the present State House stands.

to him denounce the slavery policy of the ruling party for two hours and a half. Time and again hecklers taunted him, but "he spoke boldly, proudly, his sentiments—in the face and eyes of all the contumely and insults thrown upon him . . ." and made a "GREAT HEROIC SPEECH." Thus spoke the *Journal*. But to the *Register* "sentiments more atrocious never found a place in the heart of the foulest traitor that ever meditated the destruction of his country." Editors, in 1854, were not accustomed to treat each other with any excess of politeness, but passion was behind words like these.

Two months later the campaign opened with a debate between Lincoln and John Calhoun. The issue was the Nebraska Bill, and not the personal merits of the two candidates—Thomas L. Harris, the Democrat, and Richard Yates, the Anti-Nebraska Whig. Thereafter friend and foe clashed weekly in Springfield—Harris himself and Stephen T. Logan, Murray McConnel and James C. Conkling, and many others. But the high point of the campaign came with the state fair in early October. Knowing that large crowds would gather at the capital, the politicians disregarded the publicly expressed disapproval of the fair's managers and planned to assemble in force.

Chief interest centered in the address which Stephen A. Douglas was scheduled to make. A month earlier Douglas had returned to his home city of Chicago to find himself exceedingly unpopular. When he tried to justify his course at a public meeting in Chicago on September 1, the crowd howled him down until he finally gave up the attempt. But Springfield's temper was different. Passing through the town a few days before the fair opened, Hopkins' artillery had signalized his arrival with a national salute, the German band serenaded him, and for hours crowds surged through the American House, where he stayed overnight, to shake his hand and wish him well. The friends of his youth were still faithful.

Douglas's address, a justification of the Nebraska Bill nationwide in its significance, was announced for the afternoon of Wednesday, October 3. Anticipating a huge audience, a stand and 5,000 seats had been erected in a grove southwest of the town, but because of rain the meeting had to be transferred to the State House. There the Hall of the House of Representatives, the stairways and the rotunda were all jammed, and hundreds were turned away for want of room. When the short, stocky figure of the Little Giant appeared cheer after cheer broke from the crowd. For three hours he spoke, while his hearers alternated between tense quiet and spontaneous applause. It was a masterly justification of the measure on which he had staked his political future.

When Douglas concluded, Lincoln, who had sat immediately in front of the speaker throughout the meeting, arose to announce that on the next day, at the same time and place, either he or Lyman Trumbull, or both, would speak in reply. On Thursday afternoon it was Lincoln who stood before the crowd to carry the Anti-Nebraska attack. For three hours he too held forth. When he finally finished, cheers rocketed through the Hall, for his supporters were even more delighted than the friends of Douglas had been twenty-four hours earlier. Douglas's quality was known, but heretofore Lincoln had been only one of many political speakers— shrewd, witty, sometimes boisterously funny, but so far as Springfield knew, no certain match for his great opponent. Yet this speech had a depth and seriousness about it which marked it off from those which had preceded it as clearly and sharply as the line between black and white. In three hours Lincoln had placed himself at the head of the Anti-Nebraska forces in Illinois.

When Lincoln concluded Douglas spoke briefly, and that evening James Singleton, a former Whig, and Thomas L. Harris piled up more arguments in favor of the Nebraska

Bill. The next day crowds turned out to hear Sidney Breese and E. D. Taylor attack the Nebraska policy and John Calhoun defend it. At night Trumbull, who had come up from Alton only that day, spoke to an enthusiastic audience. But the speeches of Douglas and Lincoln remained the high points of the series.

Few took seriously the "Republican" convention which was held in the State House on the afternoon after Lincoln's speech. Prominent among the participants were Ichabod Codding and Owen Lovejoy, well known abolitionists, William H. Herndon, and Erastus Wright, "who, of himself," sneered the *Register,* "has enough of the elements of a disunionist to constitute one entire abolition convention. . . . Ichabod raved," the editor continued, "and Lovejoy swelled, and all indorsed the sentiments of that [Lincoln's] speech." Fearing just that, and more serious entanglements as well, Lincoln himself had climbed into his old buggy and started for court in Tazewell County. This was not the time, he well knew, for a rising politician to have his record indelibly stained with abolitionism.

A month later the votes were counted. In the Springfield congressional district the Democrats had won and Harris was elected, but over the state as a whole a majority of Anti-Nebraska members had been elected to the legislature. In three months came the sequel, when the two houses met in joint session, with the galleries packed, to elect a successor to James Shields in the United States Senate. On the first ballot forty-four votes were cast for Abraham Lincoln. No other candidate received as many, but the number was still short of a majority. As the balloting progressed the Democrats switched to Governor Matteson, Lincoln's supporters slipped away, and Trumbull, who had started with five votes, gained in strength. Finally, on the tenth ballot, when it was apparent not only that his own election was impossible, but also that Matteson's election was imminent, Lincoln swung his remaining supporters to Trumbull, who was elected. Eight days later the *Illinois Journal* carried a short news item: "A large number of anti-Nebraska members of the Legislature met on yesterday, and partook of a dinner provided by the liberality of Mr. Lincoln. . . . The affair passed off very pleasantly."

With 1855 came reaction from the tension of the preceding year. "In political matters Springfield was never quieter than it is now," wrote a correspondent of the Chicago *Democratic Press* in the late spring. "Even that interminable theme 'Nebraska,' has ceased to be a matter of interest; while the recent outrages of 'squatter sovereignty' in Kansas, though shocking to the feeling of all good men, are scarcely thought of a moment after reading of them in the public prints." In mid-September Douglas spoke in Metropolitan Hall on the Democratic party and the elements opposed to it, but while the hall was filled to capacity, the calm was not broken. Of more interest was the visit, a few days later, of Joshua Giddings, the Ohio abolitionist, and Codding, his Illinois colleague. For once both parties were in agreement. An uncalled-for violation of the political calm, said the conservative Anti-Nebraska men; "it is not required that any such enthusiasts . . . should travel around to teach us our duty." "The usual amount of abolition rant and fustian and bare-faced falsehood!" snorted the Democrats. Only the Republicans—and they were few in number—were pleased.

But 1856, the year of a presidential campaign, promised to be different. Since the passage of the Nebraska Bill opponents of that measure had been working independently, and often as not, at cross purposes. Anti-Nebraska men of Democratic antecedents distrusted those who had formerly been Whigs only less than they distrusted the faithful Democrats; Old Whigs disliked the turn events had taken but saw no reason for abandoning their own party organization on that account; and all elements shunned the Republicans because of their radicalism. But for several months these groups had gradually been moving toward common ground, and it was apparent that the forthcoming campaign would be fought with some kind of a unified organization.

A big step in the direction of such an organization was taken on Washington's Birthday, 1856, when a number of Anti-Nebraska editors, with Abraham Lincoln as a special adviser, met at Decatur, adopted a set of resolutions, and made plans for a state convention to be held at Bloomington in the spring. On May 10 the *Illinois State Journal* published a call for a county convention to meet in Springfield and select delegates to the state meeting. Signed by Lincoln, Herndon and 130 others, the call was addressed to all who were opposed to the repeal of the Missouri Compromise and in favor of "restoring the administration of the General Government to the policy of Washington and Jefferson." Two weeks later a sizable gathering assembled at the court house and selected Lincoln, Herndon, Logan and George R. Weber as delegates. Resolutions denouncing the repeal of the Missouri Compromise and endorsing a reasonable fugitive slave law were adopted, but the most significant declaration was one which stated "that in the attempt to prevent the consummation of the wrong of the repeal of the Missouri Compromise, and to restore the authors of that repeal to the peaceful walks of private life, we will unite with all who are willing to unite with us—but we distinctly state that we will go no further in any agitation of the question of slavery."

On May 29 the convention assembled at Bloomington. Something of the atmosphere which pervaded the meeting may be gathered from the editorial which appeared in the *Illinois State Journal* on the same day. "They [the delegates]," said the editor, "are there to take steps for the protection of those liberties which have been, and are now threatened by the party in power. Aggression has followed aggression, until a period has arrived when, in order to preserve their own rights, the freemen of the North must rise in their majesty and say to the monster: 'Thus far shalt thou go, and no farther.'"

In framing a platform and laying plans for the ensuing campaign, however, the moderates prevailed, but after the business of the convention was finished, Lincoln stirred the delegates with the most impassioned speech of his career. Reporters, carried away by his fervor, forgot to take notes, but words alone could never have recorded the passion which caused the audience to explode in cheers, and fired those in attendance with an enthusiasm which carried them through the entire campaign.

Ten days later a meeting to ratify the action of the Bloomington convention was held in Springfield. The court house was crowded.[2] Calmly, slowly, Lincoln related what had happened at Bloomington and asked for the approval of the meeting. After he had finished, John M. Palmer of Carlinville took the stand and added his own appeal. The audience responded with three cheers for the ticket and three for Lincoln and Palmer, and then dispersed.

Meanwhile, on June 6, the news of the nomination of

[2] Of this meeting William H. Herndon wrote as follows: "The Bloomington convention and the part Lincoln took in it met no such hearty response in Springfield as we hoped would follow. It fell flat, and in Lincoln's case drove from him many persons who had heretofore been his warm political friends. A few days after our return we announced a meeting at the court-house to ratify the action of the Bloomington convention. After the usual efforts to draw a crowd, however, only three persons had temerity enough to attend. They were Lincoln, the writer, and a courageous man named John Pain. Lincoln, in answer to the 'deafening calls' for a speech, responded that the meeting was larger than he *knew* it would be, and that while he knew that he himself and his partner would attend he was not sure anyone else would, and yet another man had been found brave enough to come out. 'While all seems dead,' he exhorted, 'the age itself is not. It liveth as sure as our Maker liveth. Under all this seeming want of life and motion, the world does move nevertheless. Be hopeful, and now let us adjourn and appeal to the people." (Herndon, *Life of Lincoln,* II, 385-86.) But in view of the contemporary account in the *Journal,* and in the light of the *Register's* admission that two hundred had been in attendance, Herndon's account cannot be accepted. For a somewhat fuller discussion of these contradictory accounts, see *Herndon's Life of Lincoln* (Paul M. Angle, Ed.), 315n.

James Buchanan as the Democratic candidate for President
had reached Springfield. As soon as the word was received
a national salute was fired, and that evening the Democratic
Association met and ratified the nomination by acclamation.
But to many a Springfielder the news came like a breath of
chilly fog. For months the *Register* had carried at its masthead the slogan, "For President, Stephen A. Douglas," and
the rank and file of the party looked upon the dynamic
Senator as their very own. Moreover, Douglas had seemed
to be the outstanding contender for the honor, which could
not have been said of him four years earlier. Now he was
passed by again, and for an elderly time-server who was
his complete antithesis. Genuine enthusiasm could hardly
have been expected. "In this community," sneered the
Journal, ". . . the nomination of Buchanan has fallen like
a wet blanket."

However, the Democrats took comfort in the belief that
Douglas would be the certain victor in 1860, and set out
to organize for the task at hand. Following time-honored
forms, a rally was scheduled for June 26. Throughout the
morning of that day delegations from nearby towns and
villages crowded Springfield's streets. At noon a procession
formed and marched northward to Edwards' Grove.[3] There
several rounds from Hopkins' Artillery and music from the
German band signalized the opening of the meeting. On a
stand hung with flags and decorated with mottoes like,
"The Union as it was—The Union as it is—The Union Forever," were gathered the party notables—Ex-Governor
French, Governor Matteson, Lt. Governor Moore, A. G.
Herndon and others. First on the program came John Hogan
of St. Louis, an Old Whig. John A. McClernand followed,
and C. H. Constable, another Old Whig, concluded. (The
Whig party was breaking to pieces, and the wooing of the

[3] The present Edwards Place, now occupied by the Springfield Art Association.

more conservative among their former opponents was a prominent phase of Democratic strategy.) That evening there was speaking at the State House, and more Old Whigs who had joined the Democratic ranks were put forward.

Tactics of this sort were made more fruitful when the first Republican National Convention nominated John C. Fremont on June 19. (Springfield was chary of the word, "Republican." For two years the opponents of the administration called themselves "Anti-Nebraska" men, and even in this campaign they shunned the national party label and preferred to be known as "the supporters of Fremont and Dayton.") Though personally popular, the character and antecedents of the candidate were not likely to reassure those who feared that the new party would take an extreme position. Radicals like William H. Herndon were undismayed, but the majority were better pleased by the honor accorded to Abraham Lincoln, when 110 votes were cast for his nomination for the vice-presidency, than they were over the principal nomination.

Nevertheless, the Fremont men, like the Democrats, resolved to do their utmost, for state and local offices were tangible prizes no less real because one had only a lukewarm admiration for the head of the ticket. Both parties organized clubs which held frequent meetings throughout the campaign, supplied speakers for meetings in villages and country schoolhouses, and sent delegations to gatherings in nearby towns.

But the favorite device of the campaign was the rally, which drew the faithful from many miles around for a field day of political oratory. Sometimes several were staged during a campaign, but usually there was one which the party workers labored to make larger and more impressive than anything of the kind which the town had ever witnessed. Such was the Democratic demonstration which took place on September 18, 1856.

As early as the evening of the 17th there were crowds of strangers in Springfield. Among the visitors was a band from St. Louis which serenaded the Governor and other prominent Democrats, and then, not yet tired, struck up tune after tune in front of I. B. Curran's jewelry store. In a short time a crowd had gathered, cheers for Buchanan, Douglas, Richardson and other favorites rang out, and speechmaking started, to continue far into the night.

Early the next morning Springfield bloomed with flags and banners. Lines were strung from the State House dome to the buildings on the four corners of the square and hung with Buchanan and Breckenridge banners and party slogans. Stores and residences were festooned with bunting. By railroad, by carriage and wagon, on horseback and on foot people poured into the town. The day became a holiday, and business, except at the bars and restaurants, was suspended.

Late in the morning the inevitable procession formed and proceeded to the grove of P. P. Enos and A. Kessler northwest of the city. There, after one other speaker, Stephen A. Douglas took the stand. "Time and again we have heard him, but never before was he greater . . . ," Lanphier wrote in the *Register*. "He reviewed the entire political field, and showed up, in glowing light, the shape of the contest now pervading the country. . . . Shout upon shout followed the homethrusts and happy hits he made at the abolition enemy. He showed up their designs. He dissected the machinery of their organization. He tore off their hypocritical mask, and exposed to his hearers the corruption of the tricksters who trade in negro sympathy and Kansas roorbacks. His discourse was overwhelming, and carried conviction to the mind of every hearer of the justice of the democratic cause, and the utter corruption and demagogism of those who advocate the cause of Fremont."

After Douglas, W. A. Richardson of Quincy, the Democratic candidate for Governor, and Thomas L. Harris spoke briefly. When they had concluded, representatives of the German and Irish voters held forth until six o'clock. Even then the crowd was not satiated, for that night there were still more speeches, punctuated by salvos from Hopkins' Artillery and music from the St. Louis band and the German band of Springfield.

Seven days later the Fremont men tried mightily to outdo their opponents. Again the town was crowded with strangers —seven carloads from Chicago, and five each from Decatur, Alton and Jacksonville, besides many smaller delegations. Again flags and streamers waved above the streets. Once more a procession formed, heading this time for a grove west of the city. Behind a band from Chicago came a "beautifully ornamented car" in which were seated thirty-one white-garbed girls representing the states of the Union. Banners expressed the temper and tenets of the party—"Our glorious Union: it must and shall be preserved"; "Down with the compromise breakers"; "Fremont, the people's candidate"; and "Bissell, the hero of Buena Vista."

There was no Republican Douglas, but Lyman Trumbull, Owen Lovejoy, B. S. Edwards, Brown of Jacksonville and Bross of Chicago held the crowd until late afternoon. That night Representatives' Hall was jammed to capacity while Abraham Lincoln delivered "a most masterly speech," and John Wentworth and Edwards, who was doing double duty, added their eloquence to the cause. Throughout the day German speakers had appealed to their countrymen in their own language.

By demonstrations such as these, Democrats and Fremont men all but monopolized public attention, but actually the election was to turn on a smaller, less demonstrative group —the Know Nothing and Old Whig remnants which had rallied to Millard Fillmore as a third party candidate. In Springfield this group had taken shape at a meeting held late in July. At that time a Fillmore Club was organized, one or two rallies were held, and Shelby M. Cullom, then at the beginning of his political career, raised enough money to start a campaign newspaper, the *Conservative*.

Astute politicians in both of the larger parties realized that in Illinois at least, this was the group which held the balance of power. Impelled by the necessity of winning a large part of those whose natural tendency was to follow the Fillmore banner, Abraham Lincoln resorted to an ingenious device. Having drafted a persuasive argument to the effect that a vote for Fillmore was really a vote for Buchanan, he wrote it in the form of a personal letter, carefully making an interlineation or two so that its appearance would be perfectly natural, and then had it lithographed. After he had filled in the date and the name of the addressee, and had written the word "Confidential" in a conspicuous place, only the keenest eye could have detected its true character. Dozens of these letters went out to Old Whigs of Lincoln's acquaintance. All went well until near the end of the campaign. Then, at a rally in the country, one old farmer called several of his friends together to talk over something which troubled him deeply. After swearing them to secrecy—for the matter was "confidential"—he pulled one of Lincoln's letters from his pocket and handed it to one of his friends. The second man read a sentence or two, laughed, and handed it to a third, who was soon laughing also. Each pulled an identical letter from his pocket. The story soon reached Springfield, and Lincoln became the object of both ridicule and denunciation.

Other Fremont men attempted in their public speeches to make the same point at which Lincoln had aimed. For arguments of this sort the Democrats were as keenly alert as the Fillmore men themselves, for they knew very well that their opponents were a majority, and that their only hope of success lay in maintaining the division between them. Typical of the Democratic attitude was the *Register's* comment on one of the speeches of Benjamin S. Edwards. "On Wednesday night," said the editor, "Mr. B. S. Edwards shrieked for several hours, to prove that he was a better whig than those of that party who support Fillmore. He satisfied himself, doubtless, and the corporal's guard of Fremonters about town, who have hitherto wailed with Garrison and Wendell Phillips; but on Thursday evening the Fillmore club was addressed by Hon. John T. Stuart, Matheny and others who, in reply, placed Ben. as a Whig, in anything but an enviable attitude. His sudden conversion to 'Lovejoy or the devil,' in preference to a maintenance of the constitution, and the rights of the states, was severely commented on, and he and his new associates shown up in a light repulsive to any national man, whig or democrat."

By this time Stuart's position had become too much of an irritant to the Fremont men to be endured in silence. In the organization of the Fillmore group he had played a prominent part, declaring that although he deprecated Know Nothingism only less than Republicanism, Fillmore's personal integrity and public character were such that he would support him for the Presidency. Because of his prominence in the old Whig party and his high standing as a citizen, his example was a weighty one. For weeks his old associates ignored his defection, but when he took Edwards to task, the *Journal* scuttled caution and gave him a piece of its mind.

"Our old friend Major Stuart," the editor wrote, "is a very clever, honest sort of an old gentleman—who likes his ease, and who, no doubt, thinks his 'strength is to lie still.' In the last great contest of 1852, when Whigs in this State were alive, he *slept*. No effort could arouse him. Since 1844, when he retired, having been the recipient from the *Whigs* of all the honors he desired, he has literally in every Whig contest been almost, if not altogether an idle spectator. His heart, his real political feeling is with the principles as laid down in the Republican platform. The only trouble with

him is, he is mad because his laziness has been disturbed. . . .
His conscience is with us, but if he yielded to its dictates, he
would have to *work*—and he is *mad*. He tries in vain to
satisfy that conscience, by ebullition against the very doctrines his heart advocates."

Election day—marked by one shooting, one stabbing and
a number of street fights—gave statistical proof of the importance of the Fillmore vote. In Springfield 912 votes were
cast for Buchanan, as against 549 for Fremont and 403 for
Fillmore, but in the county as a whole, Fremont dropped
to third place.[4] Over the state, however, Fremont received
only 8,000 votes fewer than Buchanan. If only a fourth of the
37,451 votes given to Fillmore could have been won for him,
he would have been victorious in Illinois. To the Democrats,
however, the presidential victory was small compensation for
the other losses they had suffered. Although Richardson carried both Springfield and Sangamon County,[5] Bissell swept
the state and carried the other Republican candidates for
state offices with him. Even in Sangamon County, which gave
large pluralities to the Democratic candidates for both President and Governor, Republicans were elected to all except
one of the county offices.

The Republicans were jubilant, for with a party organization perfected only a few months earlier, they had routed
their opponents in all except the presidential contest. The inauguration of Bissell, on January 12, 1857, gave them an
opportunity to manifest their joy. At two o'clock in the
afternoon the guns of the Springfield Artillery thundered
a national salute. Then the general assembly, the judges of
the supreme court, the city officials and a large number of
citizens marched to the Mansion, where the new Governor

[4] The vote was as follows: Buchanan, 2,475; Fillmore, 1,612; Fremont, 1,174.

[5] Springfield gave Richardson 933 votes, Bissell 865, and Morris (Fillmore
candidate) 58. In Sangamon County the figures were: Richardson, 2,519;
Bissell, 2,232; Morris, 390.

and the other state officers held a formal reception and were sworn into office. The procession then returned to the State House, where Bissell read his inaugural address. That evening the Republicans assembled in the Hall of the House of Representatives to listen to their leaders congratulate the party on its achievements. "The speeches were all characterized by great good feeling," the *Journal* reported, "and the enthusiasm of the audience often vented itself in rounds of applause. The interest continued unabated until a late hour, and many expressed themselves 'that it was good to be there.'"

Normally, interest in politics would have abated until the next presidential contest, but the shadow of slavery was deepening too rapidly to make peace possible even for four short years. In March the Supreme Court of the United States announced its decision in the case of Dred Scott. Stated in its simplest terms, the question at issue involved the ability of a negro, once a slave, to become a citizen of the United States and bring suit in its courts. Chief Justice Taney, voicing the opinion of the majority of the court, declared that Dred Scott was not and could not, under the constitution, become a citizen. Unwisely, the court went beyond the immediate issue, and declared further that Congress could not exclude slavery from the national domain, and therefore the Missouri Compromise was illegal.

The immediate effect of this decision was to bring the slavery question once more before the country. Only the South was satisfied. In the North, the decision robbed the Anti-Nebraska forces of their one tangible remedy for the Nebraska Bill—the restoration of the Missouri Compromise. The Democrats were hardly less happy, for if slavery could not be excluded from the national domain, how could a territorial legislature choose between freedom and bondage? In view of the Dred Scott decision, what became of popular sovereignty?

A few weeks after Congress adjourned, Douglas was in Springfield. Promptly the grand jury of the United States court invited him to speak on the political issues of the day. He accepted, and set June 12th as the date.

The Democratic dilemma was still unsolved, so interest in what he would say was even greater than usual. Long before dark the Hall of the House of Representatives was jammed. In prominent places were Abraham Lincoln, William H. Herndon, Shelby M. Cullom (who by this time had come into the Republican organization) and other well-known opponents. At eight o'clock Douglas mounted the rostrum. Speaking slowly but with all his usual force, he laid down the platform of the Northern Democrats—the right of the master to his slave, affirmed in the Dred Scott decision, was "a barren and worthless right, unless sustained, protected and enforced by appropriate police regulations and local legislation, prescribing adequate remedies for its violation. These regulations and remedies must necessarily depend entirely upon the will and wishes of the people of the territory as they can only be prescribed by the local legislatures." By deciding that the Missouri Compromise was unconstitutional, the court had actually vindicated the principle of popular sovereignty. When the speaker concluded at ten o'clock, the audience burst into prolonged cheers. The Democrats had been given an escape from their corner, and their opponents were downcast.

For nearly two weeks Republican leaders tried to get the grand jury to invite Lincoln to speak on the other side of the question, but to no avail. Finally he decided to reply to Douglas, invitation or no invitation, and announced his speech for the evening of June 26. "We think the Dred Scott decision is erroneous," he declared. "We know the court that made it has often overruled its own decisions, and we shall do what we can to have it overrule this." When important decisions were made unanimously, he went on to say, and in accord with established precedent and unquestioned historical fact; or, lacking some of these elements, when they were affirmed and reaffirmed over a course of years, not to acquiesce in them would be factious or even revolutionary. But when a decision lacks all these supports, he asserted, "it is not resistance, it is not factious, it is not even disrespectful, to treat it as not having yet quite established a settled doctrine for the country." But although the fair-sized crowd applauded the speaker, there was some truth in the *Register's* observation that "he fell immeasurably short of even making an impression on any position taken by Judge Douglas."

A month later slavery was lifted from the realm of political argument and placed squarely on Springfield's doorstep as a living, human problem. Late in July, a few miles south of the city, the United States Marshal arrested a negro who was alleged to be a fugitive slave from Missouri. As it was Springfield's first case of the kind since the passage of the fugitive slave law of 1850, interest was widespread. When the U. S. Commissioner, S. A. Corneau, heard the case a few days later, the courtroom was crowded; but there were no threats of violence, and the general attitude was that if a fair trial should show the fugitive to be a slave, he should be returned to his owner. After W. H. Herndon and John E. Rosette had argued the case for the defendant, and E. B. Herndon and John A. McClernand had appeared for the claimant, the commissioner took it under advisement. A few days later he decided that the negro should be returned to Missouri. The crowd which had gathered to hear the decision quietly dispersed.

For the balance of the year the panic crowded both politics and slavery to secondary places in the public mind. But early in 1858 politics were in the foreground again. By that time the stern problem of making a living had eased somewhat, while there had been startling developments in the national scene. On the question of the admission of Kansas

Douglas had broken irrevocably with President Buchanan, and it was apparent that the full strength of the administration would be thrown against his re-election to the Senate, which would be in the hands of the next legislature. It was also apparent that the Republican candidate would be Abraham Lincoln—the most dangerous opponent he could have. But defeat for Douglas would be an inglorious end to a political career whose full promise had not yet been realized. The campaign for seats in the general assembly, it was quite obvious, would be worth watching.

The campaign started in April, when both branches of the Democratic party—the Douglas men and the followers of Buchanan—met in Springfield on the 21st. The Douglas men assembled in the Hall of the House of Representatives and proceeded to nominate W. B. Fondey for state treasurer and A. C. French for superintendent of public instruction, the only two state offices to be filled. Across the hall in the Senate chamber the Danites,[6] as they soon came to be called, spent the day in "schemes of party disorganization, and in giving vent to sorehead feeling"—or so the Douglas organ reported—and postponed their nominations until a second convention to be held later. "The Democracy parted in not a very encouraged frame of mind," Lincoln informed Elihu B. Washburne. Far different was the temper of the group of Republican leaders who gathered informally in the evening. Among them all was harmony and hope, and each felt that if the party failed to triumph, they had only themselves to blame.

Six weeks later—on June 9—the Buchanan men met again at the State House and nominated candidates for the state offices. Two hundred delegates were in attendance, but a third of them came from Cook County, while more than half of the state was not represented at all. Obviously the Bu-

[6] The term went back to the Mormon troubles, and the band of followers sworn to do the bidding of Joseph Smith regardless of law or morality.

chanan men had little popular backing, but they controlled the patronage of the national administration, and that was sufficient to make them a dangerous factor.

Seven days later the State House was the scene of the Republican State Convention. From all parts of Illinois the delegates assembled, more than a thousand in number. Cheered by their victory of two years earlier, they were confident of success. Speedily they adopted a platform, selected a state central committee, nominated James Miller for state treasurer and Newton Bateman for superintendent of public instruction, and passed unanimously a resolution declaring "that Abraham Lincoln is the first and only choice of the Republicans of Illinois for the United States Senate, as the successor of Stephen A. Douglas." Then they adjourned until eight o'clock.

That night, after Gustave Koerner had called the packed audience to order, Lincoln mounted the speaker's stand. Slowly, impressively, he opened his speech with fateful words:

"Mr. President and Gentlemen of the Convention: If we could first know where we are, and whither we are tending, we could better judge what to do, and how to do it. We are now far into the fifth year since a policy was initiated with the avowed object and confident promise of putting an end to slavery agitation. Under the operation of that policy, the agitation has not only not ceased, but has constantly augmented. In my opinion, it will not cease until a crisis shall have been reached and passed. 'A house divided against itself cannot stand.' I believe this government cannot endure permanently half slave and half free. I do not expect the Union to be dissolved—I do not expect the house to fall— but I do expect it will cease to be divided. It will become all one thing, or all the other. Either the opponents of slavery will arrest the further spread of it, and place it where the public mind shall rest in the belief that it is in the course of ultimate extinction; or its advocates will push it forward till it shall become alike lawful in all the States, old as well as new, North as well as South."

With this as an introduction, Lincoln delivered a short, compact argument to show that the national trend was towards the expansion of slavery, and closed with a plea for Republican solidarity. The delegates cheered, but many of them had misgivings. Lincoln's had been a "radical" utterance—some of them called it "a damned fool speech." But they listened to the other speakers who followed, cheered them also, and scattered to their homes with confidence high.

Soon after the conventions, active campaigning commenced. On July 9, in Chicago, Douglas made his first speech.[7] A week later, on the 16th, he set out for Springfield. At Bloomington, where he spoke that night, a large delegation from Springfield greeted him. On the next day the ovations along the route were so continuous that six hours elapsed before the sixty-odd miles were covered. Finally, at three in the afternoon, the booming of minute guns announced the Senator's arrival. As the train stopped at the Edwards' Grove, a cannon mounted on a platform car answered the salute, and the thousands who had gathered in the driving rain did their best to drown out the sound of both guns.

Escorted to the stand by the Capital Guards and the Capital Band, Douglas was greeted by Benjamin S. Edwards, now in the Democratic fold. Though a recent convert, Edwards expressed perfectly the peculiar fervency of the Sangamon Democracy's regard for the Little Giant. "In other places," he said, "political attachment dictates the public manifestation. Here personal friendship claims the prominent position. We cannot forget, nor do we desire to

[7]Lincoln was in the audience, and spoke on the following night at the same place.

forget, that here was once your home; that here among us were spent the days of your early manhood, and before position and fame had deservedly made you the Douglas of the United States you were the Douglas of 'Old Sangamon.' In short, sir, while assembled multitudes may receive you to cities, here and here only can your friends give you a *'welcome home.'* "

"My heart is filled with emotions," Douglas replied, "at the allusions which have been so happily and so kindly made in the welcome just extended to me—a welcome so numerous and so enthusiastic, bringing me to my home among my old friends, that language cannot express my gratitude. I do feel at home whenever I return to old Sangamon and receive those kind and friendly greetings which have never failed to meet me when I have come among you; but never before have I had such occasion to be grateful and to be proud of the manner of the reception as on the present." And then he went on to deliver a characteristically forceful defense of his own course and a sharp attack on his Republican opponents. Five thousand followers heard him to the end regardless of the rain, cheered him to the echo, and then escorted him to the St. Nicholas Hotel.

That night, while the jubilant Democrats touched off fireworks in honor of their chief, Lincoln spoke at the State House. A goodly crowd gathered to hear him repel the charges of disunion sentiment, resistance to the Dred Scott decision, and negro equality which Douglas had made. It was an able address—in a letter he called it the best he had so far made—but while it heartened his friends, it caused no consternation among Democrats flushed by the presence of their invincible leader.

A few days later Lincoln challenged his opponent to a series of joint debates and Douglas accepted. While the contestants were planning their itineraries, local leaders started to perfect their organizations. Summoned by William H.

Herndon, the younger Republicans formed the Young Men's Republican Club, elected C. C. Brown president, and prepared to supply speakers for meetings in the county and hold frequent gatherings of their own. Soon afterwards their opponents organized the Democratic Club, with John A. McClernand at its head. After mid-August not a week passed without a meeting of one or both of these organizations.

By this time both candidates were actively stumping the state. Springfield watched their progress with never-lagging interest. The local papers reported each of the joint debates in full, printed many accounts of the other addresses of the candidates, and in the interim filled their columns with partisan matter of diverse kinds. As time went on the editors lost restraint and indulged in personalities to the limit. Typical of many a newspaper report was the *Register's* account of a Buchanan meeting in which W. H. Herndon, for reasons obvious to all parties, played a prominent part.

"Billy Herndon, Lincoln's man Friday," said the editor, "appeared in a new character at the Court House on Tuesday night, as moderator of Danite performances. During the evening a drunken man was somewhat noisy, after Billy's own style of a few years ago, when a democrat present endeavored to quiet him, and was about taking him off, when Herndon seized the drunken man and brutally hauled him downstairs, yelling, 'God damn the Irish, I want it distinctly understood that *we* (the Danites and Republicans) are willing to have war with them.' The man hauled out by Herndon is an American, but his remark only tends to show up the new move of woolydom to catch American votes. Republicanism cannot secure the votes of Irishmen, and wants it now 'distinctly understood' that they are for war with them."

In its attacks on Benjamin S. Edwards the *Journal* was equally abusive. Although no Republican had been more active than he in 1856, Edwards went over to the Democratic party the following year—motivated, he said, by the increasing radicalism of his former associates. In his new alignment he was outspoken against his former friends. At frequent intervals throughout 1858 the *Journal* raked him with its hottest fire. Morover—and this did not often happen, even in days when politics were a serious business—many of his personal friends ignored him, and ill-feelings developed which took many years in the healing.

In at least one instance newspaper intemperance resulted in physical violence. Early in September E. L. Baker, the editor of the *Journal,* charged John A. McClernand with the authorship of a *Register* article which he had found offensive. Shortly afterward McClernand met Baker on the street, denied that he had written the article in question, and demanded that he publish a correction of his statement. Baker answered that he had nothing to retract, whereupon McClernand belabored him with his cane until bystanders stopped the fracas.

Before the campaign was over, another honored name was the subject of political recrimination. A month before the election the St. Louis *Republican* announced that John T. Stuart, whom it described as the one-time opponent of Douglas and the long-time friend of Lincoln, would support the Democratic candidate. The *Journal* denied the report at once, but a few days later the *Register* announced that Stuart had authorized it to state that he agreed with Douglas on the slavery question and that he was wholly opposed to the Republican party, but that because of his personal relations with Lincoln he was taking no part in the senatorial contest and would not vote for members of the legislature.

Besides the meetings of the political clubs, there were larger rallies at frequent intervals. When Douglas stayed in Springfield over a week-end in early September a large crowd greeted him at the railroad station, escorted him to his hotel, held a formal ceremony of welcome, and saw him

off when he left for Jacksonville on the following Monday.
When he spoke in the capital on October 20th, the town was
decorated with flags and mottoes, bands played, cannon
boomed, and 5,000 braved roads and streets made almost impassable by rainy weather to hear him speak. When Lincoln
spent the week-end of September 25th at home, Springfield
Republicans procured a band and serenaded him. Only the
Buchanan men failed to draw crowds. A meeting at the court
house in early October drew only a small audience, and the
Register charged that this was made up in the main of Republicans. "Seven, all told, were Reynolds'[8] gang," the paper
sneered "—four of them holding office and the other three
waiting for tits. Never was an honest cow tugged by such
lousy calves."

But with all the meetings, large and small, the frenzied
partisans were not satisfied. Let a big rally be scheduled at
any city within a reasonable distance, and special trains
would be made up to carry fervid supporters within the sound
of the speakers' voices. Thus in early September two hundred
Democrats, accompanied by Merritt's Cornet Band, went
to Jacksonville to hear Douglas. Later in the same month the
Republicans filled a special train of eleven cars for a Lincoln
rally in the same city. After a whole afternoon of oratory
they were able to return to Springfield, assemble on the court
house yard, and listen to speeches by Milton Hay, James C.
Conkling and Richard Yates!

At last the campaign neared its close. The Douglas meeting of October 20th was the last big effort of the Democrats,
and the final Republican rally took place on the 30th. Its
pattern was familiar—delegations from nearby cities, flut-
tering flags and banners, parades and fireworks. During the
afternoon Lincoln spoke from a stand on the east side of the
square, concluding with an eloquent and touching reference

---

[8] John Reynolds was the Buchanan candidate for Superintendent of Public
Instruction.

to his own part in the contest. "In some respects the contest has been painful to me," he said. "Myself, and those with whom I act have been constantly accused of a purpose to destroy the Union; and bespattered with every imaginable odius epithet; and some who were friends as it were but yesterday have made themselves most active in this. I have cultivated patience, and made no attempt at a retort.

"Ambition has been ascribed to me. God knows how sincerely I prayed from the first that this field of ambition might not be opened. I claim no insensibility to political honors; but today could the Missouri restriction be restored, and the whole slavery question be replaced on the old ground of 'toleration' by *necessity* where it exists, with unyielding hostility to the spread of it, on principle, I would, in consideration, gladly agree, that Judge Douglas should never be *out,* and I never *in,* an office, so long as we both or either, live."

After Lincoln came Richard Yates, who spoke until six o'clock, and that evening a succession of speakers held forth in the rotunda of the State House. Late that night, when finally the town was quiet, the campaign came to an end.

On November 2 rain fell throughout the day and the streets were in a terrible condition, but the largest vote ever polled in the city was turned out in spite of the weather. The next day it was apparent that Douglas had won his re-election. Over the state as a whole the Republican candidates had received a majority of the popular vote, but the apportionment favored their opponents, and Douglas's re-election was a certainty. In Springfield and Sangamon County the vote was close, but the Douglas candidates had clear majorities over their Republican and Danite opponents.[9]

[9] Springfield's vote for representatives was as follows: Barrett, 1207, Short, 1227 (Douglas Democrats); Cook, 1128, Brown, 1111 (Republicans); Watts, 25, Wright, 26 (Buchanan Democrats). For the same candidates the totals in Sangamon County were: Barrett, 3050, Short, 3052; Cook, 2745, Brown, 2730; Watts, 113, Wright, 125.

Two months later the general assembly of Illinois met in joint session. Before crowded galleries James W. Barrett of Sangamon nominated Stephen A. Douglas for the United States Senate; Norman B. Judd of Cook nominated Abraham Lincoln. A few minutes later the vote was announced: Douglas, 54; Lincoln, 46. "Glory to God and the Sucker Democracy," Lanphier wired to his chief in Washington. A short time afterward he sent a second telegram: "Announcement followed by shouts of immense crowd present. Town wild with excitement. Democrats firing salute. Guns, music, and whiskey rampant." Back from Washington came the message: "Let the voice of the people rule."

CHAPTER XI

The Republicans Elect a President

IN the office of the *Illinois State Journal* sat a small group of men. Their conversation came in scraps, their faces were drawn, and an unmistakable tension pervaded the room. Suddenly a boy banged through the door and handed a scrap of paper to one of them. For what seemed hours to the observers the recipient stared at the writing, his face expressionless. Then he lifted his long, gaunt figure from the chair and quietly remarked that there was "a little woman down at our house" who would be interested. On the slip was written: "Mr. Lincoln, you are nominated on the third ballot."

As Abraham Lincoln made his way to the square frame house at the corner of Eighth and Jackson streets, bedlam broke loose. By the time he reached his destination the first guns of an hundred-gun salute were rattling the windows. Around the square men were shouting for joy, shaking each others' hands, slapping backs. Flags soon fluttered from the State House, the Republican headquarters, the *Journal* office. Before long all the bells in town were clanging, while in the Lincoln parlors, as friend after friend called to offer congratulations, the pistol shots and cheers of the more exuberant could be plainly heard.

That evening, by common understanding, a crowd gathered at the State House. One or two speeches were made, but for once the excitement was too intense for political oratory. The meeting adjourned, the audience lined up behind the Young America band, and, growing like a rolling snowball, started for the Lincoln residence. There, in response to a shout for "Mr. Lincoln," the tall form of the candidate was soon silhouetted in the doorway. At his appearance cheer after cheer broke from the crowd. When the noise had subsided, Lincoln spoke a few words to the effect that he took the demonstration as a tribute to a cause rather than as a personal compliment, and concluded by inviting in as many as his house would hold. Above the noise a voice rang out: "We'll give you a larger house on the fourth of next March!" Laughing and cheering, the crowd pushed through the door, and as many as could clasped the large, rough hand of the man whom they hoped to make the next President.

That night, after the last of his noisy guests had departed, Lincoln must have marvelled at his fortune. With a few close friends he had hoped for this result, but he was too much of a realist in politics to have expected it. In truth, not only Lincoln, but almost every political forecaster in the land as well, was taken by surprise.

And yet, in retrospect, it is hard to imagine a different outcome. By his debates with Douglas, Lincoln had acquired a national reputation. In the following year, through speeches in Iowa, Ohio, Indiana, Wisconsin and Kansas, his name had been kept before the public, and thousands had had a chance to measure him for themselves. Early in 1860, in his Cooper Union address, he had made a mark on the East which he had quickly impressed the more deeply by a speaking tour through New England. At the same time, because he had held no office and because his fame was young, he had stirred up none of the animosities which men long in public life arouse. The tenor of his speeches had been consistently conservative, which was reassuring to the timid; but radicals were cheered by the remembrance of his "house divided" statement. His humble birth and early struggles with adversity could be counted on to arouse no less enthusiasm than Harrison's log cabin and cider gourd. And he came from the doubtful state of Illinois which, with Indiana, Pennsylvania and New Jersey, had to be carried if the party were to be victorious.

On the other hand, each of his prominent competitors was under some serious disadvantage. Seward, the idol of the rank and file, was too "radical," and would surely go down to defeat in the doubtful states. Chase, even more radical, could not even get the undivided support of his own state. Bates of Missouri suited the conservatives, but he had been a Know Nothing, and the Germans would revolt if he were chosen. John McLean, a justice of the Supreme Court, could carry the doubtful states, but he was a colorless old man, and about as capable of arousing enthusiasm as a marble statue.

Even so, the result of the convention might have been different if it had not been held in Chicago, vibrant with Lincoln sentiment; and if Lincoln's interests had not been entrusted to as shrewd a group of manipulators as existed anywhere in the United States. Norman B. Judd, David Davis, Leonard Swett, O. H. Browning, Stephen T. Logan, Ward H. Lamon—these were the men who, with skill seldom equalled, struck just the right balance of forces to make inevitable the selection of the Springfield lawyer.

On the evening of the day following the convention the official notification committee reached Springfield. A huge crowd greeted the special train at the station. Behind a band from Philadelphia, reputed to be the best in the country, and escorted by two hundred members of the visiting delegation with rails over their shoulders, the committee marched to the Chenery House. There the crowd veered off to the State House where, in the Hall of Representatives, the marchers stacked their rails like muskets, and settled down to listen to speaker after speaker hot from the convention.

Shortly after eight o'clock the committee reached the Lincoln home. Two boys seated on the steps hailed them as they passed through the gate.

"Are you Mr. Lincoln's son?" asked William M. Evarts of the elder.

"Yes, sir," said the boy.

"Then let's shake hands," Evarts proposed. Seeing the attention accorded his older brother, young Tad spoke up:

"I'm a Lincoln too!"

Whereupon, with much laughter, the delegates saluted him and knocked on the door.

Collecting in the north parlor, George Ashmun, the chairman of the Chicago convention, stepped forward and read the formal notification address. Lincoln responded with a few words of appreciation, and a promise to reply to the address in writing very soon. Ashmun then introduced the delegates. When Kelly of Pennsylvania was presented, Lincoln asked,

"What is your height?"

"Six feet three; what is yours, Mr. Lincoln?"

"Six feet four."

"Then," said Kelly, "Pennsylvania bows to Illinois. My dear man, for years my heart has been aching for a President that I could *look up to,* and I've found him at last in the land where we thought there were none but *little* giants!"

Various other men were presented, but Ashmun soon tired of introductions, and asked the visitors to present themselves. "Come up, gentlemen," Judd called out, "it's nobody but Old Abe Lincoln!" Soon the delegates were gathered in small groups, talking in undertones. Apparently they had expected a sort of human monstrosity, for one of them was heard to remark: "I was afraid I should meet a gigantic rail-splitter, with the manners of a flatboatman, and the ugliest face in creation; and he's a complete gentleman!"

The delegates were presented to Mrs. Lincoln in the south parlor, and then they started back to the hotel. As they walked along the sky was bright with rockets, cannon boomed at intervals, bonfires blazed on corners, and homes and stores were illuminated from basement to attic. In the State House orators were holding forth before an overflowing audience. The Republican celebration, begun the day before, was still in progress.

That same evening an anxious group of Democrats gathered in the court house to hear John A. McClernand, fresh from the national convention, speak on the condition and prospects of the party. It was not a happy meeting. For four years they had taken for granted the nomination of Douglas in 1860. He had been a factor in 1852; in 1856 he was the outstanding contender; in 1860, they felt, his selection was inevitable. But in the national convention, which assembled in Charleston, South Carolina, on April 23rd, discord soon ran rampant. Southerners insisted that the platform contain an affirmation of the federal government's duty to protect slave property in the territories by legislation, and when the Northerners refused the demand, delegations from several of the slave states withdrew. With the seceders gone, the convention attempted to nominate a candidate. For fifty-seven ballots Douglas received more votes than any other, but he was never able to muster the necessary two-thirds majority. Finally, on May 3rd, the convention adjourned, to reconvene at Baltimore six weeks later.

News of the adjournment fell on angry ears in Springfield. Said the *Register:* "Mr. Douglas may again be defeated in the nomination by the devices, machinations, and intrigues of a corrupt set of political traders, but he will enjoy the consciousness, from unmistakable evidences, that he was the choice of the masses of his party, and that their confidence in him is stronger and more abiding than falls to the lot of a statesman oftener than once in a generation." As the weeks passed, the conviction that Douglas must be nominated grew ever deeper. On the night of May 19th, after McClernand's address, the Springfield Democrats asserted, by resolution, "that in the repeated triumphs of *Stephen A. Douglas* over *Abraham Lincoln,* the nominee of the republican party for president, we have the assurance of a renewed and decisive democratic triumph in the event of the nomination of the former for the same office by the democratic convention at Baltimore." Relieved somewhat by this declaration, the participants in the meeting procured the Union Band, marched around the square, and then proceeded to serenade McClernand and Charles H. Lanphier at their residences.

On the appointed day the national convention reconvened, this time at Baltimore. For days the members wrangled over the seating of delegates, and tension reached the breaking point. Finally this convention, like its predecessor at Charleston, split in two. Relieved of the irreconcilables, the regular Democracy proceeded to nominate Douglas by acclamation.

At three-thirty on the afternoon of June 23rd the telegraph wire in the *Register* office brought the long-expected news. A shout that shook the building gave notice to the town that the Little Giant had won the prize he had been seeking for eight long years. A few minutes later Hopkins' Artillery was banging out a national salute. That night the German Band summoned the Democrats to the court house yard. Again the artillery thundered, and then Benjamin S. Edwards stepped forth to eulogize Douglas as "the representative man of the age—the bold, able, and honest statesman, the friend and upholder of the constitution, the vindicator of the laws of the land, and the defender of the rights of the people." After Edwards' speech, the crowd paraded through the streets. Throughout the evening bonfires blazed and rockets flared, while the homes of prominent Democrats were illuminated from top to bottom.

But for all the high spirits of the rank and file, the leaders of the party must have been sick at heart. The proud Democracy was hopelessly split, and they knew it. The seceders

from the Baltimore convention whose withdrawal had made
Douglas's nomination possible had chosen John C. Breckenridge of Kentucky as their own candidate. Moreover, in John
Bell of Tennessee the remnant of the Old Whig Party had
presented a fourth aspirant. To any clear-headed observer
it was apparent that in a four-cornered contest of this kind
the odds were all with the Republicans, and that only a
miracle could prevent the election of Lincoln.

In 1860, however, politicians were not accustomed to
yield passively to the inevitable. On the contrary, with one
candidate a resident and the other a former citizen, leaders
of both parties prepared to give Springfield a campaign the
like of which she had never seen.

Organization proceeded quickly. Political clubs sprang up
like mushrooms, and grew no less rapidly—German Republican and German Democratic clubs, the British Republican
Club, the Hickory Buds (for young zealots between the ages
of twelve and eighteen), and the Lincoln Young Americas
for boys of Republican proclivities. But most popular of all
were the Wide-Awakes. Beginning by accident in Hartford,
Connecticut, the idea of groups of young men in uniform,
parading in military formation by torchlight, took the North
by storm. In Springfield the Wide-Awakes, garbed in glazed
fatigue caps and rubber capes, made their first appearance
in early June. The *Register* commented acidly that they
looked "as terrible as a squad of smooth-faced juveniles in a
Sabbath-school procession," but within a month the Hickory
Club, also in uniform, turned out for its first torchlight
parade. Thereafter long rows of marching men, each with
a flaming torch over his shoulder, could be seen every few
nights on the downtown streets.

Marching clubs were only one distinctive feature of the
campaign. Another was the construction of elaborate headquarters. By early summer "Wigwams" in imitation of the
structure in which Lincoln had been nominated were spring-

ing up in hundreds of towns and cities. Early in July Springfield Republicans secured the vacant lot on the southeast corner of Sixth and Monroe streets[1] and started to build a circular frame building ninety feet in diameter. Inside, at the east end, was a speaker's stand, on each side of which were small galleries for the accommodation of glee clubs and bands. Around two-thirds of the circumference ran a wide gallery. On this, and the main floor, more than 3,000 people could be seated.

While the Wigwam was going up at one end of the business district, carpenters were working on the Democratic headquarters at the corner of Fifth and Jefferson streets. Lacking the famous prototype of the rival party, the building was nameless until the day of its dedication, when McClernand christened it "Douglas Hall." The name, however, turned out to be too staid for the turbulent summer of 1860, and was soon dropped for the less pretentious designation of "The Barn."

Both parties made a great pother over flags and flagpoles. For the Democratic headquarters James W. Barrett contributed a tall hickory shaft, and David McGinnis, an Old Whig who lived on Lick Creek, donated an ash pole to surmount it. From the ladies came a silk flag. The Republican devices were more elaborate. At the top of a pole 120 feet high a broom was lashed, to signify Lincoln's determination to sweep out the Augean stables in Washington. (In more prosaic words, to make jobs for the faithful.) A few feet below the broom was a weathervane shaped like an axe—symbolic of the candidate's early days as a laborer. Underneath that was a large silk flag.

The poles at the headquarters were the tallest in the town, but they were by no means the only ones. By mid-summer there were poles everywhere—on the public buildings, in

[1]Where the Postoffice and Federal Court Building is situated.

front of bars and stores, even on some of the residences. From all of them flew banners inscribed with mottoes or decorated with pictures of the candidates. Occasionally the temptation presented by their very existence grew too strong, and then it would be reported that "some miserable, infamous, low-flung, narrow-minded, ungodly, dirt-eating, cut-throat, hemp-deserving, deeply-dyed, double-distilled, concentrated miscreant of miscreants" had "sinned against all honor and decency" by cutting down two or three poles during the preceding night. (In this case Republican poles were the victims, but the language was no less forceful when Democratic timber was felled.)

Rails were another symbol. When John Hanks had stampeded the Republican state convention by appearing on the floor with two fence rails said to have been split by Lincoln thirty years earlier, the candidate instantly became the "Rail-Splitter." After the nomination the Republican county committee was deluged with requests for rails. The demand presented possibilities too obvious to be ignored, and various citizens of Springfield began importing fence rails in wholesale quantities and selling them, authenticated with imposing affidavits, to all comers. Others made souvenirs—canes, cigar-holders, pen holders and gavels—from "authentic" Lincoln rails. The sale of rails and rail products became a regular profession.

As soon as the Wigwam and Barn were finished, zealous partisans crowded into them for almost nightly meetings. For the most part the Democratic orators were old favorites, well known in Springfield—William A. Richardson of Quincy, John A. Logan of Murphysboro, Anthony Thornton of Shelbyville, Orlando B. Ficklin of Charleston and B. S. Edwards of Springfield. Usually they harped on the radical proclivities of Republicanism. Now and then a speaker took a shot at Lincoln's Mexican War record, whereupon the audience would chant:

Mr. Speaker! Spot! Spot! Spot!
Mr. Speaker! Where's the Spot?
Is it in Spain, or is it not?
Mr. Speaker! Spot! Spot! Spot!

Ordinarily, however, the orators readily granted Lincoln's high standing as a citizen, but hammered home the question: "What has he ever done to indicate ability to handle the duties of the Presidency?"

Even more often the "Lincoln cannon," especially cast in the foundry of A. S. Booth for use in the campaign, summoned the Republicans to the Wigwam. There they soon became accustomed not only to familiar figures like Cullom, Yates and Trumbull, but also to prominent outsiders drawn to the Illinois capital by the magnet of Lincoln's presence— Galusha Grow of Pennsylvania, Corwin, Piatt and Hassaurek of Ohio, Carl Schurz of Wisconsin, Caleb B. Smith of Indiana and Zachariah Chandler of Michigan. Occasionally, if the visitor was a man of especial prominence, Lincoln himself would attend the meeting and take a seat on the platform.

Republican speakers had plenty of ammunition, for Douglas's long record presented many vulnerable points. But in the mass hysteria which quickly developed, the appeal to reason counted for little. Always there were glee clubs and bands, and audiences took delight in roaring out jingles from the paper-backed songsters with which the country was soon flooded. What mattered the merits of platforms or candidates with three thousand voices shouting the refrain:

Ain't I glad I joined the Republicans,
Joined the Republicans, joined the Republicans,
Ain't I glad I joined the Republicans,
    Down in Illinois?

Even though meetings were held every few days, several grand rallies were thought to be necessary. Three weeks after

Lincoln's nomination the Republicans scheduled the first one of the campaign. With thousands of visitors joining in the parades and listening to speakers from several different states, it was a decided success. But in comparison with the gigantic rally of August 8th, it was nothing.

For weeks the Republicans of Springfield had worked night and day for a grand "ratification" meeting. Invitations were sent out all over the state, bands and Wide-Awake clubs were summoned, calls were sent for prominent speakers, and preparations were made for a huge crowd. It was hoped that the great rally of the Harrison campaign would be definitely eclipsed.

On the appointed day the sun rose in a dense fog, but a light breeze soon cleared the air. As day broke the guns barked out a national salute. Even then the roads leading into town were filled, and many people were on the streets. By nine o'clock the downtown section was jammed. But all morning special trains brought in their hordes—180 carloads in all—until the capital was a milling mass of humanity.

At ten the procession began to form. At its head, indicating the irresistible march of Republican principles, was an immense ball, inscribed on one side,

> The People mourn insulted laws,
> And curse Steve Douglas as the cause;

and on the other,

> Westward the Star of Empire takes its way;
> We link-on to Lincoln—our fathers were for Clay.

Then came the Springfield Wide Awakes, the Springfield German Wide Awakes, the Lincoln Young Americas, and nineteen other Wide Awake clubs from as many counties and towns, including Hannibal and St. Louis, Missouri. Nearby Illinois counties sent immense delegations—1,200 came from Christian and 1,000 from Scott. Almost every imaginable sort of float was in evidence. Menard County brought a flatboat on wheels, to represent Lincoln at New Salem; the Springfield Woolen Mills had a power loom mounted on a dray, on which workmen wove several yards of jeans and made them into pantaloons for the candidate during the march; Cotton Hill appeared with a log cabin on wheels, in front of which an old settler methodically split rails; while the Republicans of Williamsville drove twenty-three yoke of oxen ahead of an immense wagon on which blacksmiths, wheelrights and railsplitters were at work. And these were only part of an infinite variety.

The procession wound through the downtown streets of Springfield to the Lincoln home, where the cheers of the marchers made an incessant roar. Not until two o'clock did it reach the fair grounds west of the city. There five speakers' stands had been erected. After the meeting had organized by electing Governor John Moore as president, the orators set to work. In a short time word spread through the grounds that Lincoln had arrived. Immediately the crowd rushed his carriage, lifted him out and carried him to an improvised stand. There he thanked the excited partisans for the demonstration, and assured them that he accepted it as an evidence of their enthusiasm for Republican principles rather than as a personal tribute. Demanding a real stump speech, hundreds eager for campaign oratory surrounded his carriage, but he escaped them by mounting a saddle horse and leaving the grounds before they realized what had happened.

That evening, after a torch-light procession, the Wigwam was filled to suffocation while thousands stood in line in a futile effort to obtain admission. "Never, we will venture to say," the *Journal* trumpeted, "have the highways and by-ways of any town, large or small, been so completely surcharged with the electric current which flows from the consciousness of being embraced in the meaning of that prayer which says, 'May God speed the right.' Hearts beating to the sublime cadence of 'freedom for the oppressed,' backed by tongues and lungs that made the very heavens echo with the glad acclaims of victory, rendered the scene one sublime, magnificent spectacle of triumph and joy."

The supreme effort of the Democrats came more than two months later. On the morning of October 17th Douglas left Chicago. At Bloomington, where he was scheduled to speak that afternoon, a delegation of eighty was on hand to escort him to the capital. Meanwhile, there was high excitement in Springfield. The fife and drum were heard throughout the afternoon, and at frequent intervals there were rounds of cheers as delegations from the county and nearby towns arrived at the Barn. At 6:30 the Hickory Club and the Hickory Buds, a thousand torches in all, drew up in line on Jefferson Street at the Alton station, but not until eight o'clock did the distant booming of cannon announce the approach of the train. As Douglas alighted, cheers rocketed from the crowd. He was escorted immediately to the American House where, from a stand in front of the hotel, he responded to the welcoming address of B. S. Edwards.

On the following morning Springfield presented a colorful appearance. Many of the visiting delegations had come in costume—the Quincy Continentals were dressed in the uniform of the Continental Line, the delegation from Lincoln was garbed in red and white, the clubs from Chatham and Cotton Hill were all on horseback. While these and others, many of them with bands, marched through the streets, Douglas spent the morning greeting callers at the American House.

At noon a procession formed, and headed for an open area at Ninth and Jefferson streets, where a platform had been erected. When Douglas mounted the stand, a wild hurrah went up from the thousands of faithful Democrats who made up his audience. For an hour he pleaded for an endorsement of his policy of leaving the slavery question to the in-

THE REPUBLICAN RALLY, AUGUST 8, 1860

The parade passing the Lincoln home. Lincoln is standing at the right of the doorway.

CAMP BUTLER, 1862

habitants of the territories. When he finished, Robert G. Ingersoll of Peoria drew rounds of applause with his wit and sarcasm. Then the meeting broke up.

In the evening there was a torch-light procession two miles long, and speaking at the Barn. Altogether, it was a big day, but the attendance was so far below that of the great Republican rally that the Democrats were secretly downcast and their opponents openly jubilant.

To the meetings and rallies and Wide Awake processions, Lincoln paid little attention. His days were full enough with other occupations. With the nomination, the interest of the country centered on Springfield. Artists came to paint the portrait of the candidate, newspaper correspondents to write of him, and the idly curious to see for themselves what manner of man he was. Realizing that his dusty law office was no fit place for the reception of visitors, Lincoln took over the Governor's room on the second floor[2] of the State House, installed John G. Nicolay as his secretary, and welcomed without formality all who chose to call.

Old friends found Lincoln unaffected by his changed position. "After breakfast called to see Hon. Abm. Lincoln, at his room in the State House," Orville H. Browning recorded in his diary on June 12th. "He was very glad to see me, and received me with great cordiality. I found Mr. Hicks, an artist of New York, painting a portrait to be lithographed in Boston, and at the request of himself and Mr. Lincoln, I remained and talked to Lincoln whilst Mr. Hicks worked on the picture." That afternoon Browning called again. "Lincoln bears his honors meekly," he wrote. "As soon as other company had retired after I went in he fell into his old habit of telling amusing stories, and we had a free and easy talk of an hour or two."

Newspaper correspondents often wrote disparagingly of

[2] Now the third floor. At present the room is the office of the master in chancery.

Springfield's heat, its mud, or its lack of hacks and elegant hotels, but they liked the Republican candidate. A correspondent of the Utica *Morning Herald* who called on Lincoln one June evening intended to stay ten minutes, but his host was so cordial that he remained two hours. In summing up his impressions he wrote: "He has all the marks of a mind that scans closely, canvasses thoroughly, concludes deliberately, and holds to such conclusions unflinchingly." A representative of the New York *Herald,* which was hostile to Lincoln, was charmed with him. " 'Old Abe' and your correspondent took a chair together," he wrote to his paper, "and talked upon almost every topic now attracting the attention of the public. . . . The conversation was lively, and occasionally interspersed with some brilliant flashes of wit and good nature from the Kentucky lady, his wife."

As the summer wore on strangers in Springfield—even important strangers—became commonplace. Nevertheless, there were two whose advent caused a real sensation. One was the Prince of Wales; the other was William H. Seward.

Traveling through the United States as Baron Renfrew, the future Edward VII of England passed through Springfield on September 26th, on his way to St. Louis. A large crowd had gathered at the station, and when the train made a ten-minute stop, the Prince obligingly exhibited himself on the rear platform. Romantic ladies who had imagined that royalty and physical perfection were synonomous were disappointed—the Prince had neither beard nor moustache, and his hands and feet were uncommonly large—but most of the crowd were pleased with him. Later in the day Lincoln confessed that he would have been glad to see the royal visitor, but that his position forbade him to take the initiative. "Not being able to take any lead in the matter," he said, "I remained here at the State House, where I met so many sovereigns during the day that really the Prince had come and gone before I knew it."

Seward's appearance five days later was unexpected. Not until ten o'clock on the morning of October 1—an hour before his arrival—was it known that his train would stop. But the Republican cannon was hastily pressed into service, and two or three thousand people were on hand to greet him. As the train stopped, all eyes were on the tall form of Lincoln as he pressed forward to greet his defeated rival. A few minutes later both men appeared on the platform of the car, where Seward, with his customary grace, promised that New York would support the Republican candidate more cordially, and ask less of him, than any other state in the Union. The audience responded with three cheers for Seward and three for Lincoln, and then the train moved on. That night a special train of eleven cars left Springfield for Chicago, where Seward was scheduled to speak on the following day.

Throughout the campaign, the Republicans counted confidently on victory. "We know not what a day may bring forth, but to-day it looks as if the Chicago ticket will be elected," Lincoln had written to his old friend A. G. Henry as early as July 4th. When the states which voted for state officers in October—Ohio, Indiana and Pennsylvania—turned in Republican majorities, all doubt was banished. Even so, November 6th, when all America went to the polls, was a day tense with expectation.

Lincoln himself took it calmly enough. For most of the day he remained in the Governor's office, making conversation with numerous visitors. About three o'clock he casually walked across the street to the court house with a few friends, cut his own name from the top of a ballot, and dropped it into the box. Five minutes later he was back in his office.

Early that evening as many Republicans as the room could contain jammed into the Hall of the House of Representatives, the Democrats gathered at the Barn, and the overflow assembled in front of the Court House. Lincoln's office at the State House was crowded almost to suffocation. Soon after seven o'clock the first dispatch came in—a bulletin from Decatur showing a large Republican gain over 1856. For an hour or more, while the nominee sat with stolid face, only a trickle of returns, and those from nearby localities, were reported.

Finally, unable to stand the tension longer, Lincoln, Dubois, Hatch and two or three others walked over to the telegraph office. Here the bulletins were coming in more rapidly—fast enough, in fact, to indicate that Illinois had gone Republican. In a short time a report from Indianapolis indicated success in Indiana as well. By ten o'clock scattered returns from other Western states were pointing to victory. Still, as time passed anxiety grew—so far there was nothing from Pennsylvania and New York, and both states had to be carried. Finally, after another hour, there came a bulletin from Pittsburgh—Lincoln had carried Allegheny County by a majority of 10,000. Shortly afterward word came that the Republicans had a clear majority of 5,000 in Philadelphia. Pennsylvania was safe.

While they were waiting for the news from New York which should clinch the victory, the little group in the telegraph office was invited to Watson's saloon, which the Republican women of the town had taken over for the night. As Lincoln walked through the door a hundred feminine voices sang out, "How do you do, Mr. President!" and as he sat down at a long table piled with food the old refrain was started:

> Ain't you glad you joined the Republicans?
> Joined the Republicans,
> Ain't you glad you joined the Republicans,
> Down in Illinois?

While the voices were still ringing the long-expected dispatch from New York was delivered. Returns from New

York City indicated certain victory in the state. The word spread through the room in a flash, and congratulations came in an avalanche.

At the New York returns the crowd at the State House went mad. Old men and young men, bankers and clerks slapped each other on the back, danced, sang, and yelled until their voices sank to hoarse whispers. Outside one long shout announced the news. From stores, from houses, even from housetops, men called out that New York was safe, while groups ran through the streets shouting their joy at having joined the Republicans. Never had Springfield seen anything like it.

Meanwhile, all was gloom at the Democratic headquarters. The first returns dashed last-minute hopes, and in a short time the crowd began to dwindle. When the news from New York was read, the faithful few who had remained throughout the evening knew that they had heard the final verdict. Quietly they put out the lights, barred the doors, and slipped home to bed.

For Lincoln there was only one regret. By the narrow margin of sixty-nine votes he had carried the city of Springfield, but once again his rival swept to victory in Sangamon County.[3]

The election made no difference in Lincoln's daily routine, except to increase the number of those who called upon him. That routine is best described in the words of Henry Villard, who came to Springfield in mid-November to supply the readers of the New York *Herald* with a daily account of the activities of the President-Elect.

Mr. Lincoln makes his appearance in the State House regularly before eight o'clock, A. M. He is often found there earlier than the State officers, and sometimes is even sooner ready for work than his private secretary, who sleeps in the building.

[3] The official figures for Springfield were: Lincoln, 1395; Douglas, 1326; Breckenridge, 31; Bell, 16. In Sangamon County Douglas led with 3598; Lincoln followed with 3556; Bell polled 130; and Breckenridge received 77.

The first thing done in the morning is the opening and reading of his daily increasing mail matter. When visitors of distinction are in town who are entitled to more attention than the ordinary crowd of callers, they usually seek his presence at an early hour, and their hearings then take place under lock. At ten A. M. the door of the reception room is opened, and the general levees commence, and continue until noon. At one P. M. Mr. Lincoln repairs to dinner, after which he allows himself to rest until three P. M., when he again receives calls until half-past five, at which time he retires from the public gaze.

After supper he engages either in conversations with intimate political friends, or works with his secretary, sifting his correspondence, inditing replies, &c., &c. Light is seen in his room very late every evening, and he hardly ever allows anything to lay over unattended until the next day.

Altogether, he cannot be said to rest on a "bed of roses," although the real duties of his position do not yet weigh upon him. The most laborious part of his present daily task is the entertainment of his numerous callers. As everybody is more anxious to hear than to be heard (place seekers excepted), he is obliged to do nearly all the talking himself. His extreme fondness of and great practice in the light tone of social chat enables him to carry this heavy burthen with comparative ease.

In one of his letters Villard gave a lively description of the daily receptions.

On entering the State House the visitor will see groups of quietly conversing individuals, occupying various portions of the spacious hall of the first story. Their conversation, of course, turns about "Old Abe." Some he will find "wondering how he looks;" others, "whether he puts on airs," and how he treats callers. Excessively bashful personages, who are altogether afraid to venture into the Presidential presence, are also never wanting. . . .

The appointed hour having arrived, the crowd moves up stairs into the second story, in the southeast corner of which the reception room is located. Passing through a rather dark sort of a doorway, the clear voice and often ringing laughter of the President usually guide them to the right door. The boldest of the party having knocked, a ready "Come in" invites to enter. On opening the door the tall, lean form of "Old Abe" directly confronts the leader of the party.   Seizing the latter's hand with a hearty shake, he leads him in, and bids the rest to follow suit by an encouraging "Get in, all of you."   The whole party being in, he will ask for their names, and then immediately start a running conversation.   In this respect he displays more than ordinary talent and practice.   Although he is naturally more listened than talked to, he does not allow a pause to become protracted.   He is never at a loss as to the subjects that please the different classes of visitors, and there is a certain quaintness and originality about all he has to say, so that one cannot help being interested.   His "talk" is not brilliant.   His phrases are not ceremoniously set, but pervaded with a humorousness, and, at times, a grotesque joviality, that will always please.   I think it would be hard to find one who tells better jokes, enjoys them better and laughs oftener, than Abraham Lincoln. . . .

No restrictions whatever being exercised as to visitors, the crowd that daily waits on the President is always of a motley description. Everybody that lives in this vicinity or passes through this place goes to take a look at "Old Abe."   Muddy boots and hickory shirts are just as frequent as broadcloth, fine linen, &c. The ladies, however, are usually dressed up in their very best. . . .

Offensively democratic exhibitions of free manners occur every once in a while.   Churlish fellows will obtrude themselves with their hats on, lighted segars and their pantaloons tucked·into their boots. Dropping into chairs, they will sit puffing away and trying to gorgonize the President with their silent stares, until their boorish curiosity is fully satisfied.

Formal presentations are dispensed with in most cases.   Nearly everybody finds his own way in and introduces himself.   Sometimes half a dozen rustics rush in, break their way through other visitors up to the object of their search, and, after calling their names and touching the Presidential fingers, back out again without delay.

The run of visitors, usually numbering 100 or 150 a day, assumed flood proportions on November 20th—the day appointed for the celebration of the Republican victory. Hardly had Lincoln arrived at the State House than he was beset by an eager horde which had been on the lookout for him since daybreak. Reception hours went by the board as the 'people' crowded into the Governor's room—timid farmers and their more timid wives, country youths with their sweethearts, boors who made a point of keeping on their hats and puffing steadily on cigars. All day long the flood continued. When the President-Elect finally made his escape late in the afternoon, it was with the knowledge that the hardest day's work of many a month lay behind him.

The celebration itself was a failure. Surfeited with the demonstrations of the campaign, only a small number of enthusiasts came in from other cities, although a capacity audience filled the Wigwam to hear Lyman Trumbull deliver the address of the occasion. The illumination was general, but the fireworks flashed before jaded eyes. Anna Ridgely expressed the feeling of the entire town when she wrote in her diary: "Some of the fireworks were beautiful, but most of them were rockets and Roman candles that we have seen all summer long, while the torch light procession was the smallest I ever saw."

Nevertheless, there were people enough in town to make the evening only less difficult for Lincoln than the day had been. The procession halted at his residence and cheered until he had to show himself and speak a few words in acknowledgment. Even after the Wigwam meeting the people gave him no rest. They crowded into his parlor, stared at Mrs. Lincoln and the invited guests, and stood about in tongue-tied embarrassment until a late hour. The next day Lincoln, with Mrs. Lincoln, was glad to escape to Chicago, leaving the place seekers to fret for his return for nearly a week, while the correspondents complained that the Illinois capital was as dull as a New England village on Sunday.

With the common people, intent upon seeing for themselves the man whom they had made President, came others on more important missions. Simon Cameron appeared, and took back to Pennsylvania the promise of a cabinet position —a promise, incidentally, which Lincoln tried unsuccessfully to recall. Thurlow Weed came on from Albany, and the President-Elect notified William H. Seward that at the

proper time he intended to nominate him as Secretary of
State. Edward Bates of Missouri was summoned, and a few
days later the *Missouri Democrat* announced that he would
be appointed Attorney General. At Lincoln's call came Sal-
mon P. Chase of Ohio, and he too went home with the knowledge that a place in the cabinet would be his. In the intervals
between visits such as these other men only less prominent
appeared on the scene—Joshua Giddings, George G. Fogg,
Amos Tuck, Carl Schurz, Horace Greeley. Sometimes they
were closeted for hours with Lincoln at his home or in his
office; on other occasions formality was disregarded, and he
called on them at their hotels. In either case, their presence
was soon known, and a new crop of rumors spread among
the politicians of the hotel lobbies and barrooms.

But on many occasions subjects more momentous than
office holding were under discussion. Ever since Lincoln's
nomination threats of secession in the event of his election
had been coming from the South. Like most Northerners,
he was not greatly impressed. Even when the legislature of
South Carolina, on the day after the presidential election,
called a convention to meet on December 17 and consider the
question of withdrawing from the Union, the Republicans
were not seriously alarmed. Lincoln, believing that only a
small number of extremists were concerned, and that actual
secession would not be attempted, took the news calmly,
although it caused something of a commotion in the Illinois
capital.

As the weeks passed, however, and few signs of strong
conservative reaction appeared in the South, Lincoln's estimate of the seriousness of the national crisis slowly changed.
A week before the Charleston convention met he admitted
that secession was a certainty, and after it had been in session
a few days he stated his belief that several other states would
follow South Carolina's lead. But he refused to exhibit any
concern. The Palmetto State passed her ordinance, and one

by one her followers took similar action, but in Springfield Lincoln remained impassive.

Nor would he give any definite indication of the course he intended to pursue when he should be given the responsibility of the government. To inquirers he freely admitted that the Union ought to be, and in his opinion would be, preserved, but beyond this general statement he would not go. He let it be known, however, that he had no intention of receding from the platform on which he had been nominated. With Thurlow Weed, William Kellogg, Duff Green, and others he spent many hours discussing the compromises which they felt would avert the crisis, but none of them carried with him any hope that one iota of what the party had won in the election would be surrendered by the President-Elect.

But though Lincoln himself was inflexible in his refusal to announce a definite policy, there were other indications of his attitude which observers lost no time in utilizing. One such was the editorial column of the *Illinois State Journal,* whose editor, E. L. Baker, was a cousin by marriage of Mrs. Lincoln and Lincoln's own friend and supporter. Disclaiming any intention of speaking for the President-Elect, Baker left no doubt of his own attitude. Neither South Carolina nor any other state could dissolve the Union by passing resolutions to that effect. "Disunion, by armed force, is TREASON," he wrote in an editorial so forceful that it was reprinted all over the country, "and treason must and will be put down at all hazards. This Union is not, will not, and cannot be dissolved until this Government is overthrown by the traitors who have raised the disunion flag. Can they overthrow it? We think not. They may disturb its peace—they may interrupt the course of its prosperity—they may cloud its reputation for stability—but its tranquility will be restored, its prosperity will return, and the stain upon its national character will be transfered and remain an eternal blot on the memory of

those who caused the disorder.' Let the secessionists understand it—let the press proclaim it—let it fly on the wings
of the lightning, and fall like a thunderbolt on those now
plotting treason in convention, that the Republican party,
that the great North, aided by hundreds of thousands of
patriotic men in the slave States, have determined to preserve the Union—peaceably if they can, forcibly if they
must!"

The correspondents expected, also, that the inaugural address of Governor Yates would point to the policy which
Lincoln intended to pursue. But the message was so radical
in tone, so sharply anti-slavery and anti-compromise, that
they regretfully concluded that it was delivered without his
sanction. Moreover, the circumstances of its delivery de-
tracted from the message itself. With both houses in joint
session, and the galleries crowded with spectators, Yates
appeared in such condition that the clerk of the House was
forced, after the first few sentences, to read the message for
him. The episode set tongues wagging near and far, and
constituted one of the state's major scandals.

In the months which followed the election little besides the
impact of national events interrupted Lincoln's orderly routine. His brief visit to Chicago over, he settled down to
await the time for his departure to Washington. The meeting of the State Electoral College on December 5th provided
a pleasant interlude, and the visit of his old friend E. D.
Baker, now a Senator-Elect from Oregon, was another welcome break, but for the most part the days were devoted exclusively to the problems of politics and to the callers who
came in unfailing numbers.

Late in December, in anticipation of the meeting of the
legislature, when the Governor would need his office for
his own use, Lincoln and Nicolay moved from the State
House to Johnson's Building across the street from the
Chenery House. There, and in a vacant room over the store

of C. M. Smith, his brother-in-law, where he could work on his inaugural address in privacy, Lincoln spent most of his time.

Late in January, 1861, the public sale of the furnishings of A. Lincoln was announced in the Springfield newspapers. On the same day Lincoln himself started for Charleston for a final visit with his stepmother. Upon his return invitations for a farewell reception were issued. On the night of February 6th the Lincoln residence was crowded with "the political elite" of the state and "the beauty and fashion" of Springfield. Seven hundred were present, and the jam was so great that in twenty minutes one could barely make his way from the door to the parlor. The next day the family moved to the Chenery House.

On the morning of February 11, 1861, Lincoln, his wife and a small number of friends rode from the hotel to the Great Western station. There, in spite of the drizzling rain, more than a thousand of his fellow citizens had gathered. For twenty minutes, his pale face quivering with emotion so deep that he could scarcely speak, he stood in the waiting room and shook the hands of those who pressed forward to say good-bye and wish him well. Shortly before eight o'clock he was conducted to the train. On reaching the platform of the last car he turned to the crowd, removed his hat, and attempted for long seconds to control his feelings. Then, slowly, impressively, he spoke the following words:

"My Friends: No one, not in my situation, can appreciate my feeling of sadness at this parting. To this place, and the kindness of these people, I owe everything. Here I have lived a quarter of a century, and have passed from a young to an old man. Here my children have been born, and one is buried. I now leave, not knowing when or whether ever I may return, with a task before me greater than that which rested upon Washington. Without the assistance of that

Divine Being who ever attended him, I cannot succeed. With that assistance, I cannot fail. Trusting in Him who can go with me, and remain with you, and be everywhere for good, let us confidently hope that all will yet be well. To His care commending you, as I hope in your prayers you will commend me, I bid you an affectionate farewell."

CHAPTER XII

War

"WE must not be enemies," said Lincoln when he took the oath of office on March 4, 1861. "Though passion may have strained, it must not break, our bonds of affection." But six weeks later, at daybreak on the 12th of April, a shell arched from the low sand hills of Charleston harbor towards the fort on which the eyes of the nation had been focussed for three long months. The hope of peace was shattered. War had begun.

Word of the bombardment of Fort Sumter reached Springfield that same evening, but not until the next day, a Saturday, did it become generally known. Then, as despatch followed despatch, all pretense of work was dropped. With faces grave and apprehensive, men formed groups before the newspaper bulletin boards and on the street corners. The next day the churches saw few worshipers, but the streets were filled with people. Already there was talk of organizing troops. The Union was in danger, and the government must be sustained no matter what the cost.

On Monday, the 15th, Adjutant General Mather, in General Orders No. 1, notified all Illinois militia to hold themselves in readiness for service. The next day the President's proclamation calling for 75,000 volunteers to serve three months was published, and the Governor called a special session of the legislature for the following week. That night thousands gathered at the State House to express their determination to preserve the Union. After the meeting had organized, and while the resolutions committee was at work, John A. McClernand rose to say that he had always been a Democrat, and was a Democrat now, but that this was no time for partizanship—all men must stand by their government and their flag. When the cheers subsided Lyman Trumbull took the floor. He had heard talk of the government defending itself and its capital against the secessionists, and it made him sick! "Let us make *them* defend Montgomery and Charleston!" he thundered, and the cheers of the crowd carried to the limits of the town. Resolutions declaring that it was the duty of every patriotic citizen to aid the government in all possible ways were passed with a shout.

The next morning the Governor called for six regiments to rendezvous at Springfield. Before the ink of the proclamation was dry, the music of fife and drum was heard on the capital's streets. At the headquarters of the Springfield Zouave Grays one man after another signed the muster roll. By afternoon, when the company was sworn into the state service, its ranks had increased from thirty to sixty; by nightfall it numbered 108, and enlistment was stopped. At the end of the next day thirty men had volunteered in a company which W. B. Sands was forming, the Germans and Irish were organizing, and the Young America Hose and Engine Company had voted to transform itself into a military unit. Jacob Bunn, N. H. Ridgely and the Springfield Marine and Fire Insurance Company had offered Governor Yates a loan of $100,000 to facilitate the organization and equipment of the troops. All day telegrams announcing the formation of companies had poured into the State House.

Two days later, on the 19th, word spread that the evening train from the north would bring the first troops to reach the capital under the Governor's call. An immense crowd gathered at the station. As the Lincoln Guards of

Lincoln stepped from the cars a wild shout rose. The fifes shrieked, the Springfield Zouaves formed in line, and behind them the Guards paraded the streets to the applause of the entire city.

Two days earlier the county fair grounds west of the city had been selected as the place of rendezvous and called Camp Yates. Here the Zouaves were already established, and here the Guards went into camp. The next morning two companies from Quincy made their appearance, and thereafter almost every train brought its contingent. At the end of a week 4,000 men were in camp. Rapidly as possible regiments were organized. First to be formed was the Seventh,[1] which included the Zouave Grays and the National Guards, and the Grays swelled with pride when their own captain, John Cook, was elected colonel.

Even before the independent companies had been formed into regiments, movement to the field commenced. First to leave were two Quincy companies, two from Jacksonville, and Hopkins' Springfield Artillery, whose guns had boomed for so many political rallies in recent years. At the Great Western station the men were formed in line, sworn into the federal service, and the officers given their commissions. Amid the tears and farewells of relatives, the train started. Four days later, on the 27th, the departure of the Seventh touched Springfield even more deeply. Early in the morning word spread that the regiment was to entrain for Alton at ten o'clock. Long before that time the station was black with people. As they stood at ease on Jefferson Street the soldiers sang, the people cheered, and the air of a holiday prevailed. But when the train started a dead silence fell. Then cheers rang out again, but as the train faded into the distance many a face was wet with tears.

The constant arrival and departure of troops was excit-

[1] Numbered thus to preserve the fame of the six regiments which had volunteered in the Mexican War.

ing enough, but when word was received that Douglas would reach the city on April 25th to address a joint session of the legislature, the town became almost delirious. On the day after the surrender of Fort Sumter the great Democrat had sought an interview with Lincoln, at the conclusion of which he had announced his determination to sustain the President, maintain the government and preserve the Union. Soon afterward he had started west. While he had spoken on the way, it was known that he was reserving a complete statement of his position for his Illinois constituents. Not merely Springfield, but the whole North, burned for his words.

That night the Hall of the House of Representatives was crowded to suffocation and hundreds packed the corridors. When Douglas entered, promptly at eight o'clock, the audience stood up and cheered, but when he rose to speak a few minutes later, the applause rocketed in volleys. Finally silence was secured, and once more the familiar voice was heard.

Secession, he declared, was unjustified and treasonable, and all men must support the government regardless of their party affiliations. "For the first time since the adoption of the Federal constitution," he declared, "a widespread conspiracy exists to destroy the best government the sun of heaven ever shed its rays upon. Hostile armies are now marching upon the Federal capital, with a view of planting a revolutionary flag upon its dome; seizing the national archives; taking captive the president elected by the votes of the people, in the hands of secessionists and disunionists. A war of aggression and of extermination is being waged against the government established by our fathers. The boast has gone forth by the secretary of war of this revolutionary government, that on the first day of May the revolutionary flag shall float from the walls of the capitol at Washington, and that on the fourth day of July the revolutionary army shall hold possession of the Hall of Independence in Philadelphia.

"The simple question presented to us," he continued, "is whether we will wait for the enemy to carry out his boast of making war upon our soil; or whether we will rush as one man to the defence of the government and its capital, to defend it from the hands of all assailants who have threatened to destroy it! . . .

"So long as there was a hope of peaceful solution," he added sadly, "I prayed and implored for compromise. I can appeal to my countrymen with confidence that I have spared no effort, omitted no opportunity to adapt a peaceful solution of all these troubles, and thus restore peace, happiness and fraternity to this country. When all propositions of peace fail, there is but one course left for the patriot, and that is to rally under that flag which has waved over the Capitol from the days of Washington, and around the government established by Washington, Jefferson, Hamilton and their compeers. . . .

"My friends, I can say no more. To discuss these topics is the most painful duty of my life. It is with a sad heart— with a grief that I have never before experienced, that I have to contemplate this fearful struggle; but I believe in my conscience that it is a duty we owe to ourselves and our children, and our God, to protect this government and that flag from every assailant, be he who he may."

As the speaker finished men wept and cheered by turns, and hundreds who, but a few months before, had looked upon him as the arch enemy of liberty, shouted in praise. Old Democrats who had broken with him on the slavery question rushed forward to shake his hand. "A triumphant call to arms in defense of country, Government and Constitutional Liberty," said the once-hostile *Journal*. "By his noble support of his country, Mr. Douglas has endeared himself to every loyal citizen in our broad land."

A few weeks later there came a day when the church bells were tolled, and business was suspended, and flags were lowered to half mast, and crêpe drooped from hundreds of door handles. Douglas was dead. Exhausted by the strain of travel and speech-making, he had fallen an easy victim to disease. On June 7, the day of the funeral, business was again suspended, stores and public buildings were dressed in mourning, and flags were again at half-mast. Except for a single cannon, booming at half-hour intervals, a Sabbath stillness prevailed. Sorrow pervaded Springfield, and the hearts of old friend and old foe alike were saddened.

Meanwhile, preparations for war were settling into a routine. At Camp Yates regiment after regiment was organizing, electing its officers, and departing for the Union lines in Missouri or at Cairo. Gradually the town was losing its zest in the spectacle. It is unlikely, therefore, that anyone paid much attention to an announcement in one of the papers in mid-June that "Capt. U. S. Grant, of Galena, and a West Point graduate," had been appointed to the command of the Twenty-First Illinois. Few citizens of the capital knew this quiet, ordinary-looking man who, two months earlier, had presented himself to Governor Yates with the simple statement that he was a West Point man who felt it his duty to offer his services in his country's need. Impressed by some intangible quality, Yates had given him a desk in his office. Before long he realized that the newcomer's knowledge of military routine was almost invaluable. Then, while Grant was visiting his father in Covington, Kentucky, trouble over discipline and promotions developed in the Twenty-First regiment. Yates offered his absent assistant the command, which was accepted at once. In a day or two the regiment was in hand, and on its way to the Missouri front.

By this time the conviction was spreading that three months, the period for which the first troops were called, would be altogether inadequate for the suppression of secession. New volunteers were signing for three years' service. In Springfield the roll of drums was heard on all sides, and nearly every hall in town was in use as a recruiting station. Nevertheless, it was not until the battle of Bull Run, on July 21, that full realization of the magnitude of the North's task sank in.

So far, the war had been a sort of exciting holiday. There had been a few casualties from illness, and the dramatic death of Elmer Ellsworth had caused a sharp pang of sorrow. But it was all far away, and perhaps one glorious Northern victory would mean the end. So, as McDowell's army advanced, confidence rose. The enemy would not even stand and fight—victory was too easy! Then, with stunning suddenness, came news of the Union defeat. Not since the bombardment of Fort Sumter had there been such excitement. All day, on July 22, throngs of anxious men stood uneasily in front of the bulletin boards. Only late at night, when the worst was definitely known, did the streets resume their customary quiet. By that time the unwelcome realization that this would be a war of years instead of months had taken firm possession.

Long-range measures were quickly adopted. One of these was the abandonment of Camp Yates and the establishment of a new concentration camp. Long before this the citizens had learned that close association with single men in barracks was not an unmixed blessing. Men from the camp were often drunk on the streets, brawls between them were frequent, and occasionally the townspeople themselves were threatened by bullies in uniform. Farmers west of the city complained of the disappearance of fruit, vegetables and fowls. On the other hand, the saloons and prostitutes had a demoralizing effect upon the men. Therefore the new camp, to be named Camp Butler in honor of the state treasurer, was to be established on Clear Lake, a safe distance east of the city. By early August it was ready for use.

Another measure was the expansion of munitions' manufacture. Soon after the outbreak of the war Lamb's foundry started to cast artillery shot and to make musket cartridges. By mid-summer 150 hands, mainly boys and girls, were working seven days a week, turning out 25,000 rifle cartridges and 400 gun cartridges a day. By fall a new building near the state arsenal (then located on North Fifth street) had been completed, more than two hundred people were employed, and the output had risen proportionately.

A third measure was the formation of soldiers' aid societies, which undertook to supply extra bedding, underclothing, delicacies, newspapers and magazines to the men in the camps, and to alleviate suffering among the sick and wounded. The men solicited money and supplies; the women and girls devoted many hours each week to sewing and knitting. But for a long time many held aloof. "I am sorry to say the democratic ladies have taken no interest as yet," Mrs. J. C. Conkling, one of the most active participants, wrote in the fall of 1861. "I think there is very little patriotism among our ladies." Nevertheless, as time went on, and the worthiness of the work was seen, personal and party animosities were dropped and most of the leading women of the town took part.

Thus, while the green troops drilled at Camp Butler and Springfield prepared for the inevitable battles of the future, months passed in relative quiet. Then, in November, came the battle of Belmont, and because several Illinois regiments were engaged, the first casualty lists of the war were published in Springfield newspapers. But not until February, 1862, when Grant attacked Forts Henry and Donelson, was the stark reality of war brought home.

Early in the morning of February 7 Governor Yates received a despatch announcing that Fort Henry had surrendered. Excitement spread like a prairie fire. In a short time the news was confirmed, the flag was unfurled above the State House, and that night the guns at the arsenal barked out a national salute.

Ten days later came similar news from Fort Donelson. As the word spread flags were raised all over town, bells were pealed, and guns and cannon spoke in impromptu salute. In the afternoon, when an official report was received, the morning's jollification was repeated, and the six guns of Captain Cheney's artillery rattled the town's windows. That night there were bonfires around the square, and an immense meeting at the State House.

But there was deep anxiety too. Many Illinois regiments had taken part in the attack, and the lists of killed and wounded would be long. All night long the women of the Soldiers' Aid Society made bandages, and many a husband joined in the task. The next day a special train, with surgeons, nurses, and hospital supplies, left Springfield for Cairo. For weeks casualty lists were printed. "We can now realize that we are in the midst of War. . . ," Mrs. Conkling wrote. "The late victories in Kentucky created great joy here, but accompanied with great mourning. . . ."

One consequence of the battle of Fort Donelson was the reception at Camp Butler of large numbers of Confederate prisoners. On February 22 two thousand arrived, and hundreds more were received during the next few days. "Let us treat them not as rebels, but as prisoners of war," admonished the *Illinois State Journal*. "It is no part of magnanimity to crow over and, least of all, deride a conquered foe." This advice was not hard to follow, for the prisoners were young, ragged, tired of fighting, and responsive to sympathy. Often there were acquaintances, even relatives, among them. "We seem all at once in close contact with our southern friends," Mrs. Conkling wrote.

Six weeks later Springfield thrilled to the news of another victory. On the afternoon of April 9th came word that on the 6th and 7th there had been fighting at Pittsburg Landing, in Tennessee, and that the Union forces had been victorious. But later despatches left no doubt that the victory had been attained at a terrible cost. Yates, with other state officers, nurses and surgeons, left at once for the battlefield. In a few days casualty lists, long beyond anything that the people had so far seen, began to appear, and many a Springfield family mourned the loss of a son or father.

For weeks editors and military critics wrangled over the responsibility for the slaughter and near-disaster. Finally, however, the movements of McClellan's Army of the Potomac diverted attention to the East. As his men landed on the peninsula southeast of Richmond and pressed forward to their goal, all Springfield watched with anxiety and hope. Finally, on the afternoon of July 2, a cannon barked in salute. One by one the bells of the town commenced to ring, and soon the Stars and Stripes was waving from every flagstaff. Richmond had fallen, and Springfield was beside itself with joy! Citizens wild with delight paraded the streets. All the fireworks in the city were engaged, and preparations were made for a torchlight procession and jubilee the like of which the prairie capital had never witnessed. While enthusiasm was highest a despatch contradicting the news of the capture was received. Others of the same tenor followed. That night there was no procession. Instead, gloom as black as the night itself hung over the anxious men who stood before the bulletin boards hoping against hope that the first glad news of the day would find final confirmation.

In the month which followed, the failure of McClellan's Peninsular campaign became clear. At the same time the determination grew that the war must be prosecuted even more relentlessly, and Springfield grimly prepared to furnish its share of the 600,000 volunteers for whom the President was calling. On July 21 seventy-seven citizens, headed by Richard Yates, published a call for a "war meeting" to be held at the State House the following day to encourage enlistment. So large was the response that the meeting had to be transferred to the street in front of the court house. There, after appeals by Yates and other speakers, resolutions supporting the war, approving the new call for troops, and calling for the appointment of a committee of ten citizens to devise means of encouraging enlistment, were passed. The committee, appointed a few days later, promptly induced the county supervisors to appropriate $50,000 for bounties and the support of soldiers' families. Recruiting offices opened, and fife and drum sounded from morning until night. All over the state men responded with fervor. Camp Butler was filled to capacity, and Camp Yates was again pressed into service, to remain in use until the close of the war.

As the new levies poured in, confidence in the might of the North was gradually restored. Pope's defeat at the second battle of Bull Run gave mounting hopes a rough shock, but two weeks later the news of Antietam dispelled the gloom. At the first news of Union victory Yates ordered a salute of 100 guns, and on the next day, when confirmation came, flags flew from the housetops and the town was in "a state of exultant excitement."

So far, the war had been fairly well supported by the people of Springfield. Upon the outbreak of hostilities the Democratic *Register* was no less insistent than the Republican *Journal* that all men, regardless of party affiliation, join in the defense of the country. However, as the first violent enthusiasm faded, and the Republicans began to identify patriotism with adherence to their own organization, the Democrats cooled. Although continuing to urge enlistment and support of the army, they refused to surrender their own party organization, and insisted on their right to criticize the administration and to nominate candidates for office.

A few leaders—mainly men like John A. McClernand, who had gone into the army—abandoned the old party for the "fusionists," or "Unionists," as the Republicans, with a scattering of War Democrats, preferred to be known, but the Democratic rank and file remained faithful. Aided by the administration's adoption of war measures of doubtful constitutionality, particularly military arrests and the suspension of habeas corpus, the party gained ground. At a county election in the fall of 1861 they carried all except two of their candidates into office and elected Democratic delegates to the constitutional convention which was to assemble early in 1862.

But as a whole, they supported the war. After the failure of the Richmond campaign, no one was more active than B. S. Edwards, the acknowledged leader of the Springfield Democracy, in urging response to Lincoln's call for troops. The overthrow of secession and the restoration of the Union were still, in their opinion, objectives worth their cost in men and money, no matter how much they might deprecate the methods by which the Republicans were attempting to attain them.

And then, five days after Antietam, Lincoln issued the Proclamation of Emancipation.

Dutifully, but with no great enthusiasm, the Republicans came to the defense of the President. *"The President must and will be sustained,"* said the *Journal.* ". . . Those who refuse to support the Government in the exercise of its necessary and just authority are traitors and should be so treated, whatever name they may wear. True patriots of every name rally around the President, determined that the Union shall be preserved and the laws enforced."

The Democrats, on the other hand, flew to violent denunciation. To transform a war for the restoration of the Union to a crusade against slavery, and by an unconstitutional proclamation at that, was itself treason. "We trust that the people of the state, in the coming election," said the *Register,* "will meet the issue proposed, and in casting their votes decide, in the choice of members of Congress especially, whether they approve or not, the proposed plan of grinding taxation for all time to come, to pay for freed negroes, the setting aside of the national constitution, and, in all human probability, the permanent disruption of the republic, a permanent standing army, endless civil war, the Africanization of the southern states, anarchy in the north, to end in despotism."

For the short remainder of the campaign then in progress the Democrats struck hard at the "abolitionism" of the administration. Before the issuance of the Proclamation the Republicans had had hopes of victory. In the summer they had so far recovered from their defeat of the preceding fall as to defeat the constitution which the Democratic convention had framed, and everywhere the signs were encouraging. In the Springfield district John T. Stuart, with Democratic support, was admittedly a strong candidate for election to Congress, but the supporters of Leonard Swett, his opponent, foresaw victory, or at worst defeat by a narrow margin. The political cost of emancipation was soon apparent, however. Voters deserted the Union party by hundreds, with the result that in both Springfield and Sangamon County the Democratic candidates were elected by sizable majorities. Over the state as a whole the result was the same. Democrats replaced Republicans in the state offices to be filled and secured a majority in the general assembly.

When the legislature assembled in January, 1863, not only had opposition to emancipation become organized, but a definite movement looking toward peace had developed. One of the first moves of the leaders was to call a public meeting to express the views of the opposition. While speaker after speaker asserted that the constitution must be observed in peace as well as war, and that any departure from it would lead either to anarchy or to subserviency as ignominious as that against which the Revolutionary Fathers had revolted, the resolutions committee, with John T. Stuart and C. H. Lanphier as local representatives, framed a blanket indictment. "The emancipation proclamation," the fruit of their labor read, ". . . is as unwarrantable in military as in civil law; a gigantic usurpation, at once converting the war . . . into a crusade for the sudden, unconditional and violent liberation of three millions of negro slaves; a result which would not only be a total subversion of the federal Union, but a revolution in the social organization of the southern states. . . . The proclamation invites servile insurrection as an element in this emancipation crusade— a means of warfare, the inhumanity and diabolism of which are without example in civilized warfare, and which we denounce, and which the civilized world will denounce, as an ineffaceable disgrace to the American name." With the unanimous adoption of this statement the meeting adjourned, with the promise to convene again three days later and consider the political situation in its more general phases.

On the night of January 8, 1863, the Democrats gathered again at the State House. Immediately a series of resolutions was presented. "Usurpations" of the administration were condemned, the creation of the state of West Virginia was characterized as "revolutionary," and a program for the re-establishment of peace was proposed. Let an armistice be declared so that a convention of representatives of all the states, North and South, could meet at Louisville and adjust the national difficulties, and let the Illinois legislature make the first move by appointing delegates at once. When H. K. S. Omelveny, speaking in support of the resolutions, declared that he was opposed to the further prosecution of the war, and in favor of the return of peace upon a basis which would secure to all the states their constitutional rights, he was cheered repeatedly. The resolutions were adopted by acclamation.

The public expression of opinions such as these brought

into the open many whose secret sympathies had long been with the South. Street fights between defenders of secession and outraged Unionists took place. One woman raised a Confederate flag above her house and with a loaded revolver in her hand, dared anyone to take it down. "You would be surprised . . . at the number of our ladies here that are wearing copperhead breastpins and even cents on their watch guards," Mrs. Conkling wrote to her son at college. "Since our traitorous legislature met secession principles and sympathy are boldly spoken of in our midst."

The Union men were not slow in countering with public demonstrations of their own. On the night after the adjourned Democratic meeting all who favored "the unconditional support of the Government of the United States against the efforts of traitors for its overthrow" were summoned to meet at the State House to counteract the "treason" meetings held there earlier in the week. There, from a stand hung with battle flags—among them the tattered banner of the old Zouave Grays—speakers asserted that the maintenance of the Union was threatened no less by armed rebellion than by "insidious and dangerous attempts of disloyal persons" in the North itself, and urged the meeting to condemn unequivocally "all disloyal language and acts derogatory of the Government." This the meeting did with a shout of acclamation. Then, with cheers for the Union, the soldiers in the field, Lincoln, Oglesby and Yates, it adjourned.

A week later the unconditional supporters of the Union were again called to the State House, and again the Hall of Representatives was crowded. After lengthy resolutions supporting the national and state administrations, the emancipation proclamation and other war measures, and condemning any compromise with "rebels" were proposed for adoption, Colonel Noble of the Second Illinois Cavalry brought out volleys of cheers by stating that if traitors attempted a revolution at home, he would bring his regiment back to fight them. "I have not a great while to live and it makes but little difference with me personally," he said; "but I want to leave the land with the old flag floating over it, with liberty and the Union preserved. I do not want to see one star taken from the flag, nor treason triumphant on one foot of the soil over which it ever waved!" The resolutions were adopted with a roar of approval.

As the weeks wore on and the legislature, intent upon adjourning as soon as its constitutional limit of six weeks was reached, spent its time in denouncing the war and the manner in which it was being conducted, tempers reached the snapping point. One day in February people on the streets outside the State House heard a harsh voice, tense with emotion, in outraged denunciation. In an instant the chamber was crowded. There, pounding his desk to splinters, was Isaac Funk of McLean County. "I can sit in my seat no longer and see so much by-playing going on," the old man shouted. "These men are trifling with the best interests of the country. They should have asses' ears to set off their heads, for they are traitors and secessionists at heart. . . . They deserve hanging, I say, the country would be better for swinging them up. . . . They have my sentiments: let them one and all make the most of them. I am ready to back up all I say, and I repeat it, to meet these traitors in any manner they may choose from a pin's point to the mouth of a cannon." As he finished, the crowded galleries cheered him to the echo, and Union men sought the reporter's notes so that the speech might be put into pamphlet form and sent broadcast over the country.

Four months later the State House was the scene of another sensation. At the regular legislative session the Democratic majority, following the actions of the meeting held in January, had determined to urge an armistice and appoint commissioners to a national convention. Resolutions carrying out these objectives were passed by the House, and failed of passage in the Senate only because of the withdrawal of the Republican members, who did not return to their seats until the regular business of the session—the apportionment and appropriation bills—came up. Then the assembly recessed until June. Convening on June 2, the Democratic majority prepared to push its program—the passage of an apportionment bill over the Governor's veto, a bill to prevent illegal arrests, a bill to prevent the immigration of negroes, and other measures likely to embarrass their opponents. Again the Republicans resorted to obstruction. In the Senate a quorum was lacking, and as a result, the two houses were unable to agree upon adjournment. Thus matters stood for two days. Suddenly, on the morning of the 10th, the Governor's secretary walked into the Hall of the House and commenced to read a proclamation proroguing the legislature because of the disagreement on adjournment. The speaker pounded with his gavel but the reading continued, and in a few minutes the House dissolved in disorder. Wild rumors of violence flew about the town, but dissipated in talk. For two weeks the House formally remained in session, but finally the members saw the futility of the proceeding, and scattered to their homes.

Yates' action gave added seriousness to the Democratic mass meeting scheduled to be held at Springfield on June 17 to protest violation of the constitution and call for an end of the war. On the 16th thousands were already on hand, and from dawn until afternoon of the day itself cannon, drums and bands, signalizing the arrival of each delegation, sounded almost continuously. The *Register* claimed an attendance of 75,000; even the *Journal* conceded 15,000.

Six speakers' stands had been erected at the fair grounds. There S. S. Cox of Ohio, Daniel Voorhees of Indiana and other prominent Democrats supported the efforts of local leaders in denouncing Republican policies and measures. Resolutions condemning the national administration and calling Yates' prorogation "a high-handed usurpation and exercise of arbitrary power" were passed, but the real significance of the meeting was expressed in a resolution passed at all stands, declaring that "the further offensive prosecution of this war tends to subvert the Constitution and the government, and entail upon this nation all the disastrous consequences of misrule and anarchy. That we are in favor of peace upon the basis of a restoration of the Union, and for the accomplishment of which we propose a National Convention, to settle upon terms of peace, which shall have in view the restoration of the Union as it was, and the securing by Constitutional amendments, such rights to the several States and the people thereof, as honor and justice demand."

Even Democratic anticipations were exceeded by the meeting. Rarely, if ever, had Springfield witnessed so large a gathering; never had seriousness and sobriety been more noticeable. Moreover, as an evidence of their fundamental loyalty, the visitors had subscribed more than $50,000 for the benefit of wounded soldiers. But to the Republicans the meeting was a shameful assemblage of "copperheads," a disgrace to Illinois. "A remarkable day in the history of our noble State," the *Journal* called it; "and if we mistake not, a memorable day in the history of the so-called Democratic party—a day from which they may date the commencement of its disintegration and ruin caused by the treasonable advice and acts of unscrupulous party leaders."

More effective, however, than mere denunciation in counteracting the movement for peace was the news which came over the wires early in July. For several days despatches describing terrific fighting at Gettysburg were received, but not until the 8th was the definite announcement of Union victory received. An hour later the surrender of Vicksburg was announced and confirmed. At five o'clock thirty-five guns were fired in honor of the Army of the Potomac, at six there was a salute for the Army of the Tennessee, at seven another for the soldiers of Illinois, and from seven-thirty until eight all the bells in the city were rung. That night, while the State House square was bright with bonfires and rockets flashed above the city, the people gathered in front of the court house, listened to speakers extol the prowess of the Union armies, sang patriotic songs and cheered for the troops in the field. Partisan animosities were forgotten, and Democrat vied with Republican in celebrating the victories.

But the Union men were not content to let the bullets of the soldiers plead their cause. Challenged by the outspokenness of the advocates of peace, and heartened by victory in the field, they determined to prove the temper of the masses by a demonstration in comparison with which the Democratic meeting of June 17 would seem insignificant. On August 14 the call was issued. Signed by several hundred men from all parts of Illinois, it summoned "the Unconditional Union men of the State of Illinois, without regard to former party associations, who are in favor of a vigorous prosecution of the war against this unholy and accursed rebellion; who are determined to sustain the Government in its endeavors to crush out treason; who intend to preserve the integrity of the Union at any cost of treasure and blood; who mean to transmit our free institutions unimpaired to our posterity; who believe that 'the further *offensive* prosecution of the war' is the only mode of securing the blessings of peace and maintaining our National honor, and who would rejoice to see the Old Fag floating over every citadel and fort and protecting every inch of territory of these United States," to meet in Springfield on September 3rd. Prominent speakers from other states were invited to be present, and the attendance of Lincoln himself was insistently sought.

On the morning of the appointed day Springfield was alive with a multitude which could be compared only with the great Republican demonstration by which, in 1860, the nomination of Lincoln had been celebrated. As bands played, and drums rolled, and cannon boomed, and banners snapped in the wind, a procession formed, marched through the downtown streets, and turned towards the fair grounds. There, from five stands, Edward Everett, Schuyler Colfax, Zachariah Chandler, John A. Logan, John A. McClernand and many others aroused the great crowd to a high pitch. But the climax, at each stand, was the reading of the letter which Lincoln had sent when he had finally decided that attendance in person was impossible. Directed to his critics rather than his supporters, it was a magnificent defense of the Emancipation Proclamation and the policy of using freed negroes in the Union armies. The conclusion, an emotional appeal of the sort of which Lincoln was a master, brought dead silence in the vast audience. "Peace," he said, "does not appear so distant as it did. I hope it will come soon, and come to stay; and so come as to be worth the keeping in all future time. It will then have been proved that among free men there can be no successful appeal from the ballot to the bullet, and that they who take such appeal are sure to lose their case and pay the cost. And then there will be some black men who can remember that with silent tongue, and clenched teeth, and steady eye, and well-poised bayonet, they have helped mankind on to this great consummation, while I fear there will be some white ones unable to forget that with malignant heart and deceitful speech they strove to hinder it."

With a will the crowd shouted endorsement of the government, the emancipation proclamation and the relentless prosecution of the war. That night thousands listened to speeches from the steps of the court house, marched in torchlight processions, and marvelled at the fireworks. Not until long after midnight did the streets of the capital resume their customary stillness.

To the double spur of victory and the renewed determination of Union leaders, popular opinion began to respond. In

the states which held October elections large Union gains
were registered. In Springfield there was rejoicing, and
once more flags waved and cannon boomed. But there was
also disgruntlement. The verdict of the elections, said the
Register, "is against the very foundations of governmental
law and strikes another blow at civil liberty in the century
which gave it to us. . . . The rejoicing of the abolitionists
today is a jubilee over the downfall of the nation; the sorrow of the democracy is mourning over the fate they are
powerless for the time to prevent." But the direful comment
was without effect, for at the November election the Union
party carried their candidates for local offices to victory in
city, county and state.

Union victories throughout the North focussed attention
on the approaching presidential election. But before the pre-
convention skirmishing attained importance, the return of
the veteran regiments provided an interlude.

With the end of their three years of service approaching,
veteran regiments were being offered a trip home and a thirty-
day furlough in return for re-enlistment. First to reach
Springfield was the town's favorite, the Seventh Illinois.
On the afternoon of January 18, 1864, the firing of cannon
and ringing of church bells heralded the approach of the
train. The schools were dismissed immediately, and by the
time the train pulled into the Great Western station the
streets were crowded. As 360 men and officers disembarked
and marched to the State House cheer after cheer rang in
their ears, but there were tears too, for Shiloh, Corinth
and many another Southern field had claimed 500 of their
comrades. At the State House Yates and John Cook, the
Seventh's first colonel, eulogized the regiment fulsomely,
but at the first opportunity Colonel Rowett reminded the
audience that his men had not eaten since the morning of the
preceding day, and that he suspected they would prefer
food to oratory. So the meeting broke up abruptly, and the

men sought the hotels and restaurants, where all they could eat was theirs without charge.

Three days later, when the Twenty-Sixth Illinois, with one Sangamon company, reached Springfield, a similar scene was enacted, except that this time the ladies were prepared, and had a "sumptuous repast" ready. A few days later the Tenth Cavalry, with three local companies, met a similar reception. After that a different regiment arrived every few days. The novelty wore off, but for various reasons the town remained in a state of constant excitement. At frequent intervals men who had been assured that nothing was too good for them decided to take the orators at their word. Small groups would march into a bar, order drinks, and smash the place when the bartender demanded payment. Others, inflamed with whiskey, indulged in deviltry just for the fun of it. A newspaper item furnishes a typical instance: "Last night at about 7 o'clock, a gang of soldiers numbering ten or fifteen, passed down Jefferson street, conducting themselves in a most disgraceful manner. They broke down the gate of the front yard fence at Gen. Anderson's residence, tore off the palings of Mr. Gather's fence, damaged the fence and gate in front of Mr. Maxcy's residence, and completely demolished the fence belonging to Mr. Samuel Runyon. It is also reported that considerable damage was done to the fence in front of Ida Johnson's house." And so it went throughout the spring. With frequent brawls, and even an occasional killing, the provost-marshal and his guard were the busiest men in Springfield.

One result of the disorder on the part of furloughed soldiers was the development of a conviction that the city must provide some sort of accommodation for the uniformed men who were constantly passing through it. Accordingly, a committee secured $2,000 from the state sanitary commission and made plans to build a soldiers' home on a lot near the Great Western station. But when property owners in the vicinity protested, the matter lagged. Finally, after several attempts to secure a location, permission to use the government lot at Sixth and Monroe streets [2] was granted. In three weeks a frame building, with lounge and sleeping rooms, was completed. The Young Ladies' Soldiers' Aid Society opened it with a fair which the *Journal* pronounced "one of the most *recherche* [3] and fashionable affairs which ever came off in this city," and which netted $1,400 for the benefit of sick and wounded soldiers.

By this time the presidential contest was gaining momentum. The Democrats, assuming that Lincoln would be the nominee, were blasting at him without restraint. He was an "obscure lawyer" who "disgraced" the position in which an accident of politics had placed him; a "czar" who had "stricken down the last privilege of freemen"; a tyrant whose acts "are only paralleled, not transcended, in enormity by the infamies of Caligula or Dionysius of Syracuse." Weak, his head turned by power, he had set himself above the law and was fast turning a constitutional democracy into a military despotism.

Ordinarily this sort of thing, common enough in political campaigns, brought quick retort from the opposing party, but now the Republicans were silent. The truth is that long before 1864 the attachment of the Illinois leaders of the party to Lincoln had become at best lukewarm. Within a few months of Lincoln's inauguration Dubois was angered by the administration's coolness towards men he had recommended for office. Herndon complained of Lincoln's slowness in attacking slavery—"Does he suppose he can crush— squelch out this huge rebellion by pop guns filled with rose water?" Conkling thought the President weak and half-hearted. Baker of the *Journal* inveighed against the "dilly-

[2] The site of the old wigwam, and the present Post Office and Federal Court Building.

[3] The acme of praise in the terminology of the day.

dallying of the Government with the Southern traitors."
D. L. Phillips, the United States marshal, charged that
Democrats were carrying off fat army contracts while the
loyal men were ignored. Yates had spent himself in putting
an Illinois army into the field, but had "no credit for it from
Mr. Lincoln."

Late in 1863 a visitor to the capital summarized the attitude of the Illinois Republican leaders. "While in Springfield some time ago," he wrote, "it was more than intimated
to me by a gentleman attached to the State Government that
it might become necessary to nominate some other man than
Mr. Lincoln at our next National Convention. . . . While
hundreds have abiding confidence in the Patriotism of Mr.
Lincoln, they have certain misgivings in regard to many
things connected with his administration; hence the eyes of
the masses are turning in all directions in search of suitable
men *whose devotion to the true principle* involved in this
great War is above suspicion."

Since this letter was written to Lyman Trumbull, there can
be little doubt about the identity of at least one of the "suitable men" whom the writer had in mind. That Trumbull
was not entirely deaf to the promptings of ambition is evident from a letter of his own, written in February, 1864.
"The feeling for Mr. Lincoln's re-election *seems* to be very
general," he said, "but much of it I discover is only on the
surface. You would be surprised in talking with public men
we meet here, to find how few when you come to get at their
real sentiments are for Mr. Lincoln's re-election. There is
distrust & fear that he is too undecided & inefficient to put
down the rebellion. You need not be surprised if a re-action
sets in before the nomination in favor of some man supposed
to possess more energy, & less inclination to trust our brave
boys in the hands, & under the leadership of Generals who
have no heart in the war."

But they all reckoned without the master-politician in

the White House, for on June 8, 1864, the wires brought word that that day, at Baltimore, the Union Convention had unanimously nominated Lincoln on the first ballot. A salute was fired and rockets were set off. The next night, before a crowd assembled in front of the court house, J. C. Conkling and others laid aside their resentment and lack of faith and eulogized the nominee.

Now that their target was revealed, the Democrats attacked with increased bitterness. Typical of many pronouncements was a *Register* editorial of July 26: "The veriest child now knows that a vote for Abraham Lincoln is a vote for war, for murder, for the impoverishment of our people now and forever, because he will not abate one jot of his determination to employ the armies of the Union to wipe out slavery. . . . Not another life need be wasted in this war; not another dollar of the people's money need be spent, if this President would but prefer the salvation of the Union and the restoration of peace to the accomplishment of schemes which he himself solemnly swore, two short years ago, he had neither the right nor the disposition to attempt."

(In comparison with what the editor had to say of the candidate for Governor, this was mild. "Elect Oglesby!" he snorted. "Talk of a 'short-boy,' a 'plug-ugly,' a harlot's 'fancy-man,' or any other synonym of all that is utterly abandoned or despicable, but for decency's sake, never mention Oglesby in connection with the chief-magistracy of Illinois.")

Strong language, however, could not conceal the fact that many of the Democratic rank and file were slipping away from the leaders. For one thing, the party was fatally handicapped by its delay in making a nomination. When a Democratic mass meeting was held in Springfield in mid-August trouble developed over the proposal to endorse in advance the nominee of the forth-coming convention, and outright schism was barely avoided. By the time McClellan was finally selected, on August 29, so much valuable time had already passed that the Springfield Democrats did not even attempt a public demonstration.

On the other hand, military success played into the hands of the Union men. Grant was moving toward Richmond, at heavy cost, to be sure, but with grim determination, while Sherman was embarked upon the most spectacular movement of the war. With proper effort, victory at the polls could surely be made to follow success in the field. So the Union men threw themselves into the campaign with enthusiasm. A wigwam was built on North Sixth Street, glee clubs sang campaign songs, and frequent meetings, with as many speeches as possible by War Democrats, were held. Rain spoiled the grand rally of the campaign, planned for October 5, but the achievements of Grant, Sheridan, Sherman and Farragut proved to be more effective than political oratory, and a sweeping Union victory resulted.

By the narrowest of margins, Lincoln carried Springfield, but once again the county of Sangamon rejected him.[4] In the national result, however, there was glory enough for the local Republicans. As soon as success was assured, they gathered in jubilation at the State House. When John M. Palmer declared that "for the leaders of the rebellion we had bullets and ropes; for the mass of the people forgiveness," they cheered him to the echo. The Democrats, however, were not inclined to let the celebrants completely escape their own lack of loyalty to their chief. The next day the *Register* tartly reminded them that Lincoln was the real choice of "the most insignificant minority," and that his election was evidence that party success, instead of national welfare, had been their goal.

The election over, military matters monopolized the interest of Springfield, along with the North in general. With

---

[4] In Springfield Lincoln received 1324 votes to 1314 for McClellan; but McClellan carried the county by 3945 to 3565.

absorbed attention the people watched Sherman penetrate farther and farther into the South. There was rejoicing when Savannah fell into his hands, and bitter glee when Columbia and Charleston were taken. Meanwhile, under the eyes of an anxious nation, Grant pressed harder and harder on Richmond.

Finally, at eleven o'clock on the morning of April 3, 1865, came the news that had been awaited for four long years. Union troops were entering Richmond! Church bells, fire bells and cannon sounded the good news, while the people spread into the streets to greet each other in wild enthusiasm. That night bands played while rockets and bonfires lighted the sky. At last the triumph of the Union and an early peace were assured.

Just one week later came word of the end. When the wires announced Lee's surrender flags flew to their places as if by magic. In a short time business was suspended, and by common impulse the entire city sought the streets and the State House square. As the crowds grew excitement became intense; cheers and singing mingled with the noise of the bells; impromptu processions marched and countermarched. Even the "Copperheads" joined in the rejoicing.

Early in the afternoon the Pioneer Fire Company, preceded by a band, appeared in uniform. Soon the other fire companies joined them. Then a masked man in ragged regimentals led out a mule with a tattered rider, while to the rear straggled a forlorn-looking escort. On the mule's blanket was the inscription, "Jeff. Davis and Suite"; over his tail was the placard, "Lee's End." Hacks, buggies, wagons and drays carrying loads of singing, shouting men joined the parade and circled the square times without end.

At 6:30 a salute of twenty guns was the signal for a fireworks display limited only by the available supply. Then the fire companies, augmented by the Fenian Brotherhood, paraded with flaring torches. But the feature of the evening

THE SOLDIERS' HOME, 1864

The present Post Office and Federal Court Building occupies this site.

BURIAL VAULT, OAK RIDGE
Where Lincoln's body was first buried

THE STATE HOUSE
Draped in mourning, 1865

OAK RIDGE CEMETERY ENTRANCE
As it appeared in 1865

was "Old Bob," Abraham Lincoln's old bay horse, colorful with a red, white and blue blanket studded with flags. As the procession ended the people jammed the Hall of the House of Representatives, where orator after orator pronounced a requiem for the rebellion. Finally the last grandiloquent period ended, the applause died away, the band played, and the people walked quietly to their homes. Peace had come again.

EPILOGUE

IN the small hours of April 15th Springfield learned the tragic news. At three o'clock in the morning, amid despatches from Grant's army in Richmond, accounts of Lee's surrender, and New York gold quotations, came the first terse flash from Washington: "The President was shot in a theatre tonight, and is probably mortally wounded." By dawn it was known that death was only a matter of hours.

In sadness and anxiety the people gathered in groups on the streets. A few stores which had opened for business closed, and the quiet of a Sunday prevailed. Flags flew at half-mast, buildings were draped with black cloth, church bells tolled. At eight o'clock came word of Lincoln's death. Four hours later the citizens met in the State House and listened to John T. Stuart speak of the dead President. That afternoon one organization after another—the Union League, the Fenian Brotherhood, the City Council—met to give formal expression to the sorrow which all men felt.

The next day, a Sunday, the churches were crowded, and ministers decried the national calamity from black-draped pulpits. On the 19th, when funeral services were held in Washington, stores and offices were again closed; again flags hung at half-mast. At noon the guns at the arsenal fired a solemn salute; that afternoon there were services in all the churches. It was another day of sadness and mourning.

By this time preparations for the funeral were under way. In Washington, on the 17th, an Illinois delegation had secured Mrs. Lincoln's consent to the burial of the body in Springfield. At the same time a local committee had been chosen to make arrangements for an appropriate site for the grave. Soon afterward, with unanimous approval from the city, the Mather property [1] was chosen, and the construction of a temporary tomb commenced. Then, just as the vault was completed, word came from Mrs. Lincoln that the body was to be deposited in the receiving vault at Oak Ridge. The people were disappointed, but the committee acceded to her wish.

Meanwhile, the funeral train had been slowly moving westward. In Philadelphia, New York, Cleveland, Indianapolis and other cities hundreds of thousands had looked upon the features of the dead President. On the first of May the cortege reached Chicago, where the body was to lie for twenty-four hours. On the third it would be in Springfield.

The day broke bright and clear. Dawn found the streets crowded—for hours special trains had been pouring thousands into the prairie capital. By eight o'clock the Alton station was an island in a human sea, and other thousands lined the tracks beyond the limits of the town. The 146th Illinois, with detachments from other regiments, was drawn up in line on Jefferson street. Minute guns, fired by a Missouri battery, sounded strangely sharp against the hushed voices of the crowd.

Shortly before nine o'clock the pilot engine arrived. A strained silence was the crowd's only manifestation. A few minutes later the funeral train, nine black-draped cars, drew slowly into the station. In absolute quiet the body was placed in the magnificent hearse which the city of St. Louis had tendered for the occasion, and the long procession started for the State House. There, in the Hall of the House of Repre-

[1] The site of the present State House.

sentatives, the coffin was placed on a velvet-covered cata-falque. The guard of honor took their places, the casket was opened, and the people started to file past. All day and all night the slow procession continued, until it was said that 75,000 had looked upon the face of Lincoln.

At ten o'clock on the morning of May 4th the coffin was closed. While minute guns sounded, and a choir of 250 voices sang hymns on the State House steps, the casket was placed in the hearse. With General Hooker at its head, the long procession started towards Oak Ridge. The cemetery reached, the choir sang again while the body was placed in the tomb. A minister offered a prayer, another read scripture, a third read the Second Inaugural. The choir sang a dirge, and Bishop Simpson pronounced the funeral oration. There was a closing prayer, the Doxology, a benediction. Slowly, silently, the vast crowd dispersed.

THE END

A NOTE ABOUT SOURCES

HAD I followed my own inclinations, I would have used footnotes to indicate the more important sources I have consulted in writing this book. I am convinced, however, that annotation irritates almost everyone except professional historians, and therefore I have yielded my personal preference. Still, if he is to play fair with his reader, the historical writer can hardly omit all mention of the materials he has used. History is a fabric of many threads, and an historian exhibits no more than common honesty when he proclaims that he has been weaver only, and not spinner as well; and besides, the reader should have some opportunity of judging for himself the quality of the raw material: whether it be long-fibred wool, or merely shoddy. Hence this note.

First and foremost, this is a newspaper history. Without the long files of the *Illinois State Register* and the *Illinois State Journal* (called also the *Sangamo Journal* and the *Illinois Journal*) which are available in the Illinois State Historical Library, this would have been a vastly different book, and I believe a much poorer one. At first glance these papers—at least for the period in which I have worked—seem barren enough. Politics was their chief concern, and even here the editors appear to have relied on their scissors rather than their brains. But if one has the patience to examine a year's run instead of a few scattered issues, the first impression changes. Local news, especially in the earlier years, is scarce, but when one goes through thousands of pages, a mass of material illustrative of every phase of community life accumulates before one realizes what is happening. So far as this book is concerned, it is no exaggeration to say that it owes more to the two Springfield newspapers than to all other sources combined. I only wish it were possible to express my gratitude to the editors, particularly Simeon Francis of the *Journal* and Charles H. Lanphier of the *Register*. Little did they suspect to what use the future would put their paragraphs on the hog nuisance and the mud about the State House square!

Though far less important, a few other sources deserve particular mention. The records of the County Commissioners' Court, as the governing body of Sangamon County was originally called, have been drawn upon heavily. Three published works were indispensable: *Sketches of Early Life and Times in Kentucky, Missouri and Illinois,* by Elijah Iles (Springfield, 1883), *History of Sangamon County, Illinois* (Chicago, 1881), and John Carroll Power's *History of the Early Settlers of Sangamon County, Illinois* (Springfield, 1876). The first, a rare little volume, is the autobiography of the man who, more than any other, made a straggling frontier settlement into a permanent community. I have used it extensively in the first three chapters of this book. The second volume is a county history far above the average—a veritable quarry from which all sorts of diverse materials have been pried. (Since the book numbers 1067 double-column pages, and has no index, the metaphor is used advisedly.) The third title, a compilation of biographical and genealogical data concerning those who settled in Sangamon County during the first ten or fifteen years of its existence, contains much about pioneer life that is unavailable in any other form.

Of one passage in *"Here I Have Lived"* I wish to make

particular mention, if for no other reason than self-defense.
Readers who are familiar with the traditional accounts of
Lincoln's life will note that the story of the wedding of
Lincoln and Mary Todd, as it is related in Chapter V, varies
materially from the commonly accepted narrative. What
I believe to be ample authority for my own treatment may be
found in the Appendix to *Mary Lincoln, Wife and Widow*
by Carl Sandburg and Paul M. Angle (Harcourt, Brace,
1932). The letters from Mary Todd to Mercy Levering,
quoted here, as well as several of the letters of James C.
Conkling which I have used in part, are also to be found
in that volume. Other Conkling letters which I have quoted
are the property of Mrs. Georgiana Conkling Reed of New
Rochelle, New York, to whom, for permission to make use of
family correspondence, I am deeply grateful.

Out of many another source I have made sometimes a
sentence or two, sometimes pages. In addition to those to
which I have already referred, the following deserve mention:

MANUSCRIPTS

Pascal P. Enos Papers, in the Illinois State Historical Library.
Recollections of Mrs. Melvina Alvey Fisher, in the files of the
    Abraham Lincoln Association.
The Journal of Jared P. Irwin, in possession of Mrs. Margaret
    McNutt, Springfield, Ill.
Pioneer Mothers of Illinois, bound MS in the Illinois State Historical
    Library.
Lyman Trumbull Manuscripts. Transcripts and photostats in the
    Illinois Historical Survey, University of Illinois.
George Williams MS, in possession of Mrs. Edna Orendorff Mac-
    pherson, Springfield, Illinois.

NEWSPAPERS

Edwardsville [Illinois] *Spectator.* Scattered issues.
Sangamo Spectator. A few copies of Springfield's first newspaper
    have been preserved in the Illinois State Historical Library.

Illinois Intelligencer (Vandalia). Scattered issues.
New York *Herald,* 1860-61.
New York *Tribune,* 1860-61.

BOOKS AND ARTICLES

Ackerman, William K., *Early Illinois Railroads.* Fergus Historical
Series, No. 23. Chicago, 1884.

Alvord, Clarence W., *Governor Edward Coles.* Illinois Historical
Collections, XV. Springfield, 1920.

Angle, Paul M., *Marine Bank; the Story of the Oldest Bank in
Illinois.* Springfield, 1931.

Arnold, Isaac N., "Reminiscences of the Illinois Bar Forty Years
Ago." *Proceedings of the Illinois Bar Association,* 1881.

Baringer, William E., "Campaign Technique in Illinois—1860."
Transactions of the Illinois State Historical Society, 1932.

Bateman, Newton, and Paul Selby, editors, *Historical Encyclopedia
of Illinois . . . and History of Sangamon County.* 3 vols., Chicago,
1912.

Beach, Richard H., "A Letter from Illinois Written in 1836."
Journal of the Illinois State Historical Society, October, 1910.

Beveridge, Albert J., *Abraham Lincoln, 1809-1858.* 2 vols., Boston
and New York, 1928.

Bidwell, Percy Wells, and John I. Falconer, *History of Agriculture
in the Northern United States, 1620-1860.* Washington, 1925.

Boggess, Arthur C., *The Settlement of Illinois, 1778-1830.* Chicago,
1908.

Brown, Caroline Owsley, "Springfield Society Before the Civil War."
Journal of the Illinois State Historical Society, April-July, 1922.

Browning, Orville H. *The Diary of Orville Hickman Browning,
1850-1881,* edited by Theodore C. Pease and J. G. Randall.
Illinois Historical Collections, XX, XXII. Springfield, 1925,
1933.

Cartwright, Peter. *Autobiography of Peter Cartwright,* edited by
W. P. Strickland. New York, 1857.

Clarke, Charles R., "Sketch of Charles James Fox Clarke, with Letters to His Mother." *Journal of the Illinois State Historical
Society,* January, 1930.

Coffin, Levi, *Reminiscences of Levi Coffin.* Cincinnati, 1876.

Cole, Arthur C., *The Era of the Civil War, 1848-1870.* Centennial
History of Illinois, Vol. 3. Springfield, 1919.

A Note About Sources

Conkling, Clinton L., "Address on February 12, 1920." *Proceedings of the Constitutional Convention of Illinois, 1920-1922.* Springfield, 1920-22.

Converse, Henry A., *Baptist Centennial Address.* Springfield, 1930.

Curtiss, Daniel S., *Western Portraiture and Emigrants' Guide.* New York, 1852.

Davis, W. W., "A Trip from Pennsylvania to Illinois in 1851." *Transactions of the Illinois State Historical Society,* 1904.

Dowrie, George W., *The Development of Banking in Illinois, 1817-1863.* University of Illinois Studies in the Social Sciences, Vol. 2, No. 4. Urbana, 1913.

Drake, Daniel, *A Systematic Treatise, Historical, Etiological and Practical, on the Principal Diseases of the Interior Valley of North America.* 2 vols. New York, 1850.

Edwards, Mrs. Benjamin S., *Some Incidents in the Life of Mrs. Benj. S. Edwards.* [Springfield, 1904.]

Edwards, Ninian. *The Edwards Papers,* edited by Elihu B. Washburne. Chicago, 1884.

Enos, Zimri, "Description of Springfield." *Transactions of the Illinois State Historical Society,* 1909.

Ernst, Ferdinand, "Travels in Illinois in 1819." Translated from *Observations Made upon a Journey Through the Interior of the United States of North America in the Year 1819,* Hildesheim, Hanover, 1823. *Transactions of the Illinois State Historical Society,* 1903.

Flagg, Edmund, *The Far West, 1836-1837.* New York, 1838.

Flagg, Gershom. "Pioneer Letters of Gershom Flagg," edited by Solon J. Buck. *Transactions of the Illinois State Historical Society,* 1910.

Ford, Thomas, *History of Illinois.* Chicago, 1854.

Fordham, Elias Pym. *Personal Narrative of Travels in Virginia, Maryland,* etc., edited by Frederick A. Ogg. Cleveland, 1906.

Giger, Henry D., *The Story of the Sangamon County Court House.* Springfield, 1901.

Gross, Eugene L., "A Sketch of Springfield." In *Springfield City Directory and Business Mirror for 1866.* Springfield, 1865.

Herndon, William H., *Herndon's Lincoln: the True Story of a Great Life.* 3 vols., Chicago, 1889.

Laws of Illinois, 1821-1860.

Illinois in 1837. Philadelphia, 1837.

Illinois State University. Catalogs, 1852, 1857-58.

Kirkland, Edward C., *History of American Economic Life*. New York, 1932.

Koerner, Gustave. *Memoirs of Gustave Koerner, 1809-1896,* edited by Thomas J. McCormack. 2 vols., Cedar Rapids, 1909.

Lincoln, Abraham. *Complete Works of Abraham Lincoln,* edited by John G. Nicolay and John Hay. 12 vols., New York, 1905.

Linder, Usher F., *Reminiscences of the Early Bench and Bar of Illinois*. Chicago, 1879.

McConnel, George M., "Recollections of the Northern Cross Railroad." *Transactions of the Illinois State Historical Society,* 1908.

Matheny, James H., "History of Springfield." In *Springfield City Directory, 1857-58*. Springfield, 1857.

Moses, John, *Illinois, Historical and Statistical*. 2 vols., Chicago, 1889-92.

Moses, John, "The Oldest Railroad in Illinois." *Fergus Historical Series,* No. 23. Chicago, 1884.

Oak Ridge Cemetery: Its History and Improvements, Rules and Regulations. Springfield, 1879.

Paddock, Gaius, "The Original Automobile." *Journal of the Illinois State Historical Society,* April, 1918.

Palmer, John M., *Personal Recollections: The Story of an Earnest Life*. Cincinnati, 1901.

Parkinson, Daniel M., "Pioneer Life in Wisconsin." *Wisconsin Historical Collections,* Vol. 2. Madison, 1856.

Parkinson, Mary W., "Travels in Western America in 1837." *Journal of American History,* Vol. 3, No. 4.

Pease, Theodore C., *The Frontier State, 1818-1848*. Centennial History of Illinois, Vol. 2. Springfield, 1918.

Peck, John Mason, *A Gazetteer of Illinois*. Jacksonville (Ill.), 1834, and Philadelphia, 1837.

Peck, John Mason, *A Guide for Emigrants*. Boston, 1831.

Peck, John Mason. *Memoir of John Mason Peck,* edited by Rufus Babcock. Philadelphia, 1864.

Power, John Carroll, *History of Springfield, Illinois, Its Attractions as a Home and Advantages for Business, Manufacturing, Etc.* Springfield, 1871.

Prince, Ezra M., "The Fourth Illinois Infantry in the War with Mexico." *Transactions of the Illinois State Historical Society,* 1906.

Rapalje, Anna R. "Diary of Anna R. Morrison [Mrs. George Rapalje], 1840-1841." *Journal of the Illinois State Historical Society,* April, 1914.

Reynolds, John, *My Own Times, Embracing Also the History of My Life.* Belleville, 1855.

Reynolds, John, *Sketches of the Country, on the Northern Route from Belleville, Illinois, to the City of New York.* Belleville, 1854.

Rickerson, F. D., *A Half Century of Baptist History in Springfield, Illinois, 1830-1881.* Springfield, 1881.

Ridgely, Anna. "A Girl in the Sixties: Excerpts from the Journal of Anna Ridgely," edited by Octavia Roberts Corneau. *Journal of the Illinois State Historical Society,* October, 1929.

Ridgley, Douglas C., *The Geography of Illinois.* Chicago, 1921.

Robinson, Solon, "Notes of Travel in the West," in *The Cultivator* (Albany), vol. 2, 1845.

Ross, Harvey Lee, *Early Pioneers and Pioneer Events of the State of Illinois.* Chicago, 1899.

Sandburg, Carl, *Abraham Lincoln: The Prairie Years.* 2 vols., New York, 1926.

Schoolcraft, Henry R., *Travels in the Central Portions of the Mississippi Valley . . . in the Year 1821.* New York, 1825.

Shirreff, Patrick, *A Tour Through North America.* Edinburgh, 1835.

Springfield. *First Annual Report of the Public Schools, 1858-59.* Springfield, 1859.

Stuart, James, *Three Years in North America.* 2 vols., New York, 1833.

Taylor, Bayard, *At Home and Abroad: A Sketch-book of Life, Scenery and Men.* New York, 1869.

Thomas, John T., *The One Hundredth Anniversary of the . . . First Presbyterian Church, Springfield, Illinois.* Springfield, 1928.

Thomas, William, "The Winnebago 'War' of 1827." *Transactions of the Illinois State Historical Society,* 1907.

Thompson, Joseph J., *Diocese of Springfield in Illinois: Diamond Jubilee History.* Springfield, 1927.

Treat, Payson J., *The National Land System, 1785-1820.* New York, 1910.

Trotter, Isabella, *First Impressions of the New World on Two Travellers from the Old, in the Autumn of 1858.* London, 1859.

Villard, Henry, *Memoirs of Henry Villard, Journalist and Financier, 1835-1900.* 2 vols., Boston, 1904.

Wied-Neuwied, Maximilian Alexander Philipp, Prince von, *Travels in the Interior of North America, 1832-1834*. In Thwaites, *Early Western Travels,* Vols. 22-25, Cleveland, 1906.

Wines, Frederick H., *Memorial of Rev. J. G. Bergen.* Springfield, 1873.

Yates, Richard, *General Grant's Military Services.* Speech of Hon. Richard Yates of Illinois, in the United States Senate, July 18, 1866. Washington, 1866.

INDEX

Abolition, 79
Adams, J. H., 169
Adams, James, buys lot, 17; buys rattlesnakes, 20; early lawyer, 25; in political controversy, 67-70
Adams, John Quincy, 31
"Agricola," 61-62
Agriculture, dependence on transportation, 35-36; unrest of farmers, 146; conditions of, 154-55; increased use of machinery, 160; greater production, 168
Alden's Hotel, 50
Alleghenians, 105, 187
Allegheny County (Pa.), 252
Allen, Robert, 66
Allen, Rowland P., 15
Alton, freight costs to, 36; cholera in, 42; produce exported from, 47; railroad to, 54, 151, 163; contender for state capital, 56; site of Lincoln-Shields duel, 123; Mexican War camp, 132; state fair at, 187
Alton & Sangamon Railroad, 159, 162-63. *See also* Chicago & Mississippi Railroad, Chicago & Alton Railroad.
Alvey, William, 53
American Hemp Co., 142
American House, theater in, 80; visitors at, 83; described, 87-88; entertainments at, 98, 99, 100, 105; Van Buren at, 106; during state fair, 186; Douglas at, 211, 248; mentioned, 92
American Protestant Society, 142
Anderson, Gen., 283
Anderson, Joseph, estate, 68-69
Antietam, Battle of, 272
Anti-Nebraska party, 213, 215, 224

"Aristocracy Hill," 176
Armstrong, Hugh M., 169
Arnold, Isaac N., 108, 150
Arsenal, 269
Ashmun, George, 239
At Home and Abroad, 187
Augusta Family, 105

Bailey, Rev. G. S., 197
Baker, Edward Dickinson, captain Sharp Shooters, 50; speech by, 51; Whig leader, 65, 110; elected to state senate, 67; at corner stone ceremonies, 74; defends Porter, 79; Jackson funeral oration, 106; in Harrison campaign, 111, 114; in Fisher murder case, 119; in Mormon War, 127; in 1844 campaign, 129; speaks on Texas and Oregon, 131; raises 4th Illinois, 132; at Cerro Gordo, 134; visits Lincoln, 259
Baker, Edward L., 232, 258, 284
Baker, ——, 107
Balls, 98-99, 183
Baltimore, conventions, 241, 286
Banks, development of, 170-72
Bank of Illinois, 121
Baptist church, 53, 197, 201
"Barn, The," 243, 244, 249
Barnett, George I., 197
Barnum, Phineas Taylor, 188
Barrett, James W., 136, 143, 208, 235, 243
Barter, 22-23, 47, 158
Bateman, Newton, 228
Bates, Edwin, 238, 257
Baxter, W. D., 148
Beach, Richard H., 46
Beam, Thomas, 22

Index

305

Ernst, Ferdinand, 4
Evarts, William Maxwell, 239
Everett, Edward, 281
Ewing, W. L. D., 71
Excursions, 99-100

Farmers' & Mechanics' Association, 185
Farming, methods, 21-22
Farragut, David Glasgow, 287
Female Bible Society, 53
Fenian Brotherhood, 288, 290
Ferguson, W. I., 136
Ficklin, Orlando B., 72-73, 244
Fillmore, Millard, 220
Fire companies, 181-83
First National Bank, 172
Fisher, Archibald, 117-20
Fisher, S. B., 174
Fisher murder case, 116-20
Flagg, Gershom, 4
Flat Branch, 20
Flood, William G., 107
Flour, export of, 168
Fogg, George G., 257
Fondey, William B., 227
Force, J. H., 169
Ford, Thomas, 107; issues warrant for Joseph Smith, 126; investigates Mormon troubles, 127; calls for volunteers, 128, 131
Forquer, George, 38, 54, 64
Fort Donelson, 269-70
Fort Henry, 269-70
Fort Sumter, 262
Fourier, Charles, 140
Fourierism, 140-41
Fourth Illinois, in Mexican War, 132-35
Fourth of July, celebrations, 28-29, 50, 105
Fox, Benjamin Franklin, 169
Francis, Simeon, on fertility of Sangamo Country, 40-41; in Young Men's Lyceum, 52; predicts growth of Springfield, 57; editor *Journal,* 65; on building activity, 88-89; quarrel with Douglas, 115-16; on Portuguese aid committee, 143; on effect of railroads, 166. *See also Sangamo Journal, Illinois Journal.*
Francis, Mrs. Simeon, 97
"Franklin Festival," 189
Fraternal orders, 196
Freeman, J. D., 175
Fremont, John C., 218

French, Augustus C., 205, 217, 227
Frink & Walker, stages, 149
Frontier, stages in development of, 25
Fugitive slave law, adopted, 205; endorsed, 207, 215; case under, 226
Funk, Isaac, 277

Galena, 31, 149
Gambling, 49-50, 195-96
Gas, introduction of, 178
Gather, ――, 283
Gear, Charles, 15
Geographical Center, considered for capital, 56
German Band, 211, 217, 220
German Democratic Club, 242
German Methodist Church, 197
German Republican Club, 242
Gettysburg, Battle of, 279
Giddings, Joshua Reed, 214, 257
Gillespie, Joseph, 116
Gilmore, Dr., 118-19
Glaciers, in Illinois, 1-2
Globe Tavern, 87, 97
Goodell, R. E., 177n
Governor's Mansion, 19, 86n, 176, 191
Grant, Ulysses S., 267, 269, 287, 288
Graves, William, 125n
Great Western Railroad, 162, 163, 168, 260. *See also* Sangamon & Morgan Railroad.
Greece, independence toasted, 29
Greeley, Horace, 140, 188, 257
Green, Bowling, 107
Green, Duff, 258
Grimshaw, Jackson, 191
Grimsley, William P., 159
Grow, Galusha, 245
Grubb & Lewis, 89 and note

Hale, Rev. Albert, 143
Hamilton, Alexander, 14n
Hamilton, George, 198
Hamilton, Robert, 6
Hamilton, William Stephen, 9n, 12n, 14-15
Hancock County, Mormon troubles, 125-28
Hanks, John, 244
Hannan & Ragsdale, 176
Hannibal (Mo.), 246
Happy, Captain, 50
Hardin, John J., captain military company, 50; speeches by, 51, 131; in

Index

Index

McGinnis, David, 243
McLean, John, 238
McNabb, James C., 17
McNeely & Radford, 45
Madeira, Island of, 142-43
Mails, 23, 48, 150
"Maine Law," agitation, 195
Manning, G. S., 169
Manning, William, Jr., 45
Manufacturing, beginnings, 46; importance, 155-56; trade in products, 160; stimulated, 169
Market house, 90, 157, 179
Marshall, Thomas F., 125n
Mason, James, 15
Masonic Hall, 26, 175
Masonic Order, 196
Matheny, Charles R., settles at Springfield, 7; advertises lot sale, 16-17; residence, 28, 43; Adams supporter, 31; in Colonization Society, 52
Matheny, James H., 162, 205, 222
Mather, Lamb & Co., 45
Mather, Thomas, 108, 152, 153, 192
Mather, Mrs. Thomas, 291
Mather, Thomas S., 262
Matteson, Joel A., 176, 177n, 191, 213
Maxcy, ———, 283
May, William L., 60-62, 64, 107
Mechanics & Farmers Bank, 167, 172
Mechanics Institute, 74, 202
Mechanicsburg, 163
Menard County, 73
Mendel, ———, 27
Merchandising, 156-59. *See also* Business, Trade.
Meredosia, 144, 145, 146
Merritt's Cornet Band, 233
Merryman, Elias H., captain Springfield Artillery, 50; in Springfield society, 93; in Lincoln-Shields duel, 123-25; in Mormon War, 127; supports Mexican War, 132
Merryman, James H., 134-35
Messersmith, John, 13
"Meteor shower," 49
Methodists, 28, 53, 86n, 197
Metropolitan Hall, 175, 189
Mexican War, 131-36; 244-45
Military companies, 50-51
Militia, ordered out, 262
Miller, Rev. E., 200
Miller, James, 228
Miller, Major, 107

Mills, Benjamin, 60-62
Mississippi River, 145-46
Missouri Compromise, 209, 215, 224
Missouri Democrat, 132
Mitchell, Edward, 33, 36, 43, 45
Mobley, Mordecai, 13
Moffett, Thomas, 37, 52
Money, 23. *See also* Barter.
Montez, Lola, 188
Moore, John, 206, 217, 247
Morgan County, 73
Mormons, 78, 125-28
Morris, Achilles, 132
Mt. Vernon (Ill.), 161
Mud, 90-91
Munitions, manufacture, 269
Music and musicians, 102-05, 187, 245

Naples (Ill.), 153
National Guards, 264
Nauvoo, Mormons at, 125-28
Neale, Thomas M., Clay supporter, 31; in Winnebago War, 32-33; pilots *Talisman,* 37; advocates improvement of Sangamon River, 39; in Black Hawk War, 39; at corner stone ceremony, 74
Nebraska Bill, 209-13
Negroes, indentured, 29
New Berlin (Ill.), 151, 162
New England Society, 189
New Mexico, 204-05
New Orleans, 145-46
New Year's Day, observance, 190
New York, returns from, 253
New York *Herald,* 99, 250, 253-55
Newhall Family, 187
Nicolay, John G., 249, 259
Noble, Silas, 276-77
Norris, John, 127
Novel reading, 81
Northern Cross Railroad, 99, 144-48, 152, 153. *See also* Sangamon & Morgan Railroad, Great Western Railroad.

Oak Ridge Cemetery, 179-80, 291, 292
Oats, amount raised, 155
Occupations, range of, 24-25; multiplication of, 44-46
Oglesby, Richard, 286
Ohio, admitted to Union, 3; Lincoln in, 237; goes Republican, 251
Old Tavern, 181
"Omnibus Bill," 205

Index